Henry V

HENRY V

A Guide to the Play

JOAN LORD HALL

Greenwood Guides to Shakespeare

Greenwood Press
Westport, Connecticut • London

822.33 W4

Library of Congress Cataloging-in-Publication Data

Hall, Joan Lord.
    Henry V : a guide to the play / Joan Lord Hall.
      p. cm.—(Greenwood guides to Shakespeare)
    Includes bibliographical references (p.) and index.
    ISBN 0–313–29708–8 (alk. paper)
    1. Shakespeare, William, 1564–1616. Henry V. 2. Historical
drama, English—History and criticism. 3. Henry V, King of England,
1387–1422—In literature. 4. Kings and rulers in literature.
5. Great Britain—In literature. I. Title. II. Series.
PR1812.H35 1997
822.3′3—dc20   96–24174

British Library Cataloguing in Publication Data is available.

Library of Congress Catalog Card Number: 96–24174
ISBN: 0–313–29708–8

First published in 1997

Greenwood Press, 88 Post Road West, Westport, CT 06881
An imprint of Greenwood Publishing Group, Inc.

Printed in the United States of America

The paper used in this book complies with the
Permanent Paper Standard issued by the National
Information Standards Organization (Z39.48–1984).

10 9 8 7 6 5 4 3 2

CONTENTS

PREFACE

Shakespeare scholars rarely express unqualified enthusiasm for *Henry V*. While most readers would disagree with the nineteenth-century commentator who patronizingly called it "the dull play of a great artist,"[1] few critics place *Henry V* in their top ten. Yet the play is almost always successful in the theater, and it is more accessible to students—easier to grasp as a text that invites heated discussion—than some of the playwright's more critically esteemed works. In the early 1990s its fortunes surged with the release of Kenneth Branagh's movie version (1989), a hit with audiences on both sides of the Atlantic. This film has inspired students and teachers alike to examine the play afresh and to discover (or rediscover) that it can be read, interpreted, and performed in sharply different ways. Because *Henry V* invites a dialectical approach, it is ideal for classroom debate.

Henry V: A Guide to the Play is organized as an objective reference work to help students, as they engage in this debate, to examine what scholars and critics have already contributed. It provides a broad overview of textual and contextual issues, reviews the play's critical heritage, and covers significant productions of *Henry V* on stage and screen. Each chapter, or chapter section, stands on its own and can be consulted independently.

Chapters 1 and 2 of this work discuss the various texts of *Henry V* and the historical and cultural contexts that inform the play. Chapter 3 covers the play's dramatic structure and its use of different styles. In particular, it centers on the ambivalent presentation of Henry's character, an aspect of the play that has invited the most critical controversy. *Henry V* need not be read either as a full endorsement of a heroic monarch triumphing in a splendid military campaign or as a sustained ironic critique of the King and his war; the play is more subtle than that. One helpful approach to the apparent contradictions in Henry's character is to examine the way that the drama unfolds as the testing of a king, revealing what is required of a strong leader. *Henry V*, the site of contesting versions of kingship, war, and political order, has continued to raise questions rather than provide answers. This is the focus of Chapter 4: the themes of the play.

It is a truism that we interpret a dramatic work according to our own interests and biases; current presuppositions inevitably shape our reading of past literature. Chapter 5 examines different critical perspectives on *Henry V*, covering a spectrum of approaches from the earlier character studies up to the most recent methodologies: cultural materialist and feminist. Because of their importance in current theory and the teaching of dramatic literature, these recent approaches are covered in more detail than traditional ones. Nevertheless, the bibliographic essay at the end of the book offers a balanced assessment of older as well as newer work on *Henry V*. My aim in these chapters is to chart the history of critical responses to the play and, by showing what each method can offer, to suggest directions that will prove illuminating for individual readers.

The history of *Henry V* in performance, a fascinating study in itself, is the subject of Chapter 6. Once upon a time, the play on stage celebrated the image of the ideal warrior king, enhancing the patriotic appeal of the play. Laurence Olivier's 1944 film, made before the end of World War II, certainly does that on one level, although its complex cinematography achieves much more. Distaste for war, especially in the post-Vietnam era, has altered the tenor of more recent productions. Because the energies of the play radiate from Henry as a successful warrior, a relentlessly anti-war version of *Henry V* could scarcely work in the theater; yet several productions from the 1960s on have recognized the darker elements of the drama by deemphasizing the play's epic spectacle and chauvinism. The 1975 version mounted by the Royal Shakespeare Company at Stratford-upon-Avon, discussed first in this chapter, stresses Henry's painful growth into successful leadership. Kenneth Branagh's movie, in some ways a demystifying of kingship, crystallizes this drive toward realism. Branagh's adaptation, so different in style from Olivier's and yet so clearly aware of and, in many ways, indebted to it, has revitalized interest in that earlier movie. This chapter analyzes these two film versions of *Henry V*—how they handle certain cruxes in the text, what they leave out, and what they add—as well as the more traditional 1979 BBC/Time Life video production of the play.

Though primarily a systematic reference work, this study is also a critical exploration that aims to open up *Henry V* for students: to probe its ambiguities and offer insight into its various nuances. After using the play in the classroom, in conjunction with filmed versions, I can verify that both text and performance provoke lively discussion and strong clashes of opinion. *Henry V* is anything but dull.

All quotations from *Henry V* are taken from John Russell Brown (ed.), *The Signet Classic Shakespeare* (New York and Toronto: The New American Library, 1965; 1988). Quotations from Shakespeare's other plays are from G. Blakemore Evans (ed.), *The Riverside Shakespeare* (Boston: Houghton Mifflin, 1976). Journal titles are abbreviated in accordance with the *MLA International Bibliography*.

My thanks go to Professor Richard Dutton, University of Lancaster, for his encouragement during the early stages of this project, and to Nancy Mann, University of Colorado at Boulder, whose editing skills guided it to completion. Students at the University of Colorado led me "once more" into the text and its film adaptations, sharpening my appreciation for Kenneth Branagh's talents as an actor and director. And Clifton Hall's computer wizardry helped stiffen the sinews of the enterprise, proving again that "All things are ready, if our minds be so."

NOTE

1. Barrett Wendell, *William Shakespeare* (New York: C. Scribner's, 1894; 1909), p. 185.

ABBREVIATIONS OF CITED WORKS

CE	College English
CollL	College Literature
CompD	Comparative Drama
CritQ	Critical Quarterly
ELH	English Literary History
ESC	English Studies in Canada
FLQ	Literature/Film Quarterly
JEGP	Journal of English and Germanic Philology
JHI	Journal of the History of Ideas
MLQ	Modern Language Quarterly
MMLA	Midwest Modern Language Association
PMLA	Publications of the Modern Language Association
PQ	Philological Quarterly
RenD	Renaissance Drama
SEL	Studies in English Literature
SFNL	Shakespeare on Film Newsletter
ShS	Shakespeare Survey
ShStud	Shakespeare Studies
SP	Studies in Philology
SQ	Shakespeare Quarterly
UTQ	University of Toronto Quarterly
WS	Women's Studies
YES	Yearbook of English Studies

Henry V

1

TEXTUAL HISTORY

DIFFERENT TEXTS: QUARTO AND FOLIO

Readers who arrive at the play by way of *The Complete Works of Shakespeare*—perhaps the Peter Alexander edition or the *Riverside Shakespeare*—may not be aware of the vagaries of textual transmission during Shakespeare's time. There is no "true text" emanating directly from the author, as we have come to expect with the work of twentieth-century writers. Between Shakespeare's manuscript and its first emergence as a published work, all kinds of changes could occur: theatrical modification if it served as a prompt book in the playhouse (where the script became a collaborative venture between playwright and actors) and guesswork, omissions, or errors when it was being deciphered and set up by compositors in the Elizabethan printing house. Shakespeare's composition of the play, at least, can be dated fairly precisely. The tribute to the Earl of Essex in the Chorus to Act V ("the general of our gracious Empress") places *Henry V* in the spring or early summer of 1599. Essex left London in March 1599 to quash Tyrone's rebellion in Ireland and returned, the campaign in ruins, on September 28; the failure of his mission was clear from the summer on. Shakespeare's play was first performed in 1599, probably at the Curtain but possibly at the Globe Theatre. This new theater, home to Shakespeare's company, was in operation by September 21 of that year, when Thomas Platter reported seeing *Julius Caesar* staged there.[1]

By 1623, *Henry V* existed in two versions: the Folio (F) of 1623, a collection of thirty-six of Shakespeare's plays; and the Quarto (Q) of 1600. (The second and third Quartos, of 1602 and 1619, were reprints of this first one.) Heminge and Condell, the editors of the Folio, claimed that their edition of Shakespeare's plays was based not on "stolen and surreptitious copies" but on Shakespeare's own papers. The Quarto, however, appears to be one of these surreptitious copies—a so-called Bad Quarto, not licensed to be printed from the script belonging to Shakespeare's company, the Lord Chamberlain's Men, but a reconstruction of the play from memory. While the play as it appears in the Folio is called *The Life of Henry the Fift*, the title page of the Quarto reads:

THE
CRONICLE
History of Henry the fift,

With his battell fought at *Agin Court* in
France. Togither with *Auntient*
Pistoll.

As it hath bene sundry times playd by the Right honorable
the Lord Chamberlaine his servants.

Probably this text of the play was put together by the actors playing the characters of Exeter and Gower (whose lines correlate most closely with those in F), after they had performed in a shortened version of *Henry V* designed to tour the provinces in the summer. Because of the nature of the text—most likely written down from memory and not authorized by the acting company—there are errors and transpositions, though Q (*The Chronicle History*) has none of the interpolations from other contemporary plays that are often found in Bad Quartos. It is just over half as long as F. Some of the cuts in the text apparently reflect the smaller cast of such a touring company,[2] while others, as I shall discuss, may represent significant dramatic choices.[3] But although its 1993 editors urge readers to regard *The Chronicle History of Henry Fift* as an "independent cultural object," an "extremely good play in its own right,"[4] most of the standard editions of *The Complete Works of Shakespeare* follow the Folio, accepting that "Q is more frequently and more seriously corrupt than F."[5]

The Folio version, however, also presents some difficulties. Scholars agree that F is based on Shakespeare's "foul papers"— his manuscript draft of the play, sometimes written in illegible handwriting and presumably given to the Lord Chamberlain's Men before the play went into rehearsal. As is common with authorial drafts before their rough edges have been smoothed by performance in the theater, F shows signs of being provisional, especially in the naming of characters and the stage directions. Speech prefixes are sometimes vague. In the play's final scene, Henry is first referred to simply as "King" before the prefix changes to "England" to distinguish his speeches from those of the King of France. After Agincourt (V. i. 84), Pistol bafflingly refers to the death of Doll (perhaps a slip recalling Doll Tearsheet, who is prominent in *Henry IV, Part ii*) instead of Nell (Mistress Quickly, the Hostess, who is Pistol's wife in *Henry V*). Some of the minor characters are actually redundant, as when the King's brother, Clarence, is given an entrance in I. ii but does not speak and never reappears in the play. One example of imprecise stage directions occurs at the battle of Harfleur (III. i), where F reads "Enter the King, Exeter, Bedford and Gloucester. Alarum: Scaling Ladders at Harfleur." In theatrical terms this means that the King and his army come on stage carrying ladders to scale the walls (the back wall of the stage, which was the facade of the tiring house); in the manuscript, however, Shakespeare has quickly jotted down the characters and the prop without clarifying the relation between the two. Also the printer has clumsily positioned the Folio's act divisions, so that most of Act IV, for example, is indicated as Act III.

More serious than these minor imprecisions are places where the action appears to contradict itself. The Chorus to Act II announces that the scene will be "transported" to Southampton and from there to France. Instead, scenes i and iii take the audience to London (Eastcheap); Southampton does not materialize until the second scene and France not until the fourth. Similarly, the Chorus to Act V is confusing in terms of where the action should resume. Covering a considerable time span, the Chorus describes Henry's triumphant return to England and then his journey back to France for final peace negotiations; yet V. i, where Fluellen makes Pistol eat a leek, seems to take place immediately after the battle of Agincourt. Earlier scholars (such as J. H. Walter[6]) accounted for these discrepancies by theorizing that those parts of F that do not jibe with the Chorus's narration are later additions, interpolated after Shakespeare had decided to "kill off" his popular character Falstaff and replace him with Pistol. It is true that Shakespeare, in the Epilogue to *Henry IV, Part ii,* promises to bring Falstaff back in the next play,[7] but there is no evidence that he began writing *Henry V* to fulfil that promise and then decided to change course midstream. The reader can decide whether such an assumption is fair to the play as it stands. Does Falstaff's death (recounted in II. iii) strike us as a hasty theatrical expedient? More likely it represents a careful decision not to shift the focus away from Henry by bringing the witty knight to France and not to risk allowing Falstaff's cynicism to undercut the heroics at Agincourt.

One other significant inconsistency in the Folio is the role of the Dauphin. At the end of III. v, the French King tells his son that he must remain in Rouen ("Be patient, for you shall remain with us" [66]). Nevertheless, the Dauphin appears in the French camp at Agincourt in the nighttime scene where he praises his horse (III. vii). He appears here again in IV. ii and IV. v.

Because of this sign of authorial hesitation in the Folio—Shakespeare was apparently torn between following his historical sources (and therefore leaving the Dauphin behind) and adding the dramatic color of the prince's presence at Agincourt—some recent editors have followed the Quarto's reading here. Q substitutes the Duke of Bourbon for the Dauphin in III. vii (and then in the equivalent of IV. v), after first introducing him in II. iv and giving him a few lines in III. v. It is important to remember that the Quarto, although published years before the Folio, almost certainly represents a later stage of the text, reached *after* Shakespeare's original manuscript had been through the theatrical mill. It might therefore represent Shakespeare's second thoughts, approved by the author for the staged version of the play.[8] In the same way the streamlining of speaking parts, down from F's forty-five to thirty-seven or thirty-eight in Q, helps iron out some of the theatrical redundancies in the dramatis personae. (Clarence, for instance, who appears in F but has no speaking role, replaces Bedford in Q.) Gary Taylor, the first editor to adopt Bourbon instead of the Dauphin in III. vii and then in IV, goes so far as to praise some of Q's readings as "not only theatrically expedient, but genuine improvements of the play."[9] For instance, he retains Pistol's "Couple gorge," inserted by Q at the end of IV. vi, because this exhortation to cut a throat apparently converts the King's command, "Then every soldier kill his prisoners!" (IV. vi. 37), to stage action and also crystallizes a moment of choice for Pistol (if he kills his prisoner, Le Fer, he stands to lose the 200 crowns of ransom money).[10]

There has, then, been a significant shift in recent years so that editors of *Henry V* now occasionally privilege the Quarto over the Folio text. Whereas John Russell Brown confidently asserts in the Signet Classic edition (1965) that "obviously the Folio must be the basis of any modern text of *Henry V*,"[11] Gary Taylor, in his Oxford edition (1982), recommends a "reasoned evaluation of the relative merits of the alternatives."[12] He is willing to adopt the reading of Q on the few occasions when he judges it to be "clearly superior."[13]

Even if one agrees that some of Q's streamlinings constitute improvements in the theater, it is worth examining what the Folio provides in order to arrive at a broader interpretation of the play. How does its fuller version (as we surmise, Shakespeare's first thoughts or original intentions) complicate our response to the play and, in particular, our reactions to King Henry?

Several of the omissions in Q may have been made for practical reasons if, as Gary Taylor argues, the cast playing the abridged version of *Henry V* on tour was limited to eleven actors.[14] But the effect of other cuts is to present Henry and his campaign in a less ambiguous, more nationalistic light.

The most obvious omission from the Quarto is the Chorus that opens each Act. (In view of the topical reference to Essex's expedition to Ireland in the spring of 1599, the argument that the Chorus was added sometime after the first performances of the play is not convincing.[15]) Admittedly the action of the play is perfectly clear without the signposting of the Chorus. He is useful, though, in bridging the narrative gaps, especially the several years (after Act IV) between Agincourt and the Treaty of Troyes. More important, the Chorus sets a heroic, epic tone for the play, an impassioned voice that enables Henry to assume his "port of Mars" in the Prologue and become the "conqu'ring Caesar" by the beginning of Act V. In some ways, too, the Chorus, while never a simple authorial mouthpiece, serves as a surrogate for the playwright. He voices Shakespeare's continuing preoccupation, throughout his theatrical career, with whether the audience is prepared to show good will and collaborate with the performance—concerns also expressed in Puck's Epilogue to *A Midsummer Night's Dream* and Prospero's to *The Tempest*—and it is therefore surprising that the Chorus would be left out of a stage production.[16] The Prologue works hard, though deferentially ("pardon, gentles all"), to win the services of the audience. He apologizes at length for the physical limitations of the Elizabethan stage: the "wooden O" (the round or octagonal playhouse) with its "unworthy scaffold" (the raised stage projecting into the auditorium). The rhetorical question, "Can this cockpit hold / The vasty fields of France?" (Prologue, 11–12), places the onus squarely on the audience. They must supply what is missing in realism—vast armies and actual horses—through their imaginations, transforming the technical drawbacks of the theater by "piec[ing] out . . . imperfections" with their "thoughts." This urging of the audience to fill in the gaps is articulated most fully in the Prologue but reiterated in other speeches of the Chorus: "Work, work your thoughts, and therein see a siege" (III. 0. 25), "Now entertain conjecture of a time" (IV. 0. 1), and "You may imagine him upon Blackheath" (V. 0. 16). The energetic appeal helps convey the sheer "size" of the subject.[17] In fact it works so well that "for nearly four hundred years, audiences have been seeing what is described rather than what is staged."[18]

There is clearly some mock modesty in the Chorus. *Henry V* is not as dependent on the good graces of the audience as is, say, the Mechanicals' clumsy and unprofessional production of "Pyramus and Thisbe" in *A*

Midsummer Night's Dream. Shakespeare wisely avoids battle scenes in the play, knowing well how to create the tension and heroics of a war campaign without resorting to "four or five most vile and ragged foils" (IV. 0. 50). The inspiring poetry, the sheer word power, is all-important; and the play succeeds not in spite of but partly because of the technical limitations imposed on the dramatist.[19] (Of course this has not prevented *Henry V* from translating magnificently into the resourceful, realistic medium of the film.) Through his words the Chorus not only rallies the audience but canvasses that other preoccupation of the dramatist in writing a history play: how "true things" can be created through "mock'ries" (IV. 0. 53) or a valid imitation of historical reality can be presented through stage artifice and the tawdry trappings of the Elizabethan theater.

Although the Chorus, chauvinistic in Henry's cause, presents the war mission in a heroic light, the play's larger action in some ways deflects or contradicts this idealized picture. Are the contradictions merely another aspect of the roughness of the Folio, or do they represent a subtlety lost in the touring version? Whether intentionally so or not, the Chorus is certainly misleading at times.[20] At the beginning of Act II he tells us that "all the youth of England are on fire" and "honor's thought / Reigns solely in the breast of every man"; yet straightaway we travel to Eastcheap, where the seedy characters Nym, Bardolph, and Pistol are planning to join the war so that "profits will accrue" (II. i. 115). The same discrepancy occurs in Act III at Harfleur, between the Chorus's enthusiastic description of the noble army ("culled and choice-drawn cavaliers") and the sight of the Eastcheap crew slinking away from the breach (scene ii). Chorus's Act IV eulogy of Henry cheering up his troops on the eve of Agincourt ("Thawing cold fear" with his "liberal eye") is also belied by the King's pessimistic comparison of the army to "men wracked upon a sand" (IV. i. 99).

In his own person the Chorus supports the war cause unequivocally and reveres Henry as the "mirror of all Christian kings" (II. 0. 6) throughout all five acts. Close to the King in both attitude and rhetorical intent, since he works on the audience's emotions in the same way that Henry rallies his troops,[21] the Chorus invites what Lawrence Danson calls "sympathetic participation"[22] with the King's cause. But there remains the ironic counterpoint, the clash between the picture and its frame—those parts of the action that present the war mission less favorably than the Chorus does. Is this deliberate subversion, or are both perspectives on Henry valid? Rather than dismissing the Chorus as a naive cheerleader, the audience may decide to incorporate his viewpoint and accept that there are "two sets of lenses"[23] in the play that add to its complexity. We should notice, too, that even the

Chorus is unable to sustain the ambience of heroic glory by the end of Act V. Indeed the Epilogue almost deconstructs the myth of Henry. By reminding the audience of the historical future—how England "lost" France and drifted into civil war during the reign of Henry VI—the Chorus casts a shadow over Henry's fabulous achievements, turning him, like his father, into one of "time's subjects" (*Henry IV, Part ii*, I. iii. 110). In dropping the Chorus, the Quarto text abandons an important guide and mediator; it may also forfeit an intriguing perspective on the whole play.

I. i of the Folio is also missing from the Quarto (together with its echo in I. ii. 132–33). This is the sequence where Canterbury and Ely discuss Henry's proposed bill, which would disadvantage the clergy, and plan to deflect it by offering to help finance his military campaign against France. On one level the scene *is* redundant in terms of plot. Henry's resolve to wage war appears to be contingent not on the bishops' offer of money—a "mighty sum" from the "spirituality" (I. ii. 132–33)—but rather on a convincing explanation of why the Salic law should not bar his claim to France. But this private opening before the public council provides a fuller context for Henry's decision to go to war by allowing the audience to see the element of manipulation and policy—in men of God, no less!—going on behind the scenes. It may also alter and complicate our perceptions of Henry, if we see him either as the partial dupe of the bishops (who have ulterior motives for wanting him to go to war) or as a shrewd politician prepared to make a secret deal with them and therefore masquerading throughout the debate in I. ii. Without the opening scene Henry probably impresses us as a man who listens carefully, even objectively, to the Salic law speech, without being unduly pressured by the clergy's other agenda. In losing the opening scene we also skip Canterbury's awestruck eulogy of the King's attributes—an important transition from the *Henry IV* plays in its reassurance that Henry's "reformation," his renouncing of the wild Prince Hal character, is complete.

III. i, the breach scene at Harfleur, was probably cut from the Quarto for practical reasons. (In addition to casting difficulties, the touring company might not have had access to the kind of scaling ladders used on the London stage.) The sequence in III. ii where the Irish, Welsh, and Scottish captains converse may have been left out because the presentation of the Scottish Captain Jamy was deemed politically tactless, a possible affront to James VI of Scotland, who was only a few years away from becoming King of England. Most of IV. ii, the boasting of the French, is cut in the interests of theatrical streamlining. But another group of cuts—a few lines in Act II, and parts of III. iii, IV. i, and V. ii—narrows the focus of the play somewhat by eliminating ironic qualifications of Henry's role and presenting him in a more straightforwardly favorable light. II. i, set in Eastcheap, leaves out the Hostess's words "the king has kill'd his heart" (91)—a frank assessment of how Henry's rejection of his old comrade has triggered Falstaff's final illness. Nym's critical comment on how the King "passes some humors, and careers" (129) is also cut. The Quarto excludes Cambridge's hint, in the Southampton scene, that he has motives more pressing than the bribe of French gold for wanting to dethrone Henry (II. ii. 155–60). At Harfleur, Henry's threats of what will happen if the Governor refuses to surrender the town—a sustained projection of brutal rape and carnage (III. iii. 11–41) that may reflect badly on Henry—have all disappeared. Burgundy's long anti-war description of the "unnatural" devastation of "fertile France" (V. ii. 34–62) is likewise missing from the Quarto.

The changes in IV. i, where the disguised King talks to his soldiers before Agincourt, also present a more ideal, less complicated portrait of Henry.[24] The sequence in the Quarto cuts the Folio's opening with Sir Thomas Erpingham along with Henry's explanation, "I and my bosom must debate awhile," which makes it clear that he goes into disguise in order to meditate alone. In Q he apparently uses a mask in order to mix with his men. Generally, the tone of the scene is lighter; Q replaces the somber image of the soldiers as "men wracked upon a sand" with Henry's "what cheare?" and "the king is frolike," and omits the politically sensitive passage where Williams responds to Henry's defense of his cause as "just" and his quarrel "honorable" with the blunt "That's more than we know" (131). Williams' later questioning of how men of war can "charitably dispose of anything when blood is their argument" is also missing.

The most significant cut is Henry's long soliloquy "Upon the king!" (235–89), where he meditates on "thrice-gorgeous ceremony" as nothing more than a "proud dream." Some readers and audience members find that Henry's questioning of his public role, his recognition of its hollowness and its cost in personal contentment, humanizes him. But if the Quarto is promoting the image of the King as a ruler who cares deeply for his subjects the cut makes sense, for some of the references in the speech surely suggest the opposite. Henry's almost bitter envy of the "fool, whose sense no more can feel / But his own wringing" and the "wretched slave" who goes to sleep with "body filled, and vacant mind" widens the gap between king and subject. Annabel Patterson finds F's soliloquy patently anti-populist—a "self-justifying complaint that the common people are mindlessly irrespon-sible." She concludes that the Quarto of 1600 represents a "tactical retreat" from the Folio's "complex historiography that might have been misunder-stood" in the context of the Essex crisis; instead Q provides "an *almost* unproblematic version of a highly popular monarch."[25] Whether we accept her theory—that the Quarto text, altogether less ambiguous in its support for the monarchy, was tacitly appproved by Shakespeare—it is important to be aware of the cuts and to consider in what ways the differences between the Folio and Quarto texts can enhance our understanding of *Henry V.*

DIFFERENT EDITIONS

Readers who are studying *Henry V* in depth will want to go beyond *The Complete Works of Shakespeare* and consult an edition of the play that offers a fuller introduction and critical apparatus. There are several possibilities, all of which are available in paperback. J. H. Walter's *Henry V* in *The New Arden Shakespeare* (1954) represents a solid piece of editing, with extensive discussion of Shakespeare's sources. But most critics now disagree with Walter's theory that the play was revised to exclude Falstaff, and the one-sided defense of Henry as an "ideal king" and "epic hero" will also strike many readers as dated. This text has recently been superseded by the *Third Arden*, edited by T. W. Craik (1995). Craik, too, views Henry favorably, but bases his interpretation on a "close study of the whole play" and its impact in the theater rather than on a detailed analysis of Shakespeare's sources and other Renaissance texts. The *Signet Shakespeare*'s *The Life of Henry V*, edited by John Russell Brown (1965; updated 1988), relies mainly on the Folio text, as does the Arden edition. It includes useful critical commentary and also reprints, with modernized spelling, all the relevant excerpts from Shakespeare's most important source, Holinshed's *Chronicles* (1587). The *New Penguin Shakespeare Henry V*, edited by A. R. Humphreys (1968), is another very accessible edition (pocket-sized and inexpensive), with textual commentary at the end. Its comprehensive and perceptive critical introduction considers work on the play up to 1968. Humphreys also acknowledges a special editing debt to the "dramatic, linguistic, and historical scholarship" of John Dover Wilson's original *New Cambridge* edition (1947).

A ground-breaking version of *Henry V* appears in *The Oxford Shakespeare*, edited by Gary Taylor (1982). It has a good introduction, as well as detailed textual notes and appendixes. The edition is innovative in privileging the Quarto over the Folio for a few sequences—in particular, for its version of III. vii, as well as IV. v, where Bourbon replaces the Dauphin. Even more up-to-date and comprehensive is *The New Cambridge Shakespeare*'s *King Henry V*, edited by Andrew Gurr (1992). Gurr's substantial introduction is informative and scholarly, interspersed with illustrations and photographs, and it covers some recent performances of the play, including Kenneth Branagh's film production. Like Taylor's edition, this one follows the Quarto in substituting Bourbon for the Dauphin at Agincourt. One problem in checking line references against older texts is that Gurr divides Act III into eight scenes instead of the usual seven; he begins a new scene (III. iii) at the reentrance of Fluellen with Gower after the soliloquy of the Boy (III. ii. 28–55 in most editions). Taylor also breaks that scene into two but joins Henry's threat to the Governor of Harfleur—III. iii in older editions—to his new third scene, and thus still ends up with the usual total of seven scenes in the third act. The entire Quarto version is available as *The Cronicle History of Henry the Fift*, edited and introduced by Graham Holderness and Bryan Loughrey (1993), and a photographic facsimile of the First Quarto is included in T. W. Craik's Arden edition of *King Henry V* (1995).

NOTES

1. E. K. Chambers, *The Elizabethan Stage (Oxford: Clarendon Press, 1923), vol. 2, p. 365.*

2. See Gary Taylor, "We Happy Few: The 1600 Abridgement," in Stanley Wells and Gary Taylor, *Modernizing Shakespeare's Spelling* and *Three Studies in the Text of* Henry V (Oxford: Clarendon Press, 1979), pp. 72–111.

3. Kathleen O. Irace discusses this in *Reforming the "Bad" Quartos* (Newark: University of Delaware Press, 1994). She supports the conclusion that the Quarto of *Henry V* was a memorial reconstruction rather than an adaptation by Shakespeare, but finds that it makes intelligent simplifications in plot structure, characterization, and staging.

4. Edited and introduced by Graham Holderness and Bryan Loughrey (Lanham, Md.: Barnes and Noble, 1993), pp. 13, 22. The editors consider that this version of the play, in line with popular historical drama, deliberately accentuates the comic mode (pp. 24–27).

5. Gary Taylor (ed.), *Henry V* (Oxford: Oxford University Press, 1982), p. 21.

6. J. H. Walter (ed.), *Henry V, The Arden Shakespeare* (London: Methuen, 1954), pp. xxxviii, xlv.

7. There is also the ambiguity of whether the lines "where (for anything I know) Falstaff shall die of a sweat" (*Henry IV, Part ii*, Epilogue, 29–30) refer to Falstaff's dying in France or during the action of the play.

8. See Andrew Gurr (ed.), *Henry V* (Cambridge: Cambridge University Press, 1992), p. 60. In contrast, T. W. Craik (ed.), *King Henry V, The Arden Shakespeare* (London and New York: Routledge, 1995), argues that the Folio is both "the version written by Shakespeare" and the version "performed in the playhouse" (pp. xix, 30–32).

9. "Corruption and Authority in the Bad Quarto," in *Three Studies*, pp. 124–62, 156.

10. Taylor (ed.), *Henry V*, p. 65.

11. (New York and Toronto: The New American Library, 1965; 1988), p. 168.

12. *Henry V* (ed.), p. 24.

13. "Corruption and Authority in the Bad Quarto," p. 162.

14. "We Happy Few," pp. 73–74.

15. This argument was made by W. D. Smith, "The *Henry V* Choruses in the First Folio," *JEGP*, 53 (1954), 38–57. He interprets the allusion to the "general" as referring to Lord Mountjoy (who succeeded Essex). See also G. P. Jones, "*Henry V*: The Chorus and the Audience," *ShS*, 31 (1978), 93–104, who thinks that the choruses may have been added for a performance of the play at the Royal Cockpit Theatre at the court of King James (in 1605).

16. Taylor, "We Happy Few," pp. 77–80, concludes that the Chorus was left out for casting reasons (an actor could not double that role with another).

17. Michael Goldman emphasizes this theatrical effect in *Shakespeare and the Energies of Drama* (Princeton: Princeton University Press, 1972), p. 59.

18. Sharon Tyler, " 'Minding True Things': The Chorus, the Audience, and *Henry V*," in James Redmond (ed.), *The Theatrical Space*, Themes in Drama 9 (Cambridge: Cambridge University Press, 1987), pp. 69–79, 76.

19. Robert Ornstein makes this point in *A Kingdom for a Stage: The Achievement of Shakespeare's History Plays* (Cambridge, Mass.: Harvard University Press, 1972), p. 176. Lawrence Danson, "*Henry V*: King, Chorus, and Critics," *SQ*, 34 (1983), 27–43, also comments, "If the play works, the ostensible apologies only underscore the artistic triumph of Shakespeare's theatre of poor means: the fewer means, the greater share of honor" (28).

20. Gurr, *Henry V* (ed.), notes how the Chorus often "whips up enthusiasm for his *mis*representation of what follows" (7). See also Anthony Hammond, " 'It Must Be Your Imagination Then': The Prologue and the Plural Text in *Henry V* and Elsewhere," in John W. Mahon and Thomas A. Pendleton (eds.), *Fanned and Winnowed Opinions* (London and New York: Methuen, 1987), pp. 133–50; and Anthony Brennan, " 'That Within Which Passes Show: The Function of the Chorus in *Henry V*," *PQ*, 58 (1979), 40–52. Gunter Walsh, "*Henry V* as Working-House of Ideology," *ShS*, 40 (1988), 63–68, goes further in arguing that the "unreliable" Chorus helps expose official ideology as "an illusion effectively used as an instrument of power" (67–68).

21. Goldman points out that, "like Henry, the Chorus is a man whose job is to rouse his hearers to unusual effort" (*Shakespeare and the Energies of Drama*, p. 59); Gurr also notes that Henry and the Chorus use similarly elevated diction, comparing Henry's words "portage" and "jutty" with the Chorus's "sternage" and "abutting" (*Henry V* [ed.], p. 15).

22. "*Henry V*: King, Chorus, and Critics," p. 38. In "The Myth Structure and Rituality of *Henry V*," *YES*, 23 (1993), 254–69, Brownell Salomon argues that the

Chorus draws the audience into a "collective ceremony that ritualizes . . . Henry the Fifth as the cynosure of the nation's mythic past" (268).

23. Edward I. Berry, " 'True Things' and 'Mockeries': Epic and History in *Henry V*," *JEGP*, 78 (1979), 1–16, 8. Berry analyzes how "the Chorus conceives of the play's world as epic; the world we perceive on stage is most often realistic, comic, or burlesque." Richard Lanham, *Motives of Eloquence* (New Haven and London: Yale University Press, 1976), also finds that the Chorus is a "spokesman for the serious political myth" in *Henry V* (197).

24. Taylor gives a detailed analysis of this scene in "We Happy Few," pp. 87–91.

25. "Back by Popular Demand: The Two Versions of *Henry V*," in *Shakespeare and the Popular Voice* (Cambridge, Mass.: B. Blackwell, 1990), pp. 71–92, 91, 77, 81.

2

CONTEXTS AND SOURCES

HISTORICAL CONTEXT

Henry V was composed in 1599, eleven years after the defeat of the Spanish Armada. The year 1588, that *annus mirabilis*, seems in retrospect to have been a catalyst for the Elizabethan theater, fueling the patriotic impulse celebrated in the genre of the history play.[1] By the early 1590s, Shakespeare had begun to write his *Henry VI* plays, which, together with *Richard III* (1593), compose his first tetralogy. Whether Shakespeare, at that time a novice playwright not yet thirty, already envisaged a grand cycle of English history plays—with a second tetralogy (*Richard II, Henry IV, Parts i* and *ii*, and *Henry V*) culminating in the glorious reign of the warrior king—is a moot point. But by 1598 he had finished the popular *Henry IV* plays and was ready to write the sequel, the last of his historical cycle. The time was ripe for a nationalistic play. At the turn of the century England was still at peace internally, although this was hardly a golden age.[2] There were economic crises (rising inflation as well as a series of disastrous crop failures in the 1590s) and anxiety over when the aging Queen would name her successor. Moreover the country was still engaged in military action abroad, sending supplies to help the Protestants in the Low Countries and warding off the continued threat of war with Spain. In 1599 England's costly war with Ireland was intensifying, and in early spring Essex was sent with an army of 16,000 foot soldiers and 1,300 cavalry to crush Tyrone's rebellion. The mood of the Chorus to Act V is upbeat, reflecting hope for an English victory in Ireland similar to the one that Henry V enjoyed in France in the fifteenth century. The Chorus imagines

> As, by a lower but by loving likelihood,
> Were now the general of our gracious Empress
> (As in good time he may) from Ireland coming,
> Bringing rebellion broached on his sword,
> How many would the peaceful city quit
> To welcome him! (29–34)

This explicit reference to a contemporary figure is highly unusual in Shakespeare. The parallel established between Essex and the conquering Henry compliments the popular military leader while managing to subordinate Essex's glory to that of the "gracious Empress" Elizabeth I; but by September 1599, when the Irish campaign was in ruins, the adulation of Essex would have become a distinct embarrassment.

This, then, is the historical context—an England relatively united in peace under Queen Elizabeth I for forty years, but still needing to subdue Ireland—within which Shakespeare's *Henry V* takes form. As Philip Edwards points out, *Henry V* reflects England's "expansionist policy"[3] under a strong leader. Like Elizabeth, though in more militaristic fashion, Henry needs to subjugate foreign territory (France) and unify his own baronial society at the same time. Partly because it celebrates a powerful king, but also because of its allusions to Henry IV's usurpation and to the disastrous civil war during the reign of Henry VI, the play implicitly reflects Elizabethan England's desire for a peaceful succession of the monarchy. The Tudor line was destined to end with the aging Queen, but in 1599 the Stuart King James VI of Scotland had not been officially named as her successor. *Henry V* gestures toward a firmly centralized government that might incorporate the Celtic fringe—the Irish (represented by Macmorris) and the Scots (Jamy), as well as the somewhat more tractable Welsh (Fluellen).[4]

CULTURAL CONTEXTS

While we can point to certain events in history—most notably the Essex expedition to Ireland in 1599—and correlate them with *Henry V*, it is less easy to define the cultural contexts of the play precisely. Rather than envisaging the play as a piece of performed literature that passively mirrors the cultural background of the time, it is more helpful, as new historicists and cultural materialists have stressed, to examine the play as part of that culture: a discourse that participates fully in the shifting ideology, the cultural beliefs and political practices, of the time. The principle outlined by the cultural materialist Jonathan Dollimore can serve as a guide: "What the plays signify, how they signify, depends on the cultural field in which they are situated";[5] and Elizabethan culture is grounded in material forces, economic as well as political. It is clear that the material conditions under which Shakespeare's plays were performed[6]—the fact that they were staged in a commercial theater by a group of players who also enjoyed aristocratic and royal patronage—must have affected the representation of kingship in *Henry V*. Did such conditions reinforce the politics of power (the Elizabethan status quo, with authority vested in an absolute monarch), or was there some scope, within the public playhouse, to contest that dominant image?

With its bold pageantry and the skillful performances of Henry as he builds his kingly image, *Henry V* is a particularly theatrical play. New historicist critics have found a vital link between this strongly theatrical presentation of the king as a character in the public playhouse and the British monarch's sense of being on display—revealed, for instance, in Queen Elizabeth's 1586 comment to a deputation of the Lords and Commons that "We princes are set on stages in the sight and view of all the world."[7] Stephen Greenblatt points out that because the Queen had no standing army or extensive police force to help her maintain authority, her power was "constituted in theatrical celebrations of royal glory."[8] At the Elizabethan theater, history plays might likewise be produced as an "expression of Renaissance power,"[9] helping legitimate the social order by subordinating any hints of subversiveness, such as the anti-heroic activities of the Eastcheap crew or Williams' questioning of the war, to the dominant image of authority. This appears to have worked so well that Thomas Nashe, defending the players from Puritan attacks in 1592, maintains that "no play they have encourageth any man to tumults or rebellion"; instead, the drama offers both a "rare exercise of virtue" and a stimulus to patriotic emotions.[10] He points out how the warrior Talbot, for example, is revivified in *Henry VI* as the "terror of the French."[11] Had Nashe been writing eight years later, he might well have used Shakespeare's Henry V as an even more inspiring example.

Queen Elizabeth herself patronized and protected the professional drama. Apparently her Privy Council did not view the work of the playwrights, once it had been licensed by the Master of the Revels and any overt political references removed, as inimical to the status quo. In 1597, two years before *Henry V* was produced and when the *Henry IV* plays were popular, the Lord Mayor and aldermen of London petitioned the Privy Council for the "suppressinge of . . . Stage playes."[12] But the order was never enforced.

In their petition the City Fathers, obviously much more hostile to the drama than the court was, emphasized the "corrupting" effect of plays—those aspects that singularly fail to celebrate or consolidate cultural norms. They pointed out that not only did the drama represent "lewd and vngodly practices" and the "corruption of manners" (making its content potentially subversive) but the playhouses attracted "vagrant persons" and "Maisterles men," those dangerous, marginalized elements of society that threatened the stability of the Elizabethan Establishment.[13] The actors, too, were regarded as violators of social decorum. As recently as 1572, before they gained some respectability by forming troupes under aristocratic patronage, an Act of Parliament put players in the same category as rogues, vagabonds, and sturdy beggars. Stephen Gosson, writing in 1582 as a strong opponent of the theater, is horrified that on stage a "meane person"—a player—can "take vpon him the title of a Prince with counterfeit porte, and traine."[14] Such transgression, or crossing over from one identity to another, results in "proportion . . . so broken, vnitie dissolved, harmony confounded, that the whole body must be dismembred and the prince or the heade cannot chuse but sicken."[15] This ability of the actor to cross class boundaries, or to impersonate characters with very different moral codes—the "Proteus"-like[16] actor Richard Burbage was equally adept at playing the villainous Richard III as the heroic Henry V— might prove socially and morally subversive. And the very technique of the actor, by drawing attention to the theatrical aspects of character, risked destabilizing the image of royalty itself.

Queen Elizabeth, despite her endorsement of the theater, was keenly aware that plays could be used for seditious purposes, especially if they were performed away from the public playhouse. Shortly before the Essex rebellion, some of the Earl's followers paid the Lord Chamberlain's Men 40 shillings to put on their old play *Richard II*. It was performed on the afternoon of February 7, 1601. The Queen did not fail to register the parallel between herself, the anointed monarch, and King Richard, deposed by Bolingbroke (who had obvious links with Essex[17]). A few months later, after Essex had been executed, she remarked to the antiquary Lambarde, "I am Richard II. Know ye not that?", complaining that the tragedy of *Richard II* had been played "forty times in open streets and houses"[18] just before the Essex uprising. Street performance, in the Queen's eyes, clearly posed a threat to social order. Once drama left the socially sanctioned playhouse, its subversive energy could proliferate.

Critics still debate how transgressive, or genuinely challenging to the dominant culture, a play could be if it stayed within the boundaries of the public theater. Greenblatt stresses the "conventional containment of the playhouse where audiences are kept at a safe distance both from the action on stage and from the world beyond the walls."[19] He postulates that the

Elizabethan playgoers, as when they viewed the real monarch, were both "powerfully engaged" by the spectacle—the "visible presence" of power—and "held at a certain respectful distance from it."[20] Certainly this seems corroborated by Thomas Nashe's praise for the Elizabethan history plays. But Steven Mullaney argues that because the London playhouse was built outside the limits of the city proper, in the Liberties of London, it constituted a liminal area or marginal zone where social inversions (license) might be creatively explored. Thus Prince Hal, in the *Henry IV* plays, experiments with the marginal "details of popular culture"[21] in Eastcheap, although he ends up appropriating them as part of his kingly power; in this case, subversion is finally contained. Louis A. Montrose also finds that Elizabethan drama, with its "complex" treatment of "everyday circumstances," offers some genuine scope for challenging the dominant ideology of "unchanging order and absolute obedience." Shakespeare's theater, in short, is "a paradoxical phenomenon, at once on the margins and at the center of the Elizabethan world."[22]

Where does this leave *Henry V*? Critics from the 1980s have interpreted it either as ideologically conservative or as a case of managed cultural transgression, alert to political conflicts and ambiguities within a changing society but never going too far in pursuing them. After carefully examining the conditions under which the play was produced, Annabel Patterson posits an "idealized . . . displaced portrait" of Queen Elizabeth in the truncated Quarto version, while the Folio more daringly attempts (still within the ideal image of the nation-state) to mediate the struggle for popular power between Elizabeth and Essex.[23] Graham Holderness is the one critic who emphasizes how the foregrounded medium of theater in *Henry V*—specifically the blurring of the distinction between the king and the actor—may have destabilized the sacred image of royalty.[24] On the opposite side of the argument, Greenblatt makes the point, as relevant in modern cultural contexts as in the Globe, that on stage the figure of the king is overridingly charismatic, encouraging assent from the audience, so that "it is not at all clear that *Henry V* can be successfully performed as subversive."[25] Despite its potential subversiveness, then, it is unlikely that *Henry V* radically questions the dominant culture of the Elizabethan era; rather, the play tends to reinforce or consolidate belief in social order based on the power of the monarch.

SOURCES AND ANALOGUES

Hunting for Shakespeare's sources can be a fascinating pursuit in itself. For a critical analysis of *Henry V*, source study is most helpful in uncovering what information was available to the playwright and how he selected and reshaped that material to create his play. As a playwright, Shakespeare is obviously less concerned with strict historical accuracy than with telescoping or expanding historical incidents to build dramatic tension and then resolve it within a "two hours' traffic" on the stage. Thus he follows the English *Chronicles*—mainly Raphael Holinshed (1587) but also Edward Hall (1548)—closely but not slavishly. The difference between the historian and the poet, according to Sir Philip Sidney, is that whereas the historian is bound by "the particular truth of things," the poet explores universals through concrete instances that are not strictly tied to fact.[26] Shakespeare bears this out; often the details that he excludes, or the ones he invents, tell us more about his general conception of the reign of Henry V than those he adopts from his sources.

Every historian interprets the story of events with certain presuppositions, and in the case of Hall and Holinshed this takes the form of a strong bias in favor of Henry V and his country; the chroniclers view Henry as a great king, a "pattern of princehood" and a "mirror of magnificence."[27] Apparently Shakespeare did not have access to (or did not choose to consult) the French chroniclers, who presented Henry as an aggressor who ravaged their country—a verdict renewed in Desmond Seward's 1985 comment that Henry's "conquest of France was as much about loot as dynastic succession, accompanied by more slaughter, arson and rape."[28]

Shakespeare's play is actually part of a tradition of plays about Henry V. On May 14, 1594, one called *The Famous Victories of Henry Fifth* was entered in the Stationer's Register; the edition that has survived is dated 1598. The entry in the Register tells us that the play was acted by the Queen's Majesty's Players, but other plays on *Henry V*, or versions of this one, were apparently circulating in the 1590s. Henslowe's diary records performances of a "new" play, "harey the V," performed by the Admiral's Men in 1595-96, while Thomas Nashe refers in *Pierce Penniless* (1592) to the excitement of seeing Henry impersonated on stage, forcing the French King and the Dauphin to "swear fealty."[29] The anonymous *Famous Victories*, like the Quarto of Shakespeare's *Henry V*, is probably an abridged version constructed from memory.[30] The truncated text is less than half as long as Shakespeare's play, although it covers a wider span of history, from the end of the reign of Henry IV (who dies in the middle of the play, in the ninth scene out of a total of twenty) to the betrothal of Henry V to Princess Katherine. As a prosaic version of the *Chronicles*, this play offers clarity as well as brevity. Students grappling with the Archbishop's lengthy, involved speech on the Salic law (*Henry V*, I. ii. 33–95) may well prefer *The Famous*

Victories' succinct explanation (despite one tautology and a skipped generation!): "Your right to the French throne of France came by your great grandmother Isabel" (ix. 68–69).

The Famous Victories is a comedy as much as a history play; it adds low-life characters—in particular Derick, a "poor carrier"—to give spice to the action. Shakespeare, too, uses sequences of comedy to counterbalance the more serious ones. The parting of John Cobbler from his wife, as John sets off to war with the Captain (*Famous Victories*, scene x), is mirrored in Pistol's farewell to the Hostess in *Henry V*, II. iii, while Derick's farcical capture of a Frenchman (who then manages to escape [scene xvii]) finds a partial parallel in Pistol's taking Monsieur le Fer prisoner at Agincourt (*Henry V*, IV. iv). Shakespeare's version of the wooing scene also picks up the comic heartiness of the earlier play. There are noticeable verbal parallels:

King of England	Tush Kate! but tell me in plain terms, canst thou love the king of England? (*Famous Victories*, xviii. 62–63)
King Henry	But, Kate, dost thou understand thus much English? Canst thou love me? (*Henry V*, V. ii. 200–201)
Katherine	How should I love thee, which is my father's enemy? (*Famous Victories*, xx. 57–58)
Katherine	Is it possible dat I sould love de ennemie of France? (*Henry V*, V. ii. 174–75)

Although the Dauphin speaks no words in *The Famous Victories*, the drama gives special prominence to his insulting gift of tennis balls. In scene ix the Archbishop of Bruges delivers a "tun of tennis balls" from the Dauphin, explaining to Henry that "My lord, hearing of your wildness before your father's death, sent you this" (144–45). The King does not forget the insult. At Agincourt he tells the herald that he hoped the Dauphin would be there to complete the tennis match ("I have brought tennis balls for him" [xii. 36]), and in the play's final scene the silent Dauphin is made to kiss Henry's sword. In the first act of *Henry V* Shakespeare follows this source rather than Holinshed, to connect the tense moment of Henry's receiving the present with his decision to invade France.[31] The King's ironic rejoinder in *The Famous Victories*, "My lord Prince Dolphin is very pleasant with me," is echoed in Shakespeare's version of Henry's first words after receiving the tennis balls: "We are glad the Dauphin is so pleasant with us" (I. ii. 259). But whereas the earlier play makes the gift the King's immediate incentive to act—he calls out, "Now, my lords, to arms, to arms!"—Shakespeare shows Henry already resolved to go to war, to "bend" or "break"

France, *before* the Dauphin's ambassadors bring in the tennis balls. In this way the playwright exploits Henry's controlled anger at the insult, his impassioned rhetoric on how much bloodshed the Dauphin's "mock" will produce, as a high point in the scene, but without making his decision to go to war with France rest on something as trivial as revenge for the French Prince's arrogant gesture.

Shakespeare's play, then, parallels *The Famous Victories of Henry Fifth* in developing comic sequences, the wooing episode, and the Dauphin's gift of tennis balls. His main source for the history of Henry's reign is Holinshed's *Chronicles of England, Scotland, and Ireland* (1587), which, in turn, closely follows Hall's *The Union of the Two Noble and Illustre Famelies of Lancastre and York* (1548).[32] Shakespeare appears to have consulted Hall's *Union* and used details from it, rather than from Holinshed, for the conversation between the King and his nobles in I. ii. 100–83, where they urge Henry to follow the example of his ancestors and conquer France, and for the Constable's disparaging remarks about the English army (IV. ii. 16–37).[33] Shakespeare's debt to Holinshed, though, is stronger. He uses just over a quarter of Holinshed's account—from Henry's decision to go to war to the triumph of Agincourt—for the main action of his play. We can learn more about Shakespeare's play by analyzing what he imports wholesale from this source, what he uses but modifies considerably, and what he decides to leave out.

Canterbury's lengthy exposition on the Salic law—that potential stumbling block for twentieth-century readers, audiences, and actors—is the first obvious debt to Holinshed. The speech is a virtual paraphrase of the *Chronicles*. The painstaking details that "Salique land" is in Germany, between the rivers of Elbe and Sala, and that King Pepin, Hugh Capet, and King Lewis claimed their titles through the female are all taken from this source. Even the (presumably) ironic line when the Archbishop brings his peroration to a close, "So that, as clear as is the summer's sun" (I. ii. 86), derives from Holinshed's "so that more clear than the sun. . . ."[34] Why did Shakespeare follow Holinshed so closely here? The explanation about the Salic law was certainly more topical, and of greater interest to the Elizabethans, than it is now. In 1579, when Elizabeth I was toying with the idea of marrying the French Duke of Alençon, John Stubbes probed the implications of the Salic law in his pamphlet *Gaping Gulf*.[35] Sharply critical of the proposed marriage, Stubbes pointed out that because of Salic law Elizabeth could claim no power in France; England was more likely to be subject to a Catholic prince if the Queen married a Frenchman. (As punishment for his published insult to the queen, Stubbes had his right hand cut off.) By

1599, when *Henry V* was first performed, the debate over this law was more relevant to James VI of Scotland, the probable heir to the English throne. Because his claim to the throne came through his mother, Mary Queen of Scots (her great-grandfather, also Elizabeth I's grandfather, was the Tudor progenitor Henry VII), the speech refuting the Salic law could be construed as favorable to him. If Henry V had a legitimate claim to France, then James' title to England was also valid.[36] Clearly the Elizabethans were more concerned with the niceties of inheritance—in particular, the legitimacy of a monarch—than we are; Shakespeare did not turn Holinshed into blank verse in order to bore his audience or to make Canterbury look dreary or ridiculous. (The caricature version, supplemented by the stage business of Canterbury shuffling papers and losing the thread of what he wants to say, is supplied by Laurence Olivier's film production of the play.)

Another passage that Shakespeare lifts from Holinshed details the number and names of those killed at Agincourt. Part of the chronicler's full account reads:

> There were slain in all of the French part to the number of ten thousand
> men, whereof were princes and noblemen bearing banners one hundred
> twenty and six. . . . Of Englishmen, there died at this battle, Edward
> Duke of York, the Earl of Suffolk, Sir Richard Ketly and Davy Gam,
> Esquire, and of all other not above five and twenty persons. . . .[37]

In the play Henry reads the list of prominent Frenchmen followed by "Edward the Duke of York, the Earl of Suffolk, / Sir Richard Ketly, Davy Gam, esquire" (IV. viii. 105-6). This direct borrowing seems less a passion for list-making, or a rising to the challenge of making poetry out of proper names, than Shakespeare's wish to have Henry acknowledge the bare facts in order to underline the modesty and piety of his subsequent disclaimer: "Take it, God, / For it is none but thine!" (113–14). In Holinshed, Henry's thanking God for the victory is placed well before the account of who has died in battle, and no direct connection is made between the two.

While all the modifications of Holinshed in Shakespeare's play are too numerous to analyze, a few do stand out as significant choices. As noted above, Shakespeare repositions the Dauphin's gift of tennis balls so that it becomes the dramatic finale of the council scene (I. ii); in Holinshed the incident occurs at the beginning of Henry's reign (Lent 1513). Before giving the Archbishop's speech on the Salic law, Holinshed makes explicit what Shakespeare leaves ambiguous: that the Archbishop's "pithy oration" is calculated to win Henry to the cause of war. In the *Chronicles* the clergy, nervous because the proposed bill would deprive them of property and finances, "thought best to try if they might move the King's mood with some sharp invention."[38] Hence the long speech to prove the irrelevance of the Salic law. We know from the Folio text of *Henry V* that the bishops have a hidden agenda, but it is impossible, in Shakespeare's play, to assess how far Canterbury's speech is a sincere exposition, how far a piece of special pleading.

In Act III Shakespeare also modifies Holinshed's account of the siege of Harfleur. Holinshed reports that the town was sacked: "The soldiers were ransomed, and the town sacked, to the great gain of the Englishmen."[39] By hedging on his sources (he resorts to the "Some write that" formula), the chronicler is careful not to blame the English for the distress of the townspeople. Nevertheless, his account does produce sympathy for the evicted French: "Some writing of this yielding up of Harfleur, do in like sort make mention of the distress whereto the people, then expelled out of their habitations, were driven; insomuch as parents with their children, young maids and old folk went out of the town gates with heavy hearts. . . ."[40] In *Henry V* the King's threat to sack Harfleur is never carried out. Instead the brutality of such a sacking is contained within Henry's imagined projection of it, and after the surrender of the town the King is careful to tell Exeter, "Use mercy to them all" (III. iii. 54).

One of the knottiest cruxes in the play is Henry's order to kill the French prisoners at Agincourt (IV. vi. 37). Reading Holinshed's account of this helps clarify the sequence, but some important questions remain about Shakespeare's intentions. The *Chronicles* recount how the King, after hearing an outcry from his camp (where the French "robbed the tents" and "slew" the "servants"), decides to kill the French prisoners because he fears that the French army will regroup and that the French prisoners will either help their countrymen or try to kill their English captors:

> [Henry] doubting lest his enemies should gather together again and begin a new field, and mistrusting further that the prisoners would be an aid to his enemies, or the very enemies to their takers indeed, if they were suffered to live, contrary to his accustomed gentleness, commanded by sound of trumpet that every man (upon pain of death) should incontinently slay his prisoner.[41]

Shakespeare's Henry apparently acts on the second of these reasons (the possibility that if the French regroup "the prisoners would be an aid" to them), but he makes this decision *before* he learns of carnage in his camp:

But hark, what new alarum is this same?
The French have reinforced their scattered men.
Then every soldier kill his prisoners!
Give the word through. (IV. vi. 35–38)

As a response to the "alarum," Henry's order is made to seem coldly practical, a defensive military strategy. But just as Holinshed somewhat mitigates the harshness of the order by pointing out how it contradicts Henry's usual "gentleness," so Shakespeare immediately makes Henry's apparently cold-blooded decision appear, in retrospect, to have been a passionate reaction. At the beginning of the next scene (just a few lines after Henry's command), when Fluellen and Gower discover the sacked camp and its dead guardians, Gower interprets the King's order as retribution for the savage killing: "'Tis certain there's not a boy left alive . . . wherefore the King most worthily hath caused every soldier to cut his prisoner's throat" (IV. vii. 5-10). Less than fifty lines later, the King enters "with prisoners," furiously "angry" at the slaughter of the boys, and at once tells the herald that unless the French retreat or come down to fight, he and his men will "cut the throats" of those prisoners they "have" and show no "mercy" to any additional prisoners that they subsequently "take." Some critics have thought that this second threat means that the initial order to kill the prisoners was not carried out,[42] or that Shakespeare intended to delete it. In fact Shakespeare is following Holinshed again. According to the *Chronicles*, when Henry sees the French reassemble for more combat, he threatens to kill "not only those prisoners which his people already had taken but also so many of them as in this new conflict which they thus attempted should fall into his hands."[43]

Was the initial order to kill the prisoners carried out on stage in Shakespeare's play? Holinshed does not shrink from describing the "lamentable" slaughter following Henry's "dolorous decree": "pity it was to see how some Frenchmen were suddenly sticked with daggers, some were brained with poleaxes, some slain with mauls, others had their throats cut, and some their bellies paunched."[44] But neither the Folio nor the Quarto provides a stage direction after Henry's "Give the word through." Gary Taylor (picking up on the line "Couple gorge," which the Quarto gives to Pistol at the end of IV. vi) adds one in his edition of the play, convinced that the audience was meant to see the "cold-blooded atrocity."[45] It is possible, though, that Shakespeare softens the sequence in Henry's favor. He briefly offers an impression, similar to Holinshed's, of Henry as the ruthless warrior who is prepared to kill defenseless prisoners in order to protect his own army, but the playwright does not necessarily back this up with a bloody image of massacre performed in the theater. Instead, by sleight of hand (Gower's retrospective interpretation), we are encouraged to believe that Henry orders a bloodbath only in spontaneous retaliation for the Frenchmen's cowardly killing of the boys.

Finally, Holinshed's *Chronicles* include some details that Shakespeare chooses to leave out. Apart from obvious cuts in the interests of a tighter plot (such as the Lollard rebellion early in Henry's reign or the continuing campaign after Agincourt), two of the dramatist's exclusions help enhance the portrait of Henry as a strong leader. After the unmasking of the traitors at Southampton, Holinshed explains that Richard, Earl of Cambridge, planned to kill Henry so that his brother-in-law, the Earl of March, would take over the throne and leave Cambridge next in line. The chronicler also points out that, thanks to these Yorkists, ultimately Henry's "line and stock was clean consumed to ashes."[46] In contrast, Shakespeare only hints at an ulterior motive when Cambridge mutters darkly, "For me, the gold of France did not seduce" (II. ii. 155); the dramatist is apparently reluctant to tarnish Henry's heroic achievements by reminding the audience, early in the play, that Henry's claim to the throne was not accepted by every faction and that finally his son lost the crown to the York family. Holinshed also devotes several pages to analyzing Henry's battle strategy at Agincourt. In particular, he describes the formation of the archers (the main "force" of the English army) and the hedge of stakes "bound with iron sharp at both ends" used to ward off the French cavalry.[47] *The Famous Victories* also shows Henry instructing his soldiers: "Then I will that every archer provide him a stake of a tree, and sharp it at both ends; and, at the first encounter of the horsemen, to pitch their stakes down into the ground before them, that they may gore themselves upon them" (xiv. 26–30). Shakespeare mentions none of this. Not only might it have been difficult to accomplish on stage, but a focus on tactical skills or on the accomplishments of the archers would detract from the King's charisma as a leader who energetically wills his "happy few" to victory.

Most of the evidence suggests that Shakespeare absorbed Holinshed's admiring account of Henry's reign into his play. In some cases he even improved the portrait of the King. The keynote of Holinshed's presentation of Henry V is the extended passage at the end of his account of the reign, where he eulogizes the King as a "mirror of magnificence."[48] (Hall gives the tribute a more moral twist, calling Henry a "singular mirror and manifest example of morall vertues and good qualities" and "the mirror of Christendome."[49]) Rather than a reverse image or a partial distortion, as it is in some twentieth-century contexts, "mirror" here denotes a model or an accurate reflection; this is how the term is used in that popular Elizabethan series of moralized historical exempla, *The Mirror for Magistrates*,[50] and in Hamlet's assertion that the theater "hold[s] the mirror up to nature" (*Hamlet*, III. ii. 22).

At the same time, however, Shakespeare adds some material that is critical of Henry. For example, he invents the sequence in Act IV where Henry talks to his soldiers incognito (it does not appear in the *Chronicles*). And the motif of the disguised king,[51] as it is used in this play, does little to bolster the image of Henry. Anne Barton has pointed out how several history plays from 1587 to 1600, such as the *First Part of Edward IV* and *Edward I*, show the king fraternizing with commoners in disguise; the fundamental premise of these plays is that the king is a man who can talk frankly with his people and possibly redress their grievances. *Henry V*, however, which is built on the Tudor doctrine of the king's "two bodies" (one politic and eternal, the other mortal), shows that it is impossible for Henry to "produce a natural and unforced imitation of a private man" in his conversation with Williams, Bates, and Court. In this respect the play questions rather than celebrates the folk convention of the disguised king mixing easily with his subjects. Such a convention, in the context of *Henry V*, is revealed as "false romanticism."[52]

It is quite probable that Shakespeare had in mind the work of other political theorists and historians, not just the accounts of the chroniclers, when he composed this play. The idealized portrait of Henry V—a king who was Christian, scholar, and statesman—may have been influenced by Erasmus's *Institutio Principis Christiani* (1516),[53] which was echoed in Thomas Elyot's more accessible *The Book named the Governor* (1531). In complete contrast were the political ideas of Machiavelli, which were still sending shock waves through the Elizabethan Establishment in the 1590s. While it is risky to correlate Machiavelli's *The Prince* too precisely with *Henry V*, as the English translation of the work was not published until 1640, Shakespeare would have had access to French reactions to this work and to English versions circulating in manuscript.[54] The closest trace of Machiavelli's ideas in the play comes in Cambridge's hypocritical words to Henry at Southampton: "Never was monarch better feared and loved / Than is your majesty" (II. ii. 25–26). In *The Prince*, Machiavelli concludes that it is "far better to be feared than loved if you cannot be both";[55] and by the end of *Henry V*'s II. ii, with the unmasking of the traitors, Henry has exposed love as a charade and respect for the monarch as all-important. Machiavelli's remark that the prince can afford to show "cruelty" when he is "campaigning with his soldiers and is in command of a large army . . . because, without such a reputation, he can never keep his army united and disciplined"[56] sheds light on Henry's curt comment on Bardolph's execution for stealing from a French church: "We would have all such offenders so cut off" (III.

vi. 112). There were, of course, many other treatises on warfare available to readers in 1599.[57] Andrew Gurr cites Richard Crompton's *Mirror of Magnanimitie* (published the same year that *Henry V* was written and dedicated to the Earl of Essex) as one that Shakespeare might have read; it justifies the killing of the French prisoners at Agincourt as a legitimate military strategy, albeit one of the "miseries of war."[58] But Machiavelli's notions on how the prince should act seem more likely to have contributed to that sense of opaqueness in Shakespeare's Henry—the fact that we rarely know what the King is thinking. For Machiavelli stresses the gap between seeming and reality in political figures, asserting that a prince should appear to be a "man of faith . . . a kind and religious man" but be prepared to cultivate a "flexible disposition, varying as fortune and circumstances dictate."[59] In contrast, Holinshed portrays Henry's piety—his "giving laud and praise to God"[60]—as genuine. Shakespeare's audience is left to determine whether Henry's devout behavior comes across as politic or sincere, or even a combination of both.

It seems unlikely that Shakespeare set out deliberately to subvert the message of the *Chronicles* or substantially to undermine the image of Henry as the "mirror of magnificence." The Chorus, one important voice in the play, consistently presents Henry as "the mirror of all Christian kings." Yet certain qualifications of Henry, and rival perspectives on his behavior, do emerge. Careful examination of the play suggests that it is as dangerous to endorse Harold C. Goddard's verdict that Henry V comes close to "Machiavelli's ideal prince,"[61] and thereby ignore the tenor of Shakespeare's main sources, as it is unfair to the playwright's independent artistry and maturity of vision to assume that his dramatic viewpoint was defined solely by that of the *Chronicles*.

NOTES

1. This is the view of Felix Schelling, *The English Chronicle Play* (New York and London: Macmillan, 1902), pp. 2–3. The theory is impossible to prove decisively, but Thomas Nashe, in *Pierce Penniless, his Supplication to the Devil* (1592), defends the plays "borrowed out of our English Chronicles" as a vehicle through which "our forefathers' valiant acts . . . are revived" (in Thomas Nashe, *The Unfortunate Traveller and Other Works*, ed. J. B. Steane [Harmondsworth: Penguin English Library, 1971], pp. 112–13).

2. In "Revisiting *Tamburlaine*: *Henry V* as Shakespeare's Belated Armada Play," *Criticism*, 31.4 (Fall 1989), 351–66, James Shapiro disputes the notion of *Henry V* as a patriotic celebration. He argues that in 1599, when another Armada

briefly appeared to be threatening England, Shakespeare chose to imitate Marlowe's "ironic version of heroical history" (360).

3. *Threshold of a Nation: A Study of English and Irish Drama* (Cambridge: Cambridge University Press, 1979), p. 74.

4. Michael Neill, "Broken English and Broken Irish: Nation, Language, and the Optic of Power in Shakespeare's Histories," *SQ*, 45 (1994), 1–32, points out that in *Henry V* it is Fluellen, not Macmorris, who is "received into membership of the English nation" (20).

5. Jonathan Dollimore and Alan Sinfield (eds.), *Political Shakespeare* (Ithaca and London: Cornell University Press, 1985), p. viii.

6. This is further discussed in Chapter 5, "Critical Approaches."

7. Quoted in J. E. Neale, *Elizabeth I and Her Parliaments, 1584–1601* (New York: Norton Library, 1966), vol. 2, p. 119.

8. "Invisible Bullets: Renaissance Authority and Its Subversions, *Henry IV* and *Henry V*," in *Political Shakespeare*, pp. 18–47, 44.

9. Ibid., p. 45.

10. *Pierce Penniless*, pp. 114, 112.

11. Ibid., p. 113.

12. In E. K. Chambers, *The Elizabethan Stage* (Oxford: Clarendon Press, 1923), vol. 4, p. 321.

13. Ibid., p. 322.

14. *Playes Confuted in five Actions* (1582), in *The Elizabethan Stage*, vol. 4, p. 217.

15. Ibid., pp. 218–19.

16. Described as such by Richard Flecknoe, *A Short Discourse of the English Stage* (1664), in *The Elizabethan Stage*, vol. 4, p. 370.

17. In 1599, John Hayward's *History of Henry IV* was published with a dedication to the Earl of Essex. Hayward was imprisoned in the Tower after a second edition of the book was printed that year. See Annabel Patterson, "Back by Popular Demand: The Two Versions of *Henry V*," in *Shakespeare and the Popular Voice* (Cambridge, Mass.: B. Blackwell, 1989), p. 78.

18. Quoted in Peter Ure (ed.), *Richard II, The Arden Shakespeare* (London: Methuen, 1961), p. lix.

19. Stephen Greenblatt (ed.), *The Power of Forms in the English Renaissance* (Norman, Okla.: Pilgrim Books, 1982), "Introduction," p. 4.

20. "Invisible Bullets," p. 44.

21. *The Place of the Stage* (Chicago and London: University of Chicago Press, 1988), p. 18.

22. "The Purpose of Playing: Reflections on a Shakespearean Anthropology," *Helios*, n.s. 7 (1980), 51–74, 64, 65, 71.

23. "Back by Popular Demand," pp. 81, 88.

24. *Shakespeare Recycled: The Making of Historical Drama* (Savage, Md.: Barnes and Noble, 1992), p. 187.

25. "Invisible Bullets," p. 43.

26. *The Defense of Poesie* (1595), in Albert Feuillerat (ed.), *The Prose Works of Sir Philip Sidney* (Cambridge: Cambridge University Press, 1908), vol. 3, p. 14.

27. Raphael Holinshed, *Henrie the Fifth*, in *Chronicles*, (London, 1807–8; repr. New York: AMS Press, 1976), vol. 3, pp. 60–136, 136. For convenience, the following quotations are from the excerpts given in J. R. Brown (ed.), *Henry V, The Signet Classic Shakespeare* (1965; 1988), pp. 172–210.

28. *Henry V: The Scourge of God* (New York: Viking, 1985), p. xviii.

29. P. 113.

30. All line references are taken from *The Famous Victories*, in Maynard Mack (ed.), *Henry IV, Part i, The Signet Shakespeare* (New York and Toronto: The New American Library, 1965), pp. 181–233.

31. Hall's *Union* also speculates that the Dauphin's gift might have prompted the war by placing it immediately after the return of Exeter from his embassy to King Charles.

32. For other possible echoes from *Gesta Henrici Quinti* (written by a chaplain who accompanied Henry on his first campaign to France), Pseudo-Eltham, *Vita et Gesta Henrici Quinti*, and Titus Livius, *Vita Henrici Quinti* (translated as *The First English Life of Henry the Fifth*, 1513), see J. H. Walter (ed.), *Henry V, The Arden Shakespeare* (1954), pp. xxxii–xxxiii, and Geoffrey Bullough (ed.), *Narrative and Dramatic Sources of Shakespeare* (London: Routledge and Kegan Paul, 1966), vol. 4, pp. 353–55. In *"Edward III* and *Henry V,"* *Criticism*, 37.4 (Fall 1995), 519–36, E. Pearlman points out how *Henry V* also incorporates parts of the popular earlier play, *Edward III*.

33. See Taylor, "Sources and Significances," in *Henry V* (ed.), pp. 29–30, for a fuller analysis of what Shakespeare took from Hall rather than Holinshed and where he probably followed Holinshed, not Hall.

34. Brown (ed.), *Henry V*, p. 177.

35. See Gurr (ed.), *Henry V, The New Cambridge Shakespeare* (1992), pp. 18–20.

36. C. G. Thayer, *Shakespearean Politics: Government and Misgovernment in the Great Histories* (Athens: Ohio University Press, 1983), pp. 90–92, discusses the relevance of the Salic law speech to the Stuart claim to the English throne. See also Marie Axton, *The Queen's Two Bodies: Drama and the Elizabethan Succession* (London: Royal Historical Society, 1977), pp. 112–15.

37. Brown (ed.), *Henry V*, p. 200.

38. Ibid., p. 175.

39. Ibid., p. 187.

40. Ibid., pp. 187–88.

41. Ibid., p. 197.

42. See Thayer, *Shakespearean Politics*, p. 160.

43. Brown (ed.), *Henry V*, p. 198.

44. Ibid., p. 197.

45. *Henry V*, p. 32. Taylor also alters the textual evidence by changing F's direction that Henry enters "with the Duke of Bourbon and prisoners" to "with the Duke of Bourbon . . . and other prisoners" (IV. vii. 49). Joel B. Altman, " 'Vile Participation': The Amplification of Violence in the Theater of *Henry V*," *SQ*, 42.1 (Spring 1991), 1–32, also thinks that the slaughter is shown on stage. Twentieth-century productions of the play have made various decisions. The 1975 RSC production (see Chapter 6, below) decided to have two characters, Monsieur le Fer and the Boy, killed on stage; the Boy is killed by French deserters immediately after his soliloquy (IV. iv), and Pistol cuts Le Fer's throat as soon as Henry gives the command (IV. vi). The 1994 RSC production did not shrink from staging a bloody massacre. Each of Henry's followers cut the throat of his prisoner—a realistic business that dismayed some members of the audience!

46. Brown (ed.), *Henry V*, p. 184.

47. Ibid., p. 192.

48. Ibid., p. 210.

49. Edward Hall, *The Union of the Two Noble and Illustre Famelies of Lancastre & Yorke* (London, 1550; repr. Menston: Scholar Press, 1970), fol. 1, verso; fol. xlix b.

50. Bullough, *Narrative and Dramatic Sources*, pp. 357–58, cites *Mirror for Magistrates* as one of the sources of *Henry V*.

51. Bullough thinks that Henry's visit to his troops on the night before battle was suggested by Tacitus, *Annals*, II. iii, but there Germanicus does not converse with his men (see Taylor [ed.], *Henry V*, p. 41).

52. Anne Barton, "The King Disguised: Shakespeare's *Henry V* and the Comical History," in Joseph G. Price (ed.), *The Triple Bond: Plays, Mainly Shakespearean, in Performance* (University Park: Pennsylvania State University Press, 1975), pp. 92–117, 103, 99.

53. See Walter (ed.), *Henry V*, pp. xvi–xvii.

54. See N. W. Bawcutt, "Machiavelli and Marlowe's *The Jew of Malta*," *RenD*, n.s. 3 (1970), 3–49.

55. "Cruelty and compassion, and whether it is better to be loved than feared, or the reverse," in Nicolo Machiavelli, *The Prince*, trans. George Bull (Harmondsworth: Penguin Books, 1961), p. 96.

56. Ibid., p. 97.

57. See also "The Victorious Acts of King Henry V," in Lily B. Campbell, *Shakespeare's "Histories": Mirrors of Elizabethan Policy* (San Marino, Calif.: The Huntingdon Library, 1947).

58. *Henry V* (ed.), pp. 27–28.

59. "How Princes should honour their word," *The Prince*, p. 101.

60. Brown (ed.), *Henry V*, p. 198.

61. *The Meaning of Shakespeare* (Chicago and London: University of Chicago Press, 1951), p. 267.

3

DRAMATIC STRUCTURE

THE CHORUS AS FRAMING DEVICE

One of the most striking features of *Henry V* (in the Folio text) is its use of a chorus before each act—a convention that had become somewhat out-moded in Elizabethan drama by 1599. The Chorus to Shakespeare's early tragedy *Romeo and Juliet* (1595) directs the audience's attention to the "star-cross'd lovers" but disappears after Act II. In their Prologue to "Pyramus and Thisbe" at the end of *A Midsummer Night's Dream* (1595), the Mechanicals manage to destroy any dramatic suspense and "wonder" by making "all things plain" (*Dream*, V. i. 128), while Hamlet complains about the Prologue to "The Murder of Gonzago," the play-within-a-play in *Hamlet,* for much the same reason: It seems to him laborious and dramati-cally redundant (*Hamlet*, III. ii. 141–42). A century and a half later, Samuel Johnson puzzled over *Henry V*'s use of such a device, wondering "why the intelligence given by the Chorus is more necessary in this play than in many others where it is omitted."[1] Yet in this history play, Shakespeare obviously felt a special need to mediate between the audience and the dramatic action, and the Chorus offers a sophisticated strategy for doing so. Its primary function is not to serve as a narrative bridge but to set an elevated, heroic tone for the play and, by admitting the limitations of the Elizabethan playhouse, to convince the spectators of their own essential role in recreat-ing Henry's greatness.

As a framing device, the Chorus produces some complex effects. There is the strong contrast (explored in more detail in Chapter 1) between the Chorus's glorification of the action and the more flawed reality that we see enacted on stage. As well as stimulating the audience to "make imaginary puissance" by conjuring up thousands of armed men in the "vasty fields" of France (I. 0. 25, 12), the Chorus expects, too, a sympathetic identification with Henry's cause and unqualified admiration for the King himself: " 'Praise and glory on his head!' " (IV. 0. 31). Yet his reminders of the drawbacks of the contemporary stage, its "unworthy scaffold" and "ragged foils," plus the inevitable tainting of the spectacle through the imperfect medium of the players, serve simultaneously as an alienation effect, making the spectators painfully conscious of their need willingly to suspend their disbelief. Thus the Chorus's exhortations may cut both ways, creating detachment from as well as engagement with the spectacle. At one level the audience is encouraged to respond to the poetry and rise to the occasion, entering imaginatively into the "now" of historical action; on the other hand, they are not allowed to ignore the limitations of the staging and the actors or the fact that they are, after all, stuck in a theater—"In little room confining mighty men" (Epilogue, 3).

This duality—the soaring upwards of imagination versus the sensation of coming back to earth—is actually built into the structure of the Chorus's speeches, especially the first three. The Prologue calls for a "Muse of fire that would ascend / The brightest heaven of invention" (1–2), but plummets back to solid ground at the mention of "scaffold" and "cockpit," for the "swelling scene" inspired by the poetic muse is doomed to be deflated by the "flat unraised spirits" (9) of both actors and playwright. The Chorus to Act II again creates an elevated picture of how "all the youth of England are on fire," which links back to the "Muse of fire" while adding the ethereal image of "Mercuries" (messengers to the gods) who have "winged heels." There is a partial drop back to earth when the Chorus envisages England as a "little body with a mighty heart," and a further decrescendo from "mighty heart" when he turns to the traitors, who are a "nest of hollow bosoms."

The Chorus to Act III picks up the Mercury image in its opening line: "Thus with imagined wing our swift scene flies." Although Henry's fleet is associated with "young Phoebus," the sun god,[2] the element now invoked is wind (the breath of the Muse) instead of fire, as the sails of the ships are "Borne with th' invisible and creeping wind" across the furrowed sea. By urging the spectators to collaborate with this movement through mental agility, the Chorus enhances "celerity" of "motion." His cluster of strong imperatives ("behold," "hear," "follow," "work"), reinforced by the immediacy of present participles ("fanning," "dancing," and "gaping"), culminates in his invitation to the audience to join the fleet in spirit, to "Grapple your minds to sternage of this navy." From the imagined ocean we move to the earth of "girded" Harfleur in its state of siege. A touch of fire flashes again as the "nimble gunner" holds a match to the cannon.

The keynote of the Chorus to Act IV is gloom punctuated by noise—the resonant sounds of horses neighing, hammers pounding on armor, cocks crowing, and bells tolling—and the occasional flash as "Fire answers fire." Rather than a spatial movement from heaven to earth within the poetry, a visual contrast is now established between the English soldiers with their "umbered" (shadowed) faces and "lank-lean cheeks" and their royal leader, who dispenses "A largess universal, like the sun." In Act V, the Chorus's appeal to the audience's "winged thoughts" (8) to bring Henry back to England recalls the Mercury image in the Chorus to Act II, while the reference to "forge" in "quick forge and working house of thought" (23) circles back to the muse of fire that opened Act I. In the Epilogue the final effect is again ambivalent. The Chorus both detaches the viewers from the final spectacle and earnestly exhorts them to engage in it; he reminds them of Henry's "small" time of glory (before the loss of France under Henry VI) even as he solicits their "acceptance" of the players' rendition of English history.

PLOT AND UNDERPLOTS: LINEAR PROGRESSION AND CONTRAPUNTAL MOVEMENT

In *Henry IV, Part i*, which first introduces us to the Prince who will become Henry V, three groups or centers of interest reflect on one another through a pattern of repetition with variation: King Henry and his court; Prince Hal, together with Falstaff and his Eastcheap friends; and the rebels, with the focus on Hotspur as their leader. All these characters converge at the battle of Shrewsbury, which establishes Hal as the true heir to the throne when he kills Hotspur, the imposter Harry. Before that, scenes alternate among the three groups in a purposeful, contrapuntal design. Act I, for instance, begins with the King in council, switches to Hal and Falstaff in the carefree world of Eastcheap, and then, in scene iii, presents the confrontation between Hotspur and the King that results in the coalition of the Percies against Henry. All the way through the drama we are encouraged to make thematic connections among these central figures. Thus the double-crossing at Gadshill, where Poins and Hal trick Falstaff once he has robbed the travelers ("A plague upon it when thieves cannot be true to one another!" [II. ii. 27–28]), reflects on how the rebels plan to steal the kingdom from Henry after they have helped him, as their former ally Bolingbroke, to wrest the crown from King Richard. As the action develops, Hal and Hotspur vie for center stage, with Hotspur often stealing the show in the theater; the

King, preoccupied with the rebels and his fraught relationship with his son, cuts a less dynamic figure.

In *Henry V*, however, the pattern is different, for the spotlight rests firmly on the King. He speaks more lines in the play than any other character, and he initiates the dominant action. Although it is possible to analyze five plot strands centering on different groups—Henry and his comrades, the French ruling class, the Eastcheap crew, the British soldiers (Fluellen, Gower, Williams, etc.), and Princess Katherine[3]—none of the final four is truly developed as a subplot; the action of the play is fully grounded in Henry's war enterprise. Whereas *Henry IV, Part i* crosscuts frequently among its three dominant groups, *Henry V* progresses in a more linear fashion. Some critics have found the play episodic, a sequence of ceremonial scenes rather than a tightly organized, causally connected plot.[4] But there is a strong momentum in the grand design, the building blocks that move the action forward: Act I, Henry's decision to go to war against France; Act II, the preparations for the campaign and the unmasking of the traitors at Southampton; Act III, the conquest of Harfleur; Act IV, the triumph at Agincourt; and Act V, the peace treaty and the betrothal of Henry to Princess Katherine. The climax of the play is the victory at Agincourt and the denouement, or comic resolution, is the marriage as a seal of unity and peace between England and France. *Henry V* is the only one of Shakespeare's history plays to end, like his comedies, with the fulfilment of marriage. In addition to this linear momentum, the play, as Brownell Salomon has argued, gains coherence through its pattern of alternating scenes demonstrating selfish "private cause" (among the French aristocrats and the Eastcheap men) versus "public good" (in Henry and his followers).[5]

The French have the stage to themselves for five complete scenes as well as one long sequence at the beginning of II. iv before the entrance of Exeter. Yet these scenes do not build into a subplot because France is never presented as an energetic antagonist; instead of initiating important new phases of action, the French simply react to the progress of Henry's campaign. Thus we are given the response of the French King and the Dauphin to Henry's invasion (II. iv) and to his army's crossing the River Somme (III. v); the French aristocrats' impatience to fight before Agincourt (III. vii) and contempt for the ragged English army (IV. ii); and finally their "shame" at being routed and their resolve, under Bourbon, to enter the battle once more (IV. v). The scene where Katherine learns from her waiting-woman Alice the English names for body parts (III. iv) is both a comic respite from the tension and threatened butchery at Harfleur and the first reaction of the Princess to the English presence in France; in an important sense, it is her way of accommodating to the prospect of one day marrying (or having to marry) the King of England.

The French also accentuate Henry's prowess because they can offer nothing equivalent. Even the first sequence, where the French take center stage and the Dauphin dismisses Henry as "shallow" (II. iv. 28), helps reinforce the idea of Henry's greatness rather than contriving to belittle it. The French King's recollection of the battle of Crécy and Edward the Black Prince's triumph there—his respect for Henry as a "stem / Of that victorious stock" (62–63)—directly echoes Canterbury's invocation to Henry to recall his mighty ancestors (I. ii. 102). Each speaker evokes exactly the same historical moment: King Edward III standing on a hill, smiling at his son's victory over the French at Crécy. This spot of time is indelibly etched on the folk memory, English and French alike. Similarly, the Constable's horticultural image of how, before becoming king, Henry covered "discretion with a coat of folly; / As gardeners do with ordure hide those roots / That shall first spring and be most delicate" (II. iv. 38–40) is close to Ely's explanation of how the "strawberry grows underneath the nettle" (I. i. 60) to account for Hal's apparently sudden transformation into a great king.

Then, as the war conflict develops (Acts III and IV), alternating scenes are arranged so that the French come across as arrogant dilettantes, over-confident of success, while the English are humble and serious about their endeavour. The impatience of the French to fight, their refrain of "Will it never be morning?" (III. vii. 6), contrasts with Bates' conviction that Henry would rather be "in Thames up to the neck" (IV. i. 117) than on the verge of battle. The tribute to the Dauphin's horse, a Pegasus who is "prince of palfreys" (III. vii. 28), is set against Grandpré's contemptuous description of the English cavalry as "poor jades" with "gum down roping from their pale-dead eyes" (IV. ii. 46–48). Whereas the French offer a "fair show" (17), the travel-stained English are tough "warriors for the working day" (IV. iii. 109). The stage spectacle thus pits the superficial brilliance of French appearances against Henry's courageous substance, emphasized in his admission that "Such outward things dwell not in my desires" (IV. iii. 27).

The scenes featuring the British soldier Williams (IV. i, vii, viii) are also firmly tied into the main action as a commentary on the relationship between the King and his subjects; every scene in which Williams plays a role ultimately focuses on Henry. Fluellen, who appears in six scenes, also has an important structural function in relation to Henry rather than developing within an independent underplot. On several occasions the Welshman substitutes for Henry, acting as his comic surrogate. Fluellen drives the Eastcheapers back to the breach (III. ii); because he is adamant that

Bardolph should be executed he, and not the King, bears the brunt of Pistol's angry "figo for thy friendship" (III. vi. 59); he, instead of Henry, wears Williams' glove in his cap and is challenged by the soldier, who then rejects Fluellen's small gift of money after the King has given him "crowns" (IV. viii); and finally it is Fluellen's job to confront and punish Pistol, who has insulted the disguised king as well as his Welsh counterpart (V. i).

The one strand of the play that does develop outside Henry's immediate sphere of influence is that containing the Eastcheap characters: Nym, Bardolph, Pistol, the Boy, and the Hostess. This group of five appears in two scenes, still set in England, in the second act of the play (II. i, iii). The Hostess, of course, stays at home, and we do not see her again. The four male characters take the stage only once more all together, at the assault on Harfleur (III. ii). After that Pistol and the Boy share a scene in IV. iv—the capture of the French soldier Monsieur le Fer—at the end of which the Boy mentions, in passing, that Bardolph and Nym have both been hanged. (We have learned about Bardolph's imminent execution, for stealing from a French church, in III. vi.) The Boy is presumably killed by the beginning of IV. vii, the sack of the English camp, which begins with Fluellen's asyntactical explosion (zeugma), "Kill the poys and the luggage?" Pistol is now clearly established as the dominant character of the Eastcheap group. He confronts Fluellen in III. vi, interceding for Bardolph's life, and accosts the disguised Henry in the pre-Agincourt scene (IV. i). He is still very much alive in V. i, where, after being beaten by Fluellen and forced to choke down a leek, he resolves to return to England to make his living as a bawd and war veteran—the Elizabethan "sturdy beggar." Pistol thus appears in a total of seven scenes, only one including Henry. We can assume that he went over well with Elizabethan audiences, since the title page of the Quarto gives special prominence to him; evidently they enjoyed his swaggering style, first developed in *Henry IV, Part ii*, and his mock-heroic behavior.

It is true that Pistol and his comrades do not develop the rich vein of wit and abrasive humor, the complex parody of matters both civil and military, that Falstaff provides in the *Henry IV* plays. Yet the mock-heroic emphasis is important; in particular, this plot strand establishes some fairly clear parallels between what the low-life characters do and how Henry acts. Balanced situations serve mainly to provide foils for the King (cowardice versus bravery, for example), but they may also encourage us to perceive certain features, such as aggression and acquisitiveness, which are shared by both parties, and thus to reassess our overall picture of Henry. Pistol's cynical parting words to the Hostess, "Trust none; / For oaths are straws, men's faiths are wafer-cakes" (II. iii. 51–52), mirror Henry's terrible disillusionment in the preceding scene—his sense that Scroop's treachery has tainted even the "best indued" man with "some suspicion" (II. ii. 139–40). When Pistol and his gang leave for France, one of the key questions is whether they simply provide a fuller, in most cases darker, view of the war from the "underbelly of the army,"[6] or whether, through ironic parallelism, they serve to parody Henry's war effort and deflate the King's pretensions to glory.[7] For instance, Pistol's seemingly innocuous description of the fighting Nym, "Thy spirits are most tall" (II. i. 71), is echoed in Henry's exhortation at the breach, "bend up every spirit / To his full height!" (III. i. 16–17). We are left to decide whether Pistol's phrase subtly satirizes Henry's fierce demeanor at Harfleur or enhances it by contrast.[8] Similarly, Pistol's "Base is the slave that pays" (II. i. 99) could serve as an ironic commentary on Henry's giving money to Williams to smooth over an embarrassing situation (IV. viii), or it might point up Henry's courageous refusal to be ransomed by the French.

One sequence that offers an unambiguous contrast to Henry's strong leadership is the behavior of the Eastcheap gang when they face the breach at Harfleur. Henry has roused his troops until they are like "greyhounds in the slips, / Straining upon the start" (III. i. 31–32). Bardolph seems caught up in the energy of the moment when he echoes Henry's "On, on, you noble English" (17) in his opening line to III. ii, "On, on, on, on, on, to the breach, to the breach!" Nym, though, finds "the knocks are too hot" and is more interested in saving his skin ("I have not a case of lives"). The Boy adds a very human touch by wishing he were in a London tavern ("I would give all my fame for a pot of ale, and safety"), while Pistol quickly seconds the motion. When Fluellen drives them back to the breach, Pistol ironically countermands the king's instruction to "Disguise fair nature with hard-favored rage" (III. i. 8) by begging the Welshman to "abate thy manly rage" (II. ii. 23). Cowardice, or the instinct for self-preservation, stands in clear opposition to Henry's courage in the heat of battle.

On the face of it, the Eastcheap crew's attitude to looting and exploiting the opportunities of war—"they will steal anything, and call it purchase," explains the Boy (III. ii. 42–43)—contrasts strongly with Henry's disciplined insistence that "in our marches through the country there be nothing compelled from the villages, nothing taken but paid for" (III. vi. 113–15). But a parallel also presents itself.[9] Is Pistol's "brotherhood" of thievery, his plan that "profits will accrue" (II. i. 115) and his frank admission that he goes to France "to suck, to suck, the very blood to suck!" (II. iii. 57), entirely different from Henry's campaign to acquire France through "bloody constraint"? The audience may feel that like Bardolph, executed because "he hath stolen a pax" (Holinshed mentions instead a pyx, the vessel containing the consecrated communion wafer), Henry has taken away the peace (*pax* in Latin) of France. The King resolves to win Harfleur even at the expense of violated women and slaughtered babies. He is determined, too, not to part with a single village despite the devastation which, Burgundy implies, English soldiers "That nothing do but meditate on blood" have brought about in France (V. ii. 60).

Pistol and his comrades also modify the idealized portrait of the King through their comments on the illness and death of Falstaff. Their words serve as a reminder of what Henry has had to reject in order to refine his kingly image—not much in the case of Pistol, Nym, and Bardolph; more, perhaps, with Mistress Quickly (the Hostess), Falstaff, and the Boy. The placing of the scenes referring to Falstaff (II. i and iii) is important, since they flank the sequence at Southampton (II. ii) where Henry unmasks the traitors. One betrayal mirrors another. Lamenting on the terminal illness of Falstaff, the Hostess observes that "The King has killed his heart" (II. i. 91); in a switch of roles Scroop, who knew "the very bottom" of Henry's "soul" (II. ii. 97), has devastated the King emotionally by his treachery. Both have been intimates of the King, but now the Vice-like Falstaff appears less wicked than the hypocritical Scroop. Henry associates the nobleman with the most "cunning fiend" in hell, whose betrayal is so appalling that it signifies "Another fall of man" (111, 142). Meanwhile Falstaff, the Hostess assures us, is "not in hell." Some sympathy is generated for the death of Falstaff, but not too much; he dies off stage and the Hostess's detailed account, teetering on the brink of bawdiness (his nose was "as sharp as a pen," as her hand roved "upward, and upward" [17, 26]), makes the audience smile as much as grieve. Nevertheless Shakespeare reinforces the sense of personal betrayal—that Henry *has* coldly rejected his former friend—later in the play, when Fluellen ponders, "as Alexander killed his friend Cleitus, being in his ales and his cups, so also Harry Monmouth, being in his right wits and his good judgments, turned away the fat knight" (IV. vii. 47–50). Fluellen's parallel, which points up the King's icy self-control and calculating streak (a side of him we see as Prince Hal), does not work to Henry's advantage. Even Henry's heroic counterpart, Alexander the Great, is demoted somewhat by Fluellen's Welsh accent, which turns him into Alexander the Pig.

In addition to both enhancing and qualifying Henry's greatness, the Eastcheap characters underscore a significant pattern in the main action of the play: the arousal of violence that is then averted or displaced in some way. After the Salic law explanation, Henry is eager to go to war to regain what he considers to be his by right—the kingdom of France. Yet instead of admitting his imperial ambition to the French messengers, he displaces it onto anger at the Dauphin for his insulting gift of tennis balls, in effect turning the French Prince into the warmonger: "And some are yet ungotten and unborn / That shall have cause to curse the Dauphin's scorn" (I. ii. 287–88). Nym, in the following scene, also feels robbed of what is rightfully his (Pistol, as well as owing him money, has married Nym's fiancée), but he proceeds to threaten his "host" without revealing the underlying cause of his anger. When Pistol rises to the bait in swaggering style ("Pistol's cock is up, / And flashing fire will follow" [II. i. 55–56]), it is his turn to mirror Henry's aggressive response to the Dauphin's insult. But just as the rivals Nym and Pistol fail to reach "conclusions" once Bardolph intervenes to stop the fight, so Henry, despite setting up the Dauphin as his personal antagonist, does not actually encounter him at Agincourt. The rhythm of the opening Eastcheap scene, where underlying hostility never quite turns into violence on stage, may also shed light on that crux in Act IV: Henry's order to kill the French prisoners. Nym's veiled threat "men may sleep, and they may have their throats about them at that time" (II. i. 22–24), Pistol's "Couple a gorge!" (74), and Bardolph's "Why the devil should we keep knives to cut one another's throats?" (94–95) all foreshadow the sequence at Agincourt. If we accept the closing line that the Quarto gives to Pistol in IV. vi, "Couple gorge," as a legitimate part of the text, this might indicate some bloodletting on the stage after Henry orders, "Then every soldier kill his prisoners!" (IV. vi. 37). But the Folio is reticent here, and neither text provides a clear stage direction after Henry's command. It is just as likely, therefore, that violence is underplayed in the main action too, and is simply reported afterwards by Gower when he tells us that "the King most worthily hath caused every soldier to cut his prisoner's throat" (IV. vii. 9–10).

The pattern of averted violence is plainest at Harfleur. Although Henry threatens terrible consequences if the city does not surrender, his images of fierce slaughter never materialize. Similarly, Pistol's aggressive tendencies fail to translate into action. In reality a cowardly bully, he quickly backs down from his fight with Nym, conceding "fury shall abate" when confronted with a tougher opponent in Bardolph. (The Boy later explains that Pistol is less brave[10] than Nym and Bardolph, who were prepared to steal "adventurously" in France and have paid the price [IV. iv. 77].) Henry's genuine fierceness at Harfleur is caricatured by Pistol's bravado and the obscene gesture of the "figo"—a version of the flip-off performed by thrusting the thumb between the fingers or into the mouth—that Pistol uses whenever he is crossed. He resorts to this impotent gesture of defiance after he is unable to persuade Fluellen to intercede for Bardolph's life (III. vi. 59–60) and when, disgusted to find that "Harry le Roy" is a friend and kinsman of Fluellen, he rudely dismisses the disguised King with "The figo for thee then!" (IV. i. 60). Pistol gets his comeuppance for these petty acts of aggression in the final act of the play. Violence transforms into comedy when Fluellen, indirectly avenging the insult to the King as well as venting his own spleen, beats Pistol and forces him to eat a leek.

The audience also expects a violent climax after the terrific buildup of the Crispin's Day speech. But Henry's command, "Now, soldiers, march away," is not followed by a huge confrontation of the English and the French on stage, or even a few "ragged foils" to depict the battle of Agincourt. Instead we are shown Pistol taking Monsieur le Fer prisoner in a bloodless victory (IV. iv) and arranging to ransom him for 200 crowns: a comic instance of a cowardly Englishman finding an even more craven French counterpart. The scene may deflate the heroic intensity of Henry's war effort, but other parallels in it work to the King's advantage. The alacrity with which Le Fer (ironically his name is a homonym for "fire") submits to "Egregious ransom" contrasts with Henry's absolute refusal to consider being ransomed, even when Montjoy again offers this option just before battle (IV. iii. 80). In addition, Pistol's mercenary bias in this episode—he is prepared to save his prey if the price is right—contrasts with the King's resolve, two scenes later, to kill the prisoners and thereby forfeit much ransom money.[11]

It is true that not all the parallels between Pistol and Henry enhance the King's image. Yet Pistol is usually so unscrupulous and predatory that we are not, in general, encouraged to interpret his actions as a sustained critique of the King's enterprise; particularly toward the end of the play, they are the shadow that makes Henry appear all the brighter.[12] Pistol is, in Gower's phrase, the "counterfeit cowardly knave" (V. i. 72) whose brash words are at variance with his deeds, while Henry is genuinely courageous, a man whose speeches lead to action. While the opportunistic approach of the Eastcheap crew does lend the war a darker perspective, these characters never radically undermine Henry V's cause in the way that Falstaff's memorable soliloquy near the end of *Henry IV, Part i* ("Can honor set to the grief of a wound?") cuts through pretensions to glory in battle. Most critics agree that they provide what Larry S. Champion calls "divergent angles of vision,"[13] or a burlesque of the war effort, rather than a damaging undercutting of the military heroics.

MINOR CHARACTERS

Henry is such a dominant presence that it may be surprising to discover that he appears in only about half the scenes of the play (eleven out of twenty-three). While by no means as subtle in its counterpointing as the preceding history plays (the two parts of *Henry IV*), *Henry V* does contain a wide variety of dramatis personae who enlarge the dramatic viewpoint beyond that of the King. One way of approaching the minor characters is to interpret them in allegorical terms, as representing different vices or virtues. On this schematic level, the Dauphin symbolizes pride (he assumes that he can easily crush the "vain, giddy, shallow, humorous" young King Henry [II. iv. 28]), while Williams represents plain speaking. Scroop symbolizes treachery; Fluellen, loyalty; Pistol, a mixture of cowardice and greed. Some of these characters serve as partial reflections of Henry, whereas others offer undesirable alternatives to kingliness. Henry must steer a firm course among these personifications, testing and refining his own qualities. He resists the temptation to be as proud as his antagonist the Dauphin (he prays, "Yet forgive me, God, / That I do brag thus!" after praising his soldiers to Montjoy in III. vi. 158–59) and learns, insofar as it is possible for a public leader, to be an "honest man" like Williams.

Elizabethan drama was indeed rooted in the late medieval morality play, a contest between moral abstractions. Yet Shakespeare nearly always goes beyond this schematic framework to portray character through naturalistic, lifelike details. Granted, the Dauphin is never fully developed as Henry's foil; his role at Agincourt is not a crucial one, and he disappears from the Quarto text at this point. But strong characteristics do emerge in him, especially if we take into account his appearance in III. vii and IV of the Folio text. Like Hotspur, Hal's foil in *Henry IV, Part i*, the Dauphin is impulsive (II. iv), eager to join battle against the wishes of his father (III. v), and absurdly infatuated with his horse (III. vii. 11–18). He can be played as callow in his dismissal of Henry's England as "idly kinged," but also, with more depth, as a young man eager to prove himself and furious at being outdone, militarily and sexually, by the English youth whose prowess attracts the French "madams" (III. v. 28).

Because the French are broadly sketched as Henry's opponents, they sometimes speak in an undifferentiated chorus, as in IV. ii, when the Constable and Grandpré deride the English army in boastful speeches that are virtually interchangeable. On other occasions, in contrast to the unified English nobles, they are "bickering" and self-assertive.[14] The French King, however, stands out as a dignified character. He shows good sense in dealing with Henry's invasion ("It fits us then to be as provident / As fear may teach us" [II. iv. 11–12]), since he respects Henry as a descendant of the "victorious" Edward III. Shakespeare avoids any signs of the "disease of frenzy"[15] that Holinshed notes in the French monarch and that Laurence Olivier incorporates in his film version of King Charles as a bewildered depressive. While the other French aristocrats rant about the English as "bastard Normans," the King calmly and magisterially summons the princes to the field, sending Montjoy to offer "sharp defiance" to Henry (III. v. 37).

The Constable at times emerges as the wisest of these aristocrats. He rebukes the Dauphin for misjudging Henry—"You are too much mistaken in this king" (II. iv. 30)—and shrewdly satirizes the Prince's love for his "most absolute and excellent horse" (III. vii. 26–27) in the nighttime scene before Agincourt. Once the Dauphin has left the stage, the Constable wittily derides his empty boastfulness with "I think he will eat all he kills" (96). Yet although he understands and respects King Henry's "constant resolution" (II. iv. 35), he is often depicted, like the French in general, as vainglorious (proud of his armor) and overconfident (in his "haste" to join battle) (IV. ii. 62). He mistakenly scorns the English army as a "poor and starved band" and grossly underestimates what is required of the French at Agincourt:

> A very little little let us do,
> And all is done. (IV. ii. 33–34)

Montjoy, the French herald, appears in only three scenes of the play (III. vi; IV. iii; IV. vii), but his role is often extended in the theater by giving him the part of the French ambassador who delivers the taunting gift in I. ii. In this way he becomes a barometer for the changing attitude of the French toward Henry; he progresses from arrogance (as the spokesman of the Dauphin) to grudging respect for Henry's defiant refusal to be ransomed, even though he remains utterly confident that his countrymen will win (III. vi; IV. iii). Finally he shows humility after Henry's amazing victory, when he comes to request permission from the "great king" (IV. vii. 72) to collect and bury the French dead.

With the exception of Exeter, whose role in offering powerful moral and physical support to Henry is particularly prominent in Kenneth Branagh's film, the English nobles are not strongly differentiated. There is more individuality among the lower-class characters and the British soldiers; in particular, they are given idiosyncratic traits of speech, discussed later in this chapter. Fluellen is carefully characterized as a somewhat old-fashioned but intensely loyal officer—one who goes by the book in following the "disciplines of war" but is immensely proud of his Welsh kinship with Henry. Interestingly, he is more gullible than his sidekick Captain Gower, who is not fooled for a moment by the empty bravado of Pistol at the bridge; it is Gower who has to point out to his comrade that Pistol is a "gull, a fool, a rogue" (III. vi. 69). In fact the obtuse Fluellen carries a good portion of the humor in the play. His obsession with military discipline is amusing in itself, especially in the sequence where he shushes Gower, forbidding any "tiddle taddle" that the enemy might overhear (IV. i. 70–71). The scenes where he confronts Williams (IV. viii) and chastises Pistol by making him eat a leek (V. i) offer a broader comedy, verging on slapstick.

The trio of British officers—the pedantic Welshman Fluellen, the irascible Irishman Macmorris, and the conciliatory Scotsman Jamy—encounter each other in only one scene, at Harfleur. Their sharply distinguished speech patterns promote opportunities for misunderstanding and antagonism rather than suggesting unity in diversity. Macmorris's defensive question, "What ish my nation?" (III. ii. 126), leaves us with a strong impression of unresolved differences (the English and Welsh will find it hard to coexist with the outsider Irish[16]). Fluellen invites discussion of the "disciplines of war" as a possible route to establishing "friendly communication" (100) or some neutral territory among them, but this suggestion is never pursued.

More comradeship is established among the three regular soldiers—Michael Williams, John Bates, and Alexander Court—in their one scene by the campfire (IV. i). It is significant that Shakespeare endows the soldiers with both Christian and last names, instead of giving them purely comic titles, as he does for Mouldy, Bullcalf, and Feeble, the conscripts in *Henry IV, Part ii*; he also creates distinctive voices for Bates (who speculates that the King "could wish himself in Thames up to the neck" rather than on the verge of battle) and for Williams. With simple eloquence, Williams imagines how the severed limbs of soldiers killed in battle will join together on the Day of Judgment (IV. i. 136–43). His humane and Christian outlook, an appealing alternative to the callous pursuit of military glory that never considers the consequences for ordinary folk, tests the King's morality to the quick. In IV. viii, explaining that Henry's disguise as a common man was misleading, Williams again puts the onus on the King to accept responsibility for any insult he received: "I beseech you take it for your own fault, and not mine" (53–54). His role as the King's conscience is vital to the play. Yet in keeping with the pattern of averted violence, a full confrontation between them is comically deflected when Fluellen, acting as the

King's surrogate, accepts a challenge from Williams, only to have Henry quickly stall the fight.

THE CHARACTER OF KING HENRY V

Analyzing the character of Henry V poses special challenges. While *Henry V* can be read and enjoyed as self-contained drama, it is also the culmination of those history plays that cover the previous reigns of Richard II and Henry IV. There are illuminating contrasts between Richard II, presented as a weak and irresponsible king but also as a man who gains insight and maturity through experiencing loss, and Henry V, a strong, successful ruler whose inner self is often subsumed within his public role.

In choosing to portray a person who actually ruled fifteenth-century England for ten years, Shakespeare is bound by certain historical facts. Yet his Henry is still a fictive construct, a dramatic character revealed through speech and action within the conventions of the Elizabethan theater. While the chronicle sources set up certain parameters, it is important not to read the "real" historical character back into the dramatic one or to interpret Shakespeare's Henry V too much in terms of what sixteenth-century documents tell us. In any case, these are constructs too; and while the chroniclers' idealized version of Henry can be a useful point of reference, it should never displace the meanings generated by the play script itself.

Prince Hal and Henry

In any full analysis of the character it is helpful first to consider the wider dramatic context: the fact that Henry V has appeared (in a different guise, as Prince Hal) in the two preceding plays, *Henry IV, Parts i* and *ii*. Is King Henry V a credible extension of Prince Hal? One intriguing question for readers or audience members who have arrived at *Henry V* by way of the *Henry IV* plays is whether the characters are continuous—with Henry V emerging from the chrysalis of Hal—or whether the dramatic conception of the King constitutes a new departure. E.M.W. Tillyard finds no continuity. He concludes that in composing *Henry V* Shakespeare ended up "jettisoning" the subtle, often amoral character he had created in Hal, producing instead a "paragon of kingly virtue."[17] Certainly Canterbury, in the opening scene, finds an astonishing gap between the man who was prince and the exemplar who is now king. Amazed that Henry has turned into a model scholar, theologian, and statesman when "the courses of his youth promised it not," he deems the change almost miraculous:

Never came reformation in a flood
With such a heady currance scouring faults;
Nor never Hydra-headed willfulness
So soon did lose his seat—and all at once—
As in this king. (I. i. 33–37)

Canterbury speaks the language of the service of baptism in the *Book of Common Prayer*—the notion of burying the "olde Adam" and raising up the "new man"[18]—when he explains how the Prince's wildness seemed to die with his father, and "Consideration" came "like an angel" in its place. But an alternative interpretation of the King's "reformation" as gradual evolution rather than spiritual conversion is offered in the same scene by Ely. His horticultural analogy, "The strawberry grows underneath the nettle" (60), suggests natural growth, albeit growth fashioned to a deliberate game plan: The Prince was hiding his "contemplation" of kingship under a "veil of wildness" until the time was ripe to show his true self. Even Canterbury accepts this explanation, conceding, "It must be so, for miracles are ceased" (67).

The evidence is mainly on the side of those critics, such as J. H. Walter and Norman Rabkin,[19] who see Henry as a logical development from the Hal persona. When we go back to the beginning of *Henry IV, Part i* we discover that Hal has planned the surprising "reformation" all along; there is no radical conversion. In an early soliloquy after his comrades have left the stage, Hal switches from the fun-loving prince prepared to abet robbery to the detached future king who is simply marking time:

I know you all, and will a while uphold
The unyok'd humor of your idleness,
Yet herein will I imitate the sun,
Who doth permit the base contagious clouds
To smother up his beauty from the world,
That when he please again to be himself,
Being wanted, he may be more wond'red at
By breaking through the foul and ugly mists
Of vapors that did seem to strangle him. (I. ii. 195-203)

His plan is to play the reprobate to the hilt and then appear all the more impressive, like the sun breaking through the clouds, because no one expects a "glitt'ring" transformation. He takes the audience into his confidence, revealing the shrewd calculation of his strategy:

I'll so offend to make offense a skill,
Redeeming time when men think least I will. (217–18)

Having established himself early in *Henry IV, Part i* as a somewhat
cold-blooded role-player, Hal can enjoy his escapades with Falstaff and
sharpen his wits on the old man. We are always reminded, though, that he
is fundamentally distanced from the Eastcheap way of life (it is safe to say
that he and Falstaff are mutually exploiting one another) and that when the
appropriate time comes he will discard his old comrades. Hal uses a
play-acting situation to reveal this. Adopting a dramatic mask in the tavern
scene of II. iv, Hal acts the part of the king addressing the prince (played by
Falstaff) in order to remind Falstaff that he is, from a morality play
standpoint, an "old white-bearded Satan," and that in time Henry V will
banish him: "I do, I will." The sequence anticipates III. ii, Hal's real
confrontation with his father. There he also projects the future, swearing to
restore his father's tarnished opinion of him by defeating Hotspur on the
battlefield ("I will redeem all this on Percy's head" [III. ii. 132]). Hal's
vision of his destiny as a king is indeed strongly evident at Shrewsbury when
he separates himself from Falstaff's folly ("is it a time to jest and dally
now?" [V. iii. 55]) and, thinking that Falstaff has fallen in battle when he is
only shamming dead, makes his priorities quite clear: "I should have a heavy
miss of thee / If I were much in love with vanity" (V. iv. 105–6).

Henry IV, Part ii continues the pattern of Hal's separation from his old
life as he prepares to take on the new role of king. In this much less buoyant
play the Prince appears in only five scenes out of a total of nineteen, as
opposed to ten out of eighteen in *Part i*. He is marking time more heavily
now. When the audience first sees him (not until II. ii), he has become
"exceeding weary" of the role of reprobate prince; acting that part has turned
into a trap, since it keeps him in such "vile company" as that of Poins and
Falstaff and prevents him from expressing his genuine grief at his father's
terminal illness ("my heart bleeds inwardly that my father is so sick" [48]).
Increasingly he feels pressure to fulfil his own destiny—no longer to
"profane the precious time" (II. iv. 362) but to "redeem" it, as promised at
the beginning of *Henry IV, Part i*. To the audience it comes as no surprise
when he embraces the Lord Chief Justice in Act V, promising, "You shall
be as a father to my youth," instead of adhering to his temporary surrogate
father Falstaff (False-staff). With a foreshadowing of Canterbury's observation of how "The breath no sooner left his father's body / But that his
wildness, mortified in him, / Seemed to die too" (*Henry V*, I. i. 25–27), the
new King tells the Justice that "My father is gone wild into his grave; / For
in his tomb lie my affections" (*Henry IV, Part ii*, V. ii. 123–24). Echoing his

private promise in the previous play to "falsify men's hopes" (*Henry IV, Part i*, I. ii. 215), he now assures the court that Henry V lives "To mock the expectation of the world." His rejection of Falstaff—"I know thee not, old man" (*Henry IV, Part ii*, V. v. 47)—fulfils his prophecy in *Part i* and symbolizes his putting off what the *Book of Common Prayer* calls the "old man" in order that he can play the new role of Christian king.

It is because Hal is such an adroit actor that he is able to pull off this theatrical coup, staging what appears (to his brothers in court) to be an astounding transformation from wild prince to sober king. Role-playing is essential, too, in his presentation of himself as the strong king in the play that follows. Above all, he must act the soldier at the climax of Agincourt in *Henry V*; but Vernon's description of Prince Hal as "like feathered Mercury" or an angel riding Pegasus (*Henry IV, Part i*, IV. i. 105–8) has already prepared us for the King's amazing charisma on the battlefield. Moreover in this earlier play we actually see him in hand-to-hand combat; and despite having been a "truant" to "chivalry," he has no difficulty saving his father from the Douglas and then killing Hotspur at Shrewsbury. Henry V must also play the role of "king of good fellows," which he does splendidly in the Crispin's Day speech and, according to the Chorus, the night before Agincourt. We first see him practicing this part in *Henry IV, Part i*, when he tells Poins that he has become "sworn brother to a leash of drawers" by drinking with "all the good lads in Eastcheap" and acquiring their "language" (II. iv. 6–20). In *Henry IV, Part ii* Warwick suggests the cool calculation on which this social mixing is based when he points out that the Prince "studies his companions / Like a strange tongue" and is ready to discard the "immodest" part of them once he has "attained" their particular language (IV. iv. 68–71). In fact Hal is able not only to discard what he no longer needs but also to absorb the desirable characteristics of both friends and opponents, incorporating them into his future roles.[20] The brave Hotspur is his "factor" for accumulating chivalric honors that will instantly be passed to Hal when winner takes all at the battle of Shrewsbury. And Falstaff imparts to Hal a healthy skepticism, a debunking of "honor" that is is akin to Henry's deconstruction of "ceremony" in his soliloquy before Agincourt. His Eastcheap cronies also supply the common touch, the "little touch of Harry in the night" that he uses with his soldiers on the night before battle.

Shakespearean actors, admittedly biased in favor of naturalistic progression, have usually found a convincing continuity between the characters of Hal and Henry V. Alan Howard, who played the two parts in tandem in the 1975 Royal Shakespeare Company productions of *Henry V* and the *Henry*

IV plays, found a crucial link in the predilection and talent that both characters show for role-playing: "The whole question of acting, of assuming roles, which is so central to the early Hal, is carried through into *Henry V*."[21] Even the evasiveness that partly underlies Hal's choice of the prodigal son role in the first place—his desire to escape the seriousness of his father's situation and his own responsibilities as prince by allying himself with the spirit of carnival in Falstaff—may carry over into his persona as Henry V. When he is king he frequently finds it difficult to face up to the full weight of his obligations; as will be discussed in the next section, he has a noticeable tendency to slough off responsibility onto others.

Our main impression of Prince Hal, thanks to his playing double agent, is that he is calculating and usually in control, a cold fish in contrast to the spontaneous, fiery Hotspur. As Henry V he manifests the same cool efficiency as both king and military leader; moreover, he is so committed to a public facade that any complex inner self usually remains hidden. Yet Alan Howard takes as one key to Henry's character a capacity for anger, or the passionate nature that we briefly see after the slaughter of the boys at Agincourt.[22] This trait is first mentioned in *Henry IV, Part ii*, when Henry IV is advising Hal's younger brother, Clarence, to handle the future King carefully. He makes this observation about his eldest son:

> . . . being incens'd, he is flint,
> As humorous as winter, and as sudden
> As flaws congealed in the spring of day. (IV. iv. 33–35)

In *Henry V* it is Nym who gestures toward Henry's "humorous" disposition ("he passes some humors, and careers") and comments, on the king's rejection of Falstaff, that "the King hath run bad humors on the knight" (II. i. 124).

Whether or not passion is an underlying trait in Henry, one thing is certain: Henry V is singularly opaque as a hero.[23] Apart from the personal anguish he expresses over Scroop's betrayal (II. ii) and in his two soliloquies (IV. i), his motives and underlying emotions remain hidden from the audience. One sequence in *Henry IV, Part ii* that we might take as a subtext for Henry's decision to invade France (but because it is never referred to explicitly in *Henry V* it remains just that) is the advice his dying father gives him. In their final reconciliation (IV. v), Henry IV trusts that his son will inherit the throne with "better opinion, better confirmation" than his own "indirect crooked ways" warranted. Nevertheless, he counsels Hal to consolidate his position at home by pursuing war abroad:

Be it thy course to busy giddy minds
With foreign quarrels, that action, hence borne out,
May waste the memory of the former days. (213–15)

It is impossible to know whether this is a factor in Henry's decision to go to war,[24] since the only hidden agenda we are made aware of at the beginning of that play is the financial one of the clerics, Canterbury and Ely. Yet we discover from Henry's later "God of battles" soliloquy that he is still burdened with guilt over his father's usurpation, acutely aware of Bolingbroke's "fault" in taking the throne from Richard and then initiating the murder of the King. Henry's attempts to atone for the crime (a series of rituals including building chantries and paying five hundred of the poor to pray for Richard's soul) show how desperately he wants to prevent the sins of the father from being visited on the son and his army.

While *Henry V* works as a self-contained play, its roots are in the preceding histories: *Richard II* and the two parts of *Henry IV*. Similarly Henry's character, manifested through his words and behavior, can be seen as a progression of traits found in Prince Hal.[25] Shrewdness and a calculating streak; physical courage; the capacity to play roles for different occasions; a need to communicate with people from different strata of society—all these are aspects of Hal that also emerge in the powerful, successful King Henry V.

Ambivalence: Ideal Monarch or Perfect Machiavel?

How exactly does Henry V come across as a character? It is impossible to pronounce on Shakespeare's intentions, except to note that he was probably more responsive to the chroniclers' enthusiastic portrait than we are. (Our age is predisposed to ferret out irony or deconstructive tendencies within literature, but it is unlikely that Shakespeare was deliberately composing a hostile or derogatory picture of the King.) Nor can we put ourselves into the minds and emotions of Shakespeare's first-night audience, who in any case would not have formed a homogeneous unit with identical ideas and responses. As readers and spectators we are bound to respond to and judge a work from our own historical and social perspectives. And the text contains multiple possibilities.

It is hardly surprising, then, that the character of Henry V has provoked some widely divergent responses in recent years. To some critics Shakespeare's presentation of the King is relatively simple: he is modeled on the ideal Christian prince. Thus J. H. Walter focuses on Henry's "spiritual strength," "faith," and "moral courage," which are supremely manifested at Agincourt.[26] Lily B. Campbell contends that "Henry V stands as an ideal hero,"[27] while in his edition of *Henry V* (published, like Campbell's study, soon after World War II) J. Dover Wilson discusses Henry in heroic terms.[28] Others also find the King equally ideal, but by machiavellian standards, which call for ruthlessness and perfidy in the service of the state. The nineteenth-century essayist William Hazlitt was perhaps the first to call Henry an "amiable monster,"[29] morally repugnant though attractive on stage. Harold C. Goddard pushes the connections with machiavellianism further; finding Henry disingenuous and at times "savage," he thinks that the play often works to "catch the conscience of the king."[30]

In another approach, linked to the first, critics agree that Henry is depicted as an ideal monarch or epic hero but are not impressed with Shakespeare's treatment of this phenomenon. They postulate a playwright who quickly tired of dramatizing the chauvinistic enterprise and produced a hollow, strutting hero—what E.M.W. Tillyard deems a "copy-book paragon of kingly virtue"[31] and Mark Van Doren less charitably calls a "hearty undergraduate with enormous initials on his chest."[32] Convinced that Shakespeare had lost interest in the finale of his tetralogy, A. P. Rossiter finds that "war-time values demand a determined 'one-eyedness' " in the play and concludes that the King remains shallow and the play jingoistic as a result.[33]

In hindsight it becomes clear that critics interpret characters and plays through their own social and political biases. It is more than coincidental that Hazlitt, an anti-monarchist who enthusiastically endorsed the French Revolution, decries Henry's "tyranny" (declaiming that "Such is the history of kingly power to the end of the world"[34]), or that E. K. Chambers, writing shortly before World War I, finds a foreshadowing of the "blatant modern imperialist"[35] in some of Henry's utterances. Dover Wilson, who published his work soon after the Allies' victory in World War II and admired Laurence Olivier's stirring, patriotic film version (1944), dedicated his 1947 edition to "Field Marshall the Viscount Wavell, 'Star of England' in her darkest night." Ardent pacifists usually deplore *Henry V*; others, with different ideological sympathies, become caught up in the exhilarating sweep of the King's actions. Audiences conditioned to see war in terms of national honor (Shakespeare's spectators and many World War II audiences) have found Henry and his campaign more appealing than those disenchanted with military aggression.

Twentieth-century views of Henry V, then, often polarize into "celebratory" versus "ironic" or even satiric; as a protagonist this King has inspired as much dislike as praise. The view of Henry as predominantly heroic is easier to sustain than the interpretation of him as a calculating Machiavel, since to argue unequivocally for the latter, a reader must dig deep below the surface of the play, stay immune to the compelling rhythms of the Crispin's Day speech, and either ignore the Chorus or consider it seriously at odds with the rest of the play. Moreover, in the theater it has proved impossible to project a hollow or hypocritical Henry because the audience inevitably warms to him.[36] He is, above all, a winner. Settling for a single view of Shakespeare's character or setting up camps "for" or "against" Harry, in any case, risks diminishing the play.

In recent years critics have stressed ambivalence, both as a key to the presentation of Henry's character and as a mode integral to the play. In other words, the portrait of Henry may be both laudatory and ironic; as Anne Barton comments, "Celebration and denigration, heroism and irony, exist uneasily side by side"[37] in this drama. The most influential essay using this approach has been Norman Rabkin's "Either / Or: Responding to *Henry V*," a piece well worth reading in its entirety.[38] Rabkin contends that the play is what the Gestalt psychologist Gombrich terms a duck/rabbit; viewed one way, Figure 1 is a rabbit with ears, while viewed another way it is a duck with a long beak; however, it can never be perceived as both simultaneously. Similarly, argues Rabkin, *Henry V* can be seen from two opposing perspectives: either as an extension of *Henry IV, Part i*, which is hopeful that practicality and openness to experience can combine to produce the ideal ruler and man; or as a development from *Henry IV, Part ii*, which is more pessimistic in suggesting that public leaders trade their humanity for power.

Certainly *Henry V*, the play as well as the character, invites "radically different responses."[39] Before considering whether any synthesis is possible, it is helpful to review those sequences in the play that at first seem to present Henry in a good light but, on closer examination, invite more negative responses. We can begin with an interpretation favorable to Henry. In the opening scene the King, serious and purposeful, justifies beginning a war with France. Fully in command at Southampton, he exposes the treachery of his enemies and orders their execution. At Harfleur he proves

Figure 1

Source: Sarah Munson Deats, "Rabbits and Ducks: Olivier, Branagh, and *Henry V*," *Literature/Film Quarterly*, 20 (1992), 284. Reprinted with permission.

himself a strong military leader and a brilliant negotiator with the Governor; again, after the war is over, he demonstrates his shrewd diplomacy with Burgundy and the King of France (Act V). Before the battle of Agincourt Henry is a skillful communicator, addressing the concerns of his soldiers and rallying them to courageous action through the Crispin's Day speech. In battle he is disciplined and decisive (preventing a counterpunch from the French), and he shows his piety in attributing his victory, as indeed the whole progress of the war, to God. Finally, in wooing Katherine, he is successful in converting the good fellowship of a soldier into frankness and blunt charm as a lover.

Nearly all the evidence in these sequences, however, cuts two ways. Henry's sober weighing of his right to invade France may be a sham. Assuming that the opening scene from the Folio is played, the audience knows that the Archbishop has already offered a huge war chest in return for "mitigation" of the bill that would deprive the clergy of half their lands. Does Henry's decision, then, really depend on the Archbishop's Salic law speech? In any case, Canterbury's speech is full of sophistries. For one thing it conveniently ignores the fact that Henry's father was a usurper and that his claim to France through Queen Isabella (mother of Edward III and daughter of Philip of France) could be made more convincingly by the Mortimer line, descended from the third son of Edward III, Lionel, instead of the fourth son, John of Gaunt.[40] Once the speech is perceived as gamesmanship, the rest of scene falls into place as an adroit piece of stage-managed persuasion. Through his elaborate analogy between the beehive and the kingdom, the Archbishop supports Exeter's assertion that England will defend and manage herself competently while the "armed hand" fights abroad. But such arguments do not quite allay questions about why this Christian King and his spiritual adviser are promoting war in the first place.[41] Toward the end of the scene Henry shrewdly reacts to the Dauphin's gift of tennis balls as an insult that requires avenging—a specious pretext for going to war, since he has already resolved to "bend" France to his authority or "break it all to pieces." Under the smooth, persuasive surface of the scene, Henry's behavior, like that of the Archbishop, may strike the audience as "gestures in the game of power."[42]

Henry's exposure of the traitors at Southampton (II. ii) helps define him as a capable king who can uncover treachery and deal with it swiftly. Again, though, the scene is stage-managed carefully, this time to reveal Henry's godlike perspective and skillful strategy as he entraps Cambridge, Scroop, and Grey. Offering to pardon a drunkard who "railed against our person," Henry lures the three into pressing him to punish the man rather than show excessive "mercy." When their treason is subsequently revealed, the King is able to turn their own words against them:

> The mercy that was quick in us but late,
> By your own counsel is suppressed and killed. (79–80)

What is more, he appears to relish their discomfort—"Look ye, how they change! / Their cheeks are paper"—as they read their indictments. In this scene Henry's tactic is close to one recommended in the *Arte of War*, where Machiavelli advises the ruler to crush sedition by gathering all the perpetrators in a neutral place and surprising them before they guess what is afoot: "It must be doen in such a wise, that thou maiest first have oppressed them before they be able to be aware."[43]

Granted, Henry is a strong leader at Harfleur. His oration to his men at the breach, with its inhuman but exhilarating images of the tiger, the cannon, and the rock, works well as a rhetorical ploy to make them keep fighting in a tough situation. But his fantasy projection of what will happen if Harfleur does not surrender, although it can be justified as a bargaining chip, contains an excess of callous ruthlessness—especially in the vision of how the "blind and bloody soldier" will rape "fresh fair virgins" and "shrill-shrieking daughters"—that is hard to condone by complacently referring to what was expected in medieval siege warfare. Henry also damages his image by implicitly allying himself with the tyrannical King Herod (perpetrator of the Massacre of the Innocents) when he alludes to his soldiers as "Herod's bloody-hunting slaughtermen" (III. iii. 41). Henry plays a similarly ruthless role in the final scene of the play. He is prepared to remedy the "imperfections" of France (caused by him) only if the French will "buy" peace on his terms; he is even a stickler for the final article of the treaty, that the French King must always refer to him as son and heir. Echoes of his negotiating through threats of rape (at Harfleur) cast an ironic light on Henry's reference to Katherine as "our capital demand," another of the "maiden cities" to be vanquished.

On one level, Henry communicates well with his soldiers. The Crispin's Day speech, through forceful simplicity and conviction, breaks down social barriers and forges a brotherhood of shared purpose. But this is a public speech; Henry is less successful in bridging the gap when he hides his royal identity and attempts man-to-man conversation on the night before battle. He fails to convince Williams that the King will never agree to be ransomed, and their encounter ends on a contentious note, with Henry accepting a challenge from the soldier. Instead of confronting Williams directly after the battle, however, as he promises in "If ever I live to see it, I will challenge it" (IV. i. 222), Henry concocts a story about taking the glove from Alençon and sends in Fluellen as his substitute to face the challenge (IV. vii). The gap between king and commoner is reinforced rather than healed when Williams points out that Henry unfairly used the advantage of his disguise— "had you been as I took you for, I made no offense" (IV. viii. 55–56)—and Henry follows this up with a gift of crowns that looks suspiciously like a way of buying his subject's loyalty. More subtly, this act of patronage reaffirms the King's absolute authority because Williams has no choice but to accept it.

Henry shows his military discipline in approving, without hesitation, the execution of Bardolph for stealing from a church: "We would have all such offenders so cut off" (III. vi. 112). Yet there is no moment of compunction, no recognition of past ties between him and his Eastcheap companion, even though Fluellen makes a point of identifying Bardolph by his carbuncled complexion and nose "like a coal of fire" (III. vi. 109–10). As with the rejection of Falstaff, which is mentioned not only in association with his death in Act II but again by Fluellen in Act IV, this incident emphasizes Henry's emotional coldness as well as his decisiveness. Similarly, the notorious order to kill the French prisoners appears gratuitously ruthless because it is never fully explained as a justifiable military tactic; it comes too quickly after the announcement that "The French have reinforced their scattered men" (IV. vi. 36) to make much sense without the help of Holinshed's *Chronicles*. It is only retroactively linked with Henry's spontaneous and understandable anger over the massacre of the luggage attendants, an anger that then reaches excess in Henry's threat to cut more throats (IV. vii. 65). If temperance is a cardinal virtue of the ruler, Henry has failed again. His behavior on the battlefield veers confusingly between cold-blooded practicality and barely restrained fury.

Henry's piety is another moot point in the play. The sixteenth-century chroniclers stress his devotion to God; Holinshed, following Hall, mentions the King's ordering the "Te Deum" to be sung after the battle, "giving laud and praise to God,"[44] while Hall reiterates at the end of his admiring narration how Henry was "toward God most devout."[45] Indeed many of Henry's utterances can be taken as straightforwardly reverential. In his opening speech to the Archbishop (who describes him in the preceding scene as "full of grace") he mentions God three times within eleven lines: "God forbid," "For God doth know," "We charge you in the name of God" (13–23). Henry is convinced that the course of the war is providentially arranged and that human intervention counts for little: "We are in God's hand, brother" (III. vi. 177) and "how thou pleasest, God, dispose the day!" (IV. iii. 133). Often, though, the dramatic context overlays Henry's religious assertions with irony.[46] In I. ii Henry determines that the campaign against the French "lies within the will of God," but only after declaring his intention to make the Dauphin pay dearly for his ill-advised gift of tennis balls. Later Henry insists that his men give praise for their victory at Agincourt solely to God:

> And be it death proclaimed through our host
> To boast of this, or take that praise from God
> Which is His only. (IV. viii. 116–18)

This modesty and piety are reinforced by the Chorus to Act V, who describes how Henry gives "ostent / Quite from himself, to God" when he returns to London. Nevertheless, the King's behavior takes on a different cast when considered in the context of the "God of battles" soliloquy. There Henry seems frantic to appease God—"Not today, O Lord, / O, not today, think not upon the fault / My father made" (IV. i. 297–99)—in order to prevent this Old Testament deity from punishing Henry IV's sin of usurpation by allowing the English army to lose a key battle against the French. Henry's respect for God after Agincourt could, on a skeptical reading, be interpreted as gratitude for being let off the hook. With an eye to more satire, the audience might sense that Falstaff's calling out " 'God, God, God!' three or four times" just before he dies (II. iii. 19–20),[47] and Pistol's comment "Signieur Dew should be a gentleman" when he mistakes his prisoner's appeal to God ("O Signieur Dieu!") for the name of the Frenchman (IV. iv. 7), are oblique (and belittling) reflections on Henry's almost excessive deference to God.

Finally comes Henry's wooing of Katherine—again a double-edged business. After a few false starts there are moments of considerable tenderness, but Dr. Johnson is not alone in finding "grossness" and "unskilfulness" in the sequence.[48] A. R. Humphreys pinpoints the ambivalence of our response to Henry here: "One thinks first that he is hearty and honest; next that only a crude nature could be so peculiar—and also that he is shrewdly using Katherine to secure his ends."[49] Much in Henry's wooing is frank and commendable. We warm to his apology for being an unattractive "plain soldier" and his defense of his "good heart," his attempt to communicate with Katherine in French, and his occasional lapses in self-assurance, such as the tentative "Wilt thou have me?" On the other side is Henry's coarseness (his lament "I should quickly leap into a wife" and his terming the Princess a "good soldier-breeder") plus the ruthless political ambition that underlies any love for Katherine: "I love France so well, that I will not part with a village of it" (V. ii. 178–79). The crudeness, with jokes about female sexuality and deflowering maiden cities, surfaces again in the bawdy badinage with Burgundy, a part of the play usually cut in performance.

Because the play so readily generates opposing interpretations, *Henry V* in some ways fits the criteria for a "problem play." This is the term usually restricted to Shakespeare's dark comedies, *Measure for Measure*, *Troilus and Cressida*, and *All's Well That Ends Well*—plays that do not fit easily into the genres of comedy or tragedy and that explore moral questions in an unusually abstract and schematic way. Those critics who prefer to synthesize *Henry V*'s conflicting impressions (rather than resort to the label of "problem play" or choose an "either/or" interpretation) maintain that the favorable portrait of Henry is continually subject to ironic qualification without being totally undercut. Thus Robert Ornstein concedes that the play successfully celebrates English heroism while at the same time it makes "damaging admissions about the motives and methods of the conquerors of France."[50] Just as the Eastcheap characters offer a darker side of the war enterprise but do not radically undermine Henry's "cause," so the moments when we wonder about Henry's possible chicanery or question the decency and fairness of his tactics modify the portrait of him as a hero without turning him into an antihero. As Hugh M. Richmond, avoiding a one-sided approach, observes, "Henry V is shown to us as a great leader, but not an infallible one."[51]

One failing that cannot easily be translated into a virtue is Henry's evasion of responsibility. Logically it is a negative extension of his tendency to refer everything to God's will; as a king, Henry is forever passing the buck. In the council scene of Act I he does this at least twice. When he turns to the Archbishop after the long Salic law disquisition and asks, "May I with right and conscience make this claim?" Canterbury gives the expected reply: "The sin upon my head, dread Sovereign!" (This phrase is echoed when Exeter later tells the French King that Henry is "on your head / Turning the widows' tears, the orphans' cries" [II. iv. 105–6].) After the gift of tennis balls, Henry seizes the opportunity to lay the blame for any ensuing misery in France squarely on the Dauphin—"his soul / Shall stand sore charged for the wasteful vengeance" (I. ii. 282–83)—instead of accepting the implications of his earlier resolve to invade France and "break" it if necessary. In this instance, his quick assertion, "But all this lies within the will of God" (289), sounds like self-serving rationalization. Henry's speech to the Governor of Harfleur is a masterpiece of displaced responsibility as the King turns the horror of rape by British soldiers back on the Governor if he refuses to surrender:

> What is't to me, when you yourselves are cause,
> If your pure maidens fall into the hand
> Of hot and forcing violation? (III. iii. 19–21)

When he talks to Williams, he exonerates himself, as king, from any guilt if his soldiers do not make a "good end" in battle ("The king is not bound to answer the particular endings of his soldiers") and earns from Williams a grudging consent: "'Tis certain, every man that dies ill, the ill upon his own head; the King is not to answer it" (IV. i. 191–92).

Yet Henry clearly resents being expected to carry the burdens of his subjects. For the fourth time in the play, the "upon" phrase is repeated when Henry laments in soliloquy:

> Upon the King! Let us our lives, our souls,
> Our debts, our careful wives,
> Our children, and our sins, lay on the King! (IV. i. 235–37)

Even in the concluding peace treaty Henry is reluctant to admit that he has caused the devastation of France. Once again he ducks responsibility, putting the remedy in the hands of the French King when he tells Burgundy: "Well then, the peace, / Which you before so urged, lies in his answer" (V. ii. 75–76).

The most favorable gloss we can put on Henry's evasiveness or disavowal of responsibility is that the King simply finds it too disturbing to ponder the repercussions of his actions. Transferring responsibility, whether to God, the Dauphin, or the individual soldier, is a way of shutting himself off from what he knows to be the horror of war and the fact that "never two such kingdoms did contend / Without much fall of blood" (I. ii. 24–25). To remain fully sensitive to all the hurt that war entails would mean choosing not to be a statesman or a politician at all.

The Man and the Role of King

This notion is one key to a fuller interpretation of Henry. Rather than showing Henry as either a good leader to be applauded or one defined by hypocrisy or cold-bloodedness, Shakespeare's play explores the necessary gap between the sensitive human being and the shrewd politician or statesman. Humane qualities, those valued in the individual, are frequently sacrificed in the interests of public office. Alvin Kernan puts it well: "Henry V has the public virtues of a great king—magnanimity, courage, resourcefulness, energy, efficiency and a commanding presence. At the same time, certain private traits seen in him earlier—flat practicality and hard objectivity, a lack of complexity amounting almost to insensitivity, a certain coldness of heart—persist, and while contributing much to his political efficiency, raise serious questions about him as a man."[52] Una Ellis-Fermor also sees the play as a "study of the effect on the individual of the demands and privileges of the office" but emphasizes that it provides, overall, a positive study of the statesman-king who has mastered "the great art of conduct."[53] *Richard II* goes deeper in its portrayal of a sensitive, maturing consciousness—W. B. Yeats found Richard's "contemplative virtue" much more appealing than Henry V's "rough energy" and "coarse nerves"[54]—but *Henry V* completes the significant exploration, throughout the history plays, of what makes for a successful king of England and a strong leader, even if that strength often comes at the expense of other qualities prized in the individual human being.[55] That it is virtually impossible to be a successful king and a man of complete integrity is pointed up in one of Nym's teasing qualifications: "The King is a good king, but it must be as it may: he passes some humors and careers" (II. i. 128–29).

The moral contradictions within the role of king—the way that ruthlessness and even duplicity may be required of Henry if he is to maintain strong leadership—are explored more fully in Chapter 4. In the meantime, it is worth remarking that by the end of *Henry V* the decent human being and the powerful king no longer seem irrevocably at odds. It is the wooing scene that offers a synthesis of the two sides of Henry, for this encounter provides an opportunity for Henry's private self (uncomplex, blunt, distrustful of ceremony) to inform his public role. Having decided at Harfleur that the "name" of soldier becomes him best, Henry now trades on this role with Katherine. He cannot act "greenly" because he is an experienced tactician (in war, at least), and, despite his capacity for eloquence, he quickly abandons the part of the courtly lover who glibly manufactures hyberbolic compliments. He reverts to what he plays best—"a fellow of plain and uncoined constancy"—to win Katherine over with frankness. The role of "plain king," as he explains it to her, channels and activates his underlying feelings, for he finds no gap between his "good heart" (the inner self) and his public persona, but rather a natural progression from one to the other: "If thou would have such a one, take me; and take me, take a soldier; take a soldier, take a king" (V. ii. 170–71). In an earlier sequence, when Henry's guard is briefly down with Fluellen, the Welsh Captain pledges respect for him "so long as your Majesty is an honest man"; and the honest man is what comes through in Henry's wooing of the Princess. His pragmatic admission "that I shall die, is true—but for thy love, by the Lord, no" gives resonance to the words that follow: "yet I love thee too" and "By mine honor in true English, I love thee Kate." Finally, in keeping with his straightforwardness (for Henry is, after all, a man of action and not a traditional courtly lover), he bypasses the formal ceremony of "nice customs" and a "country's fashion" to kiss her on the lips. The whole sequence suggests that Henry succeeds in projecting himself authentically, releasing his genuine feelings through role-playing the soldier-king in love.

This provides a sense of resolution. The glimpses of Henry the man that we are given (mainly in the pre-Agincourt sequences of Act IV but also in II. i and III. vi) suggest anxiety about fulfilling his role, plus resentment and even self-pity at being expected to "bear" such heavy responsibility as king. But at the end of the play, when Henry turns lover, his inner self is neither fretful nor effaced. It combines with the role of king to create a new compound; for Henry remains a "fellow of plain . . . constancy" who is also a "plain king" and "the best king of good fellows."

The name "Harry" also provides some mediation between the king and the man. It may come as a surprise that, with the exception of the final scene where the King refers to himself formally as "Henry Plantagenet" and appears as "Henry" in the articles of agreement with France, he is always called Harry. (In the Quarto he is given the speech prefix "Harry" throughout this final scene.) For twentieth-century speakers, this version of the name connotes intimacy; in the play, though, it suggests informality without being overfamiliar. It encourages the audience to view Henry in more human terms, from the standpoint of his fifteenth-century subjects, who loved as well as revered their king. (Viewed at a greater historical distance, King Henry V is always referred to in the three parts of *Henry VI* as Henry.) It is the Chorus who sets the tone of warm affection as well as admiration by invoking the "warlike Harry" (Prologue, 5), the first of his six uses of the first name that in no way undercut his more reverential terms, "grace" and "mirror of kings." Sir Thomas Erpingham's heartfelt prayer, "the Lord in heaven bless thee, noble Harry!" (IV. i. 33), offers the same double perspective—the laudatory "noble" prefacing the informal "Harry"—without contradicting Erpingham's customary forms of address to the King as "your grace" and "my liege." It may be significant that on his final appearance Montjoy addresses Henry simply as "great king" and that the French monarch, in the final scene, refers to Henry only as "brother England" and, in the article confirming the English King as his heir, as "très cher fils

Henri . . . Henricus." Yet when the French, on four occasions, refer to King Harry or Harry of England, the term does not seem particularly condescending, since Henry usually refers to himself in the same way. Indeed, in the public Crispin's Day speech he realistically envisages the name of "Harry the king" becoming a "familiar" household word in years to come (IV. iii. 52–53).

LANGUAGE AND STYLE

We should not expect in *Henry V* the range and complexity of metaphor, or the rhythmic subtlety, of the great tragedies. The smooth blank verse of Henry's "'Tis not the balm, the scepter, and the ball" in his soliloquy on the penalties of kingship (IV. i. 235-89) never rises to the intensity of the mad King Lear's concentrated, arhythmic speech on the abuse of authority: "Robes and furr'd gowns hide all" (*King Lear*, IV. vi. 165). Nor does the language offer as much lively realism as does *Henry IV, Part i*—whether it is Henry IV's mimetic opening speech, "Find we a time for frighted peace to pant" (I. i. 2), Hotspur's comparison of "mincing poetry" to the "forc'd gait of a shuffling nag" (III. i. 132–33), or Falstaff's witty disquisition on Bardolph's fiery, carbuncled nose as a "perpetual triumph, an everlasting bonfire light" (III. iii. 41–42). Some of the verse in *Henry V* stays on the level of set speeches, appropriate to the occasion or mood rather than to the speaker. Exeter's lyric, almost sentimental description of how York greeted the dying Suffolk ("Tarry, sweet soul, for mine, then fly abreast" [IV. vi. 17]) and Canterbury's elaboration of the beehive analogy (I. ii. 183–204) are speeches of this kind. Yet in general the play's language is far from "mechanical" or "lethargic."[56] Not surprisingly in a play with many speaking parts for people from different regions, there is a considerable range of styles, and several characters—Fluellen, Pistol, Henry—*are* clearly distinguished by their speech patterns. *Henry V* purposefully experiments with different kinds of language to create a diverse social panorama within a European war.

Prose

Act I of *Henry V* is entirely in blank verse (iambic pentameter), but the other acts alternate between scenes of prose and ones written in poetry. Seven scenes are almost completely in prose (II. i, iii; III. ii, iv, vii; IV. iv; V. i) and five more are a mixture, with Henry speaking prose in an intimate setting but switching to poetry when he assumes his formal role (III. vi; IV.

i, vii, viii; V. ii). With the exception of Pistol, who launches into swaggering verse at the drop of a hat, low-life and even middle-class characters speak in prose. Comic, informal sequences are also presented in this mode; thus Princess Katherine, in the one scene composed all in French (III. iv), speaks to her maid Alice in prose, and the French aristocrats deviate from their usual formal verse in their edgy scene before Agincourt, where they rib the Dauphin for his attachment to his horse (III. vii).

True to form, Shakespeare individualizes several of his low-life characters through their prose styles. Nym, torn between rancor toward Pistol and the need to appear respectful, talks in a series of clauses that make a stab at decisiveness but because of their qualifications ("may," "I cannot tell") and even tautology ("things must be as they may") never firmly hit the center:

> I cannot tell. Things must be as they may; men may sleep, and they may have their throats about them at that time, and some say knives have edges. It must be as it may; though patience be a tired mare, yet she will plod; there must be conclusions. Well, I cannot tell. (II. i. 22–27)

Even more comic is the way that he deflects violence (clearly he is not brave enough to vent his spleen frankly on Pistol) and renders it innocuous through verbal qualifications: "I have an humor to knock you *indifferently well*" (58), "I would prick your guts *a little in good terms*" (61–62), and "I will cut thy throat one time or other *in fair terms*" (72–73) (emphasis added).[57] His catchphrase is "there's the humor of it"—perhaps a theatrical in-joke alluding to Ben Jonson's comedy of humors (*Everyman in His Humor* was first performed in 1599, with *Everyman out of His Humor* a year later). Although his mention of "humor" is more a verbal tic than a reference to any of the physiological imbalances or rooted psychological traits that Jonson was interested in portraying, Nym may touch on this deeper meaning of "humor" when he observes that the King "hath run bad humors on the knight" (124).

The Hostess speaks in delightfully inconsequential prose, mistaking "adultery" for bodily harm ("We shall see willful adultery and murder committed" [II. i. 39–40]) and the color "carnation" (scarlet) for "incarnate" (II. iii. 33–35). Meanwhile the Boy comes across as remarkably shrewd in his acute analysis of his companions:

> For Bardolph, he is white-livered and red-faced; by the means whereof 'a faces it out, but fights not. For Pistol, he hath a killing tongue and a quiet sword; by the means whereof 'a breaks words, and keeps whole

weapons. For Nym, he hath heard that men of few words are the best
men, and therefore he scorns to say his prayers, lest 'a should be thought
a coward; but his few bad words are matched with as few good deeds,
for 'a never broke any man's head but his own, and that was against a
post when he was drunk. . . . (III. ii. 32–42)

Here the progressive parallelism of "For Bardolph . . . For Pistol . . . For
Nym" is offset by witty antitheses: "white-livered" / "red-faced" (Bardolph), "killing tongue" / "quiet sword" (Pistol), and "few bad words" /
"few good deeds" (Nym). In this last instance, what initially seems to be a
compliment ("few bad words") turns into a deficiency when juxtaposed with
the following phrase (antithesis within parallelism) of "few good deeds."
     Prose is the medium through which Shakespeare creates an interplay of
regional dialects. Although Captain Fluellen is not a low-life character, his
melodic Welsh intonation and his verbal mannerisms ("look you," "by
Cheshu," "I warrant you") are more suited to a low-key medium than to
verse. This is how he describes Macmorris:

> By Cheshu, he is an ass, as in the world! . . . He has no more directions
> in the true disciplines of the wars, look you, of the Roman disciplines,
> than is a puppy-dog. (III. ii. 72–75)

As in his substitution of the phoneme /tʃ/ for /dʒ/ ("Cheshu" for "Jesu"),
Fluellen's Welsh accent comes through in /f/ for /v/ ("Captain Jamy is a
marvelous *f*alorous gentleman" [78–79]) and in /p/ for /b/ ("Alexander the
*P*ig" and Henry's "Welsh *p*lood" [IV. vii. 14, 110]). Fluellen is much given
to copiousness of style, often to the point of redundancy, as when he
describes the Duke of Exeter as "a man that I love and honor with my soul,
and my heart, and my duty, and my live, and my living, and my uttermost
power" (III. vi. 7–79) and repeats his condemnation of the enemy as "an ass
and a fool and a prating coxcomb" (IV. i. 78–81). Shakespeare gives
Macmorris an Irish accent that is less subtle than Fluellen's Welsh one. His
belligerence comes through in the staccato exclamations with which he
deplores the mining of Harfleur: "O tish ill done, tish ill done! By my hand,
tish ill done!" (III. ii. 94–95). The even-tempered Jamy's keyword is "gud,"
spelled phonetically (along with other words) to convey his Scottish accent:
"It sall be vary gud, gud feith, gud captens bath, and I sall quit you with gud
leve" (104–5). Princess Katherine is naturally happiest speaking in French;
when she does attempt English, Shakespeare projects her French accent
through /s/ for /ʃ/ ("sould" for "should") and /d/ for /ʃ/ ("de" for "the"), as
in "Is it possible *d*at I *s*ould love *d*e ennemie of France?" (V. ii. 174–75).

This line appears in the wooing scene, where King Henry converses with Katherine in prose. It is an opportunity for him to shed the kingly aura and use a more colloquial register, one in keeping with the role of "plain soldier" that he wants to project, as well as a vehicle for more genuine intimacy.[58] Sometimes his discourse *is* very plain, even crude: "Give me your answer, i' faith do; and so clap hands, and a bargain. How say you, lady?" (V. ii. 131–33). The down-to-earth medium also expresses Henry's frustration— "I shall never move thee in French, unless it be to laugh at me" (192–94)— and his exasperated humor, when he retorts to her evasive "I cannot tell" with "Can any of your neighbors tell, Kate? I'll ask them" (203–4). But the rhetorical finesse that Henry demonstrates in his poetry, combined with commonsense shrewdness, also appears in the controlled syntax of his prose. As he convinces her that good looks do not matter, the symmetrical clauses (identical in structure) build through repetition to the logical climax, and then amplification, of "good heart":

> a good leg will fall, a straight back will stoop, a black beard will turn white, a curled pate will grow bald, a fair face will wither, a full eye will wax hollow: but a good heart, Kate, is the sun and the moon, or rather, the sun, and not the moon, for it shines bright and never changes, but keeps his course truly. (163–70)

The other scene where many of Henry's speeches are in prose is IV. i, his encounter with that "plain" but eloquent commoner, Williams. Once again the King reveals a strong rather than a subtle mind in his conversation with the soldiers. His prose is forcefully and logically structured when he rebuts Williams' charge that "the King himself hath a heavy reckoning to make." The parallelism, emphasizing the analogies between the "king . . . father . . . master" and then evoking a range of sins in the soldiers through the "some . . . some . . . some" clauses, drives home the point that Henry needs to make: that the king is not responsible for the souls of his subjects:

> The king is not bound to answer the particular endings of his soldiers, the father of his son, nor the master of his servant; for they purpose not their death when they purpose their services. Besides, there is no king, be his cause never so spotless, if it come to the arbitrament of swords, can try it out with all unspotted soldiers: some (peradventure) have on them the guilt of premeditated and contrived murder; some, of beguiling virgins with the broken seals of perjury; some, making the wars their bulwark, that have before gored the gentle bosom of peace with pillage and robbery. (IV. i. 158–70)

The diction, too, is ornate rather than simple, with the personification of "peace" as having a "gored" bosom, and latinisms such as "arbitrament" and "premeditated." After Henry, a few lines later, reaches the forceful climax (with its clinching antithesis) of "Every subject's duty is the King's, but every subject's soul is his own," he uses the logical connective "therefore"[59] as a springboard to his next moral exhortation, that each soldier should "wash every mote out of his conscience." We are swept along in the sequence, convinced of a strong line of argument despite some glossing over the question of the rightness of Henry's "cause."

Henry's chat with Fluellen about the Welsh custom of wearing a leek on Saint David's Day (IV. vii) produces two lines that can be scanned as verse ("I wear it for a memorable honor; / For I am Welsh, you know, good countryman" [107–8]) but three other shorter ones—"They did, Fluellen," "Thanks, good my countryman," "God keep me so!"—which are more likely prose than half lines of blank verse. Unmemorable as these words are on the page, this encounter, a drop in tension after the battle, becomes an emotional high point in Branagh's *Henry V*. These are moments when the usually restrained Henry, now conversing in an informal manner about being an honest Welshman, drops his mask and breaks into tears of relief.

Overall, the sequences in prose do not suggest only "language barriers" and "noncommunication";[60] rather, they create diversity and moments of intimacy within the play. It is true that the Welshman, the Irishman, and the Scotsman, superficially brought together in the cause of fighting against the French, are separated by more than their dialects, and that the quarrelsome "yokefellows" Bardolph, Nym, and Pistol unite mainly in their quest to steal. We know, too, that the marriage of Henry and Katherine, designed to join together French and English, will be cut short by Henry's death. Nevertheless, Katherine's deficiencies in English (which she uses partly as a protective shield, not wanting to accede too quickly to Henry's overtures) do prod Henry into articulating his case more fully and trying to reach her level, even by attempting to speak her native tongue. Prose is the vehicle for this rapprochement.

Verse

At the opposite extreme from the informality of the prose is the high style of the Chorus, who speaks mainly in blank verse but departs from it to deliver a sonnet for the Epilogue. The Chorus's function in creating a heightened tone for the action and presenting Henry as a hero has already been discussed, but there are some unusual features in the language of the

Chorus that additionally foreground it from the rest of the play. Several adjectives —"vasty" (Prologue, 12), "abutting" (21), "Breasting" (III. 0. 13), and "self-glorious" (V. 0. 20)—draw attention to themselves by being nonce words. All of them are first recorded uses (in Shakespeare or elsewhere),[61] as is the noun "sternage" (III. 0.18). The inversion of noun and adjective in "crowns imperial" (II. 0. 10) and "fleet majestical " (III. 0. 16) produces a classical formality, while latinate adjectives in the Chorus to Act IV, where the English are like "horrid" ghosts with "umbered" faces by the "paly" flames, help to produce a sense of epic portentousness, a static heraldic tableau anticipating a momentous outcome. The Chorus is also resourceful in his figures of speech. The wordplay in "treacherous crowns" (coins and emblems of royalty) and "gilt" / "guilt" in the Chorus to Act II emphasizes the association between treason and wealth (the traitors have sold themselves to the French). The Chorus to Act IV develops a sustained personification of night, turning the intangible into a concrete source of irritation to both armies. To the French, impatient to join battle, night is a "cripple tardy-gaited" and an ugly "witch"; she is also endowed with a "foul womb" and a "dull ear." Yet through the transferred epithets in "weary and all-watched night" ("all-watched," meaning spent in military watches, is close in sound to "o'er-watched," or awake for too long), night also takes on the attributes of the English soldiers, especially Henry, who is tired but too anxious to sleep.

While the language of the Chorus is subtle and elevated, Pistol's "stiff armour-plated"[62] verse is overblown—in some ways a parody of the heroic register. Pistol's brash bravado in threatening Nym is pointed through extravagant figures of speech: apostrophe, alliteration (on "d" and "g"), and personification, where the standard image of the gaping grave is followed by the absurd collocation of death with "doting":

> O braggard vile, and damned furious wight!
> The *g*rave doth *g*ape, and *d*oting *d*eath is near. (II. i. 63–64)

Another source of amusement for the Elizabethan audience would be the archaic, fustian flavor of Pistol's speeches, produced here in the old-fashioned word "wight" (for man) and the classical inversion of adjective and noun in "braggard vile." Even in the stress of trying to save Bardolph's neck, Pistol does not lose his penchant for doubling and alliterating adjectives, as he expounds on "giddy *F*ortune's *f*urious *f*ickle wheel" to Fluellen (III. vi. 27).

Henry's blank verse is altogether more decorous and flexible. His verse ranges from the lofty to the naturalistic—he can "dazzle" as well as plod

"like a man for working days" (I. ii. 277–79)—but it is always rhetorical.
As befits a strong and shrewd leader, the King finds the appropriate verbal
strategy to persuade others to act on his behalf; he specializes in what Joseph
A. Porter terms "directed, practical, consequential" speech acts.[63] The first
words that he speaks to Canterbury are not the "sweet and honeyed sen-
tences" mentioned by the Archbishop in his opening eulogy (I. i. 50) but
balanced and judicious ones, carefully directed toward a practical end:

> My learned lord, we pray you to proceed,
> And justly and religiously unfold
> Why the law Salique, that they have in France,
> Or should or should not bar us in our claim. (I. ii. 9–12)

His message to the Dauphin channels fury into heavily underlined wordplay,
as he expands the tennis analogy into "matched our rackets to these balls,"
"play a set," and "courts of France" and forcefully repeats the word "mock"
as both noun and verb to make his point more incisively:

> And tell the pleasant prince this mock of his
> Hath turned his balls to gunstones . . .
> . . . for many a thousand widows
> Shall this his mock mock out of their dear husbands,
> Mock mothers from their sons, mock castles down. . . . (I. ii. 281–86)

Apart from his two soliloquies (which almost count as one) in IV. i.
235–89, 294–311, Henry is always on display. Hence his verse is public
address, a means of impressing and exhorting others rather than exploring
his inner emotions. Even the one speech where a strong personal animus
does come through—his intense disillusionment with the "Ingrateful, savage, and inhuman" Scroop—is carefully modulated, through anaphora, to
stress the gap between appearance and reality:

> . . . Show men dutiful?
> Why, so didst thou. Seem they grave and learned?
> Why, so didst thou. Come they of noble family?
> Why, so didst thou. Seem they religious?
> Why, so didst thou. (II. ii. 127–31)

When we next see Henry, at Harfleur, he is rousing his men to heroic
action through a series of strong imperatives—"imitate the action of the
tiger," "Stiffen the sinews," "set the teeth and stretch the nostril wide"

(III. i. 6, 7, 15)—that endow the soldiers with animal strength. He elaborates two epic similes (the eye as a cannonball, the forehead as a rock lashed by waves) to convey the almost inhuman resolve and fierceness that he expects of his soldiers:

> Then lend the eye a terrible aspect:
> Let it pry through the portage of the head
> Like the brass cannon; let the brow o'erwhelm it
> As fearfully as doth a galled rock
> O'erhang and jutty his confounded base,
> Swilled with the wild and wasteful ocean. (9–14)

In its heightened energy and hortatory mood Henry's speech is almost an extension of the Chorus immediately preceding it, which also works by exhortation ("Hear the shrill whistle," "behold the threaden sails," and "Follow, follow!"). It is a superb oration. Henry sweeps through and includes all the ranks of his army in his address. After the general apostrophe to "dear friends" he singles out the "noble English" (17), then the "good yeomen" (25), and finally, by implication, the lower classes: "For there is none of you so mean and base / That hath not noble luster in your eyes" (29–30). His speech to the Governor (III. iii. 1–43) is also a powerful, carefully structured piece of persuasion. Henry exonerates himself from responsibility through the repeated "What is it then to me?" formulation (followed by the grotesque vision of what "impious war," rather than King Harry, will do) and the determined logic with which he blames his opponent for the indiscriminate rape and slaughter that will ensue if the Governor refuses to yield up his town:

> If not—why, in a moment look to see
> The blind and bloody soldier with foul hand
> Defile the locks of your still-shrieking daughters. . . . (33–35)

The horror is further distanced by the conventional language that Henry uses, such as "fresh fair virgins" and "flow'ring infants," often with a formal balance of two adjectives joined by "and" in front of the noun: "hot and forcing (violation)," "cool and temperate (wind of grace)," "filthy and contagious (clouds)," and "blind and bloody (soldier)."

In contrast, Henry's Crispin Day speech (IV. iii. 18–67) is direct and distinctively colloquial in its diction, using such phrases as "hath no stomach," "stand a-tiptoe," "strip his sleeves and show his scars." The King is emotionally engaged as he appeals to his soldiers to join with him in creating a historical moment of mythic proportions. For all its simplicity of diction, often monosyllabic, the speech progresses brilliantly through its projection of a future ("will" repeated four times, "shall" nine times within twenty-five lines) in which the feats they jointly perform in this battle will be "freshly rememb'red" every year on the feast day. The repetition, with expansion, of "we" in "We few, we happy few, we band of brothers" extends into the idea of brotherhood through bloodletting ("For he today that sheds his blood with me / Shall be my brother" [61–62]). Thus Henry forges, through wordcraft, an exhilarated fellowship from which the effete aristocrats now asleep in England will forever be excluded:

> And gentlemen in England, now abed,
> Shall think themselves accursed they were not here;
> And hold their manhoods cheap whiles any speaks
> That fought with us upon Saint Crispin's Day. (64–67)

The summation of the speech comes in Henry's plain words to Salisbury, which carry absolute conviction: "All things are ready, if our minds be so" (71). This, one feels, is Henry's metier: an assured verse that effaces its rhetorical skill in a shared sense of comradeship, revealing Henry as the "best king of good fellows" (V. ii. 252).

In many ways the Crispin's Day speech is more animated and heartfelt than Henry's first soliloquy, where he laments the "hard condition" of being a king shackled by "ceremony." Here the private voice, as Henry expresses his disenchantment with the pomp of being a king through a series of apostrophes and formal questions, sounds remarkably like the public one:

> What are thy rents? What are thy comings-in?
> O Ceremony, show me but thy worth!
> What is thy soul of adoration? (IV. i. 248–50)

There is more urgency in Henry's later appeal "Not today, O Lord, / O not today" (297–98), with his simple promise "More will I do" (reinforced by stressed monosyllables) as he exhorts God not to punish him for the sins of his father in the ensuing battle. Again, though, these soliloquies are characterized by superb control of syntax; Henry is always engaged in an act of persuasion or building to a rhetorical point.

Image Patterns and Key Metaphors

Unlike the tragedies, *Henry V* does not contain a wealth of iterative imagery, such as the complex metaphors conveying sickness and corruption in *Hamlet* ("Something is rotten in the state of Denmark") or the sustained animal imagery that helps make concrete the theme of human bestiality in *King Lear*. But the images noted in the Chorus—the elements of fire and air, echoed in the Dauphin's praise of his horse as "pure air and fire" (III. vii. 21) and the reference to the "winged heels" of England's youth—connote speed; indeed the play moves along very swiftly. In the second scene, Henry hopes that "reasonable swiftness" (in arranging supplies for the war) may "add / More feathers to our wings" (I. ii. 306–7), and before Agincourt the cheerful King pays tribute to the "fresh legerity" of the body when the "mind is quick'ned" (IV. i. 20–23).[64] Sometimes the images in this play stay on the surface, briefly elaborating an idea in the ongoing argument or creating moments of visual power.[65] This is the case with Henry's extended epic similes (sometimes given a biblical twist), as when he compares "impious war" to flaming Satan in his address to the Governor of Harfleur:

> What is it then to me if impious war,
> Arrayed in flames like to the prince of fiends,
> Do with his smirched complexion all fell feats
> Enlinked to waste and desolation? (III. iii. 15-18)

Several repeated terms and images in *Henry V* tap into the war theme. In keeping with the play's military setting —a context also invoked in Mark Antony's savage resolve in *Julius Caesar*, "Cry 'Havoc!' and let slip the dogs of war" (III. i. 273)—war is sometimes associated with canines.[66] Several of these dog references form part of Pistol's abusive idiom; he puts Nym down by calling him "Iceland dog" and "hound of Crete" (II. i. 44, 76) and shouts "Yield cur" to his French prisoner (IV. iv. i). Fluellen turns the tables by referring to Pistol and his friends as "dogs" to be kicked back to the breach (III. ii. 20). The Chorus, in a loftier image that enhances Henry's status as a conquering hero, refers to "famine, sword, and fire" crouching at Henry's heels like hounds on a leash (Prologue, 6–8), while Henry envisages his soldiers as "greyhounds in the slips" (III. i. 31). The French are more derogatory about the English army, Orleans comparing them scathingly to their mastiffs: "Foolish curs, that run winking into the mouth of a Russian bear" (III. vii. 148–49). Images that associate warfare with violent death—for instance, war personified as a cruel devourer, in "this hungry war / Opens his vasty jaws" (II. iv. 104–5)—are particularly concentrated at the end of Act II and in Henry's speeches at Harfleur.[67]

Shakespeare's history plays, with their emphasis on genealogy and mortal combat, often foreground the word "blood." *Henry V* has more than its share of the word—thirty-three occurrences as opposed to thirty-two in *Richard III*, a considerably longer play. Sometimes "blood" refers simply to bloodshed, as when Henry forewarns much "fall of blood" in the kingdoms of France and England if they go to war (I. ii. 25). Often, though, it signals an appeal to famous ancestors, with Exeter urging the King to remember those "former lions of your blood" who triumphed on French soil (124). The related sense of blood as manly spirit and courage is prominent when the French Constable mistakenly contrasts the "cold blood" of the English (whom he disparages as having little "blood . . . in all their sickly veins" [IV. ii. 20]) with the "quick blood" of the French soldiers (III. v. 20–21). Henry adroitly extends the association of blood with war wounds into blood as kinship when he makes his promise at the climax of the Crispin's Day speech:

> For he today that sheds his blood with me
> Shall be my brother; be he ne'er so vile. . . . (IV. iii. 61–62)

True, this fraternity may be only temporary. Since Henry usually reserves the term "brother" or "brothers" for his siblings, Gloucester and Bedford (as in III. vi. 177 and IV. i, 24, 30), and at the end of the play addresses the French King as "brother" (V. ii. 2, 83), there is no sign that social distinctions will miraculously disappear after Agincourt. Yet Henry's forging of blood brotherhood on the battlefield does contrast strongly with the fastidious and snobbish attitude of the French immediately after their defeat. Montjoy, horrified that their aristocrats lie "soaked in mercenary blood" while the "vulgar drench their peasant limbs / In blood of princes" (IV. vii. 78–80), requests that the French be allowed to "sort" the nobles from the commoners for separate burial.

The image that gains the most resonance in the play, and correlates with the idea of Henry as both destroyer and savior, is that of the garden. Those horticultural images that Ely and the Constable use to point Henry's transformation from wild prince to perfect king each suggest an element of purposeful camouflage: Ely thinks that Henry's studying how to be a good king "Grew like the summer grass, fastest by night" under the "veil of wildness" (I. i. 64–65), while the Constable envisages Henry "Covering discretion with a coat of folly," just as gardeners cover roots with manure so that plants will flourish (II. iv. 38–40). At the beginning of the war the French still judge Henry by his "greener days" (II. iv. 136)—his apparently carefree period as Prince Hal—and Falstaff, perhaps remembering those times, on his deathbed babbles of "green fields" (II. iii. 17–18). It is significant that this kind of "wildness" rather than flourishing is also emphasized in Burgundy's long speech on how the fertile garden of France has gone to seed because of the war. Burgundy recreates details such as the hedges "Like prisoners wildly overgrown with hair" in his exploration of how "vineyards, fallows, meads, and hedges, / Defective in their natures, grow to wildness" (V. ii. 43, 54–55). But can Henry be the civilized cultivator again, restoring France to its status as the "best garden of the world"? The image that he uses when he speaks to the Governor of Harfleur, of how his soldiers will range, "mowing like grass / Your fresh fair virgins and your flow'ring infants" (III. iii. 13–14), suggests an absolute antipathy between war and fruitful cultivation. Yet one early image in the play does link Henry with the restored garden of Eden. Canterbury reminds Ely of how Henry's "wildness" disappeared when his father died; at that time the "offending Adam" was whipped out of him by an angelic presence and his body became "as a paradise / T' envelop and contain celestial spirits" (I. i. 29–31). The image is extravagant, but it suggests that Henry has somehow brought back a prelapsarian state, turning England into the "other Eden" referred to in Gaunt's eulogy of England in *Richard II* (II. i. 40–68). Nevertheless, his kingdom *is* a fallen society, as Scroop's betrayal of him a few scenes later makes clear. Bitterly envisaging his close friend as the victim of a "cunning fiend," Henry sees Scroop's act of treason as "another fall of man," resulting in the loss of Eden.

It is possible that Agincourt symbolizes a restoration of paradise to the British. Fluellen's reminder to Henry (proud of his Welsh ancestry) of how the "Welshmen did good service in a garden where leeks did grow" (IV. vii. 101–2) obliquely points in that direction, though the garden of France is utterly ruined for its natives. Henry's marriage to Katherine signals the renewal of the land. The King of France, using a horticultural image, finds in this union a hope for restoring fertility as well as peace between the kingdoms; he trusts that this "dear conjunction" may "Plant neighborhood and Christian-like accord / In their sweet bosoms" (V. ii. 364–66). Even though the Epilogue tells us that the "world's best garden" achieved by Henry will soon be lost by his son, we have briefly witnessed, through Henry, the prospect of its transformation from wildness to order and assured prosperity.[68]

NOTES

1. W. K. Wimsatt (ed.), *Dr Johnson on Shakespeare* (Harmondsworth: Penguin English Library, 1969), p. 121.

2. Andrew Gurr (ed.), *Henry V* (Cambridge: Cambridge University Press, 1992), accepts F's reading "feigning" in line 6, "With silken streamers the young Phoebus feigning," and glosses it "the English fleet pretending to be rising Phoebus," which suggests a more direct connection between the ships and the sun. Most editors adopt Rowe's emendation, "fanning."

3. See Larry S. Champion, *Perspective in Shakespeare's English Histories* (Athens: University of Georgia Press, 1980), pp. 148–49.

4. Herbert Lindenberger, *Historical Drama: The Relation of Literature and Reality* (Chicago and London: University of Chicago Press, 1975), views *Henry V* as "ceremonial drama" that avoids a tight "unity of events" (79).

5. "Thematic Contraries and the Dramaturgy of *Henry V*," *SQ*, 31 (1980), 343–56, 344.

6. This term is used in Sally Beauman (ed.), *The Royal Shakespeare Company's Centenary Production of* Henry V (Oxford: Oxford University Press, 1976), which contains interviews with the actors playing Bardolph, Nym, and Pistol in the 1975 RSC production (91–95).

7. Roy Battenhouse, "*Henry V* as Heroic Comedy," in Richard Hosley (ed.), *Essays on Shakespeare and Elizabethan Drama in Honor of Hardin Craig* (Columbia: University of Missouri Press, 1962), pp. 163–82, finds that the "antic clowning" does indeed parody the main action of the play (169).

8. This is the view of Richard Levin, *The Multiple Plot in English Renaissance Drama* (Chicago and London: University of Chicago Press, 1971): that the "negative analogies" provided by the clowns "augment" the "seriousness of the main action" (119).

9. Harold C. Goddard, *The Meaning of Shakespeare* (Chicago and London: University of Chicago Press, 1951), comments on the thievery parallels (259–60).

10. It is ironic that Pistol is first styled "Ancient" (ensign) when, according to Paul Jorgensen, *Shakespeare's Military World* (Berkeley and Los Angeles: University of California Press, 1956), this office of standard-bearer "called for courage and honor" (81). Pistol's self-appointed office of sutler (or victualler), with its reputation for cheating and exploitation, is more appropriate to his character (83).

11. This is not emphasized in Shakespeare's play, but it was deplored in the historical campaign. According to Desmond Seward, *Henry V: The Scourge of God* (New York: Viking, 1985), Henry's "men were horrified" at the King's order to kill the prisoners, "not from compassion but at the prospect of losing such valuable ransoms" (81).

12. William Babula, "Whatever Happened to Prince Hal? An Essay on *Henry V*," *ShS*, 30 (1977), 47–59, stresses the "moral criticism" of Henry through the Eastcheap counterparts, but concedes that by the end of the play Pistol serves not as a parallel but "as a contrast to a matured king" (57).

13. *Perspective in Shakespeare's Histories*, p. 154.

14. Gary Taylor (ed.), *Henry V* (Oxford: Oxford University Press, 1982), p. 61.

15. In J. R. Brown (ed.), *Henry V, The Signet Classic Shakespeare* (1965; 1988), p. 180.

16. Jorgensen notes that one additional source of contemporary friction between the English and the Irish was that by 1599 the Queen had ordered that no more Irish captains were to be commissioned in her army (*Shakespeare's Military World*, p. 79).

17. *Shakespeare's History Plays* (1944; London: Chatto and Windus, 1959), pp. 305–6.

18. See J. H. Walter (ed.), *Henry V, The Arden Shakespeare* (1954), p. xviii.

19. *Shakespeare and the Problem of Meaning* (Chicago and London: University of Chicago Press), pp. 33–62.

20. James L. Calderwood, *Metadrama in Shakespeare's Henriad* (Berkeley; Los Angeles; London: University of California Press, 1979), points out how Prince Hal goes about "collecting something from each as he prepares to pay England the debt he never promised" (59).

21. *The Royal Shakespeare Company's Centenary Production of* Henry V, p. 53.

22. Ibid., p. 57.

23. Anne Barton, "The King Disguised: Shakespeare's *Henry V* and the Comical History," in Joseph Price (ed.), *The Triple Bond* (University Park: Pennsylvania State University Press, 1975), comments on how "the mind and heart of the king are essentially opaque. . . . His true thoughts and feelings remain veiled behind a series of royal poses" (102). Andrew Gurr also discusses this "opaque self" (*Henry V*, [ed.], p. 12), as does John D. Cox, *Shakespeare and the Dramaturgy of Power* (Princeton: Princeton University Press, 1989), pp. 111–13.

24. A. C. Bradley, "The Rejection of Falstaff," *Oxford Lectures on Poetry* (1909; London: Macmillan, 1965), assumes that his father's advice—to go to war "to keep factious nobles quiet and unite the nation"—was Henry's motive for pursuing his claim to France (257).

25. In *A Kingdom for a Stage: The Achievement of Shakespeare's History Plays* (Cambridge, Mass.: Harvard University Press, 1972), Robert Ornstein speculates that Shakespeare worked backwards from Henry V to Prince Hal and deduced from "Harry as the hero of Agincourt . . . the personality of the Prince who appears in the *Henry IV* plays" (183).

26. *Henry V* (ed.), p. xxxi.

27. *Shakespeare's "Histories" as Mirrors of Elizabethan Policy* (San Marino, Calif.: The Huntingdon Library, 1947; 1968), p. 255. More recently, C.W.R.D. Moseley, *Shakespeare's History Plays*, Richard II *to* Henry V (London: Penguin Books, 1988), argues that Henry develops into a credible "mirror of all Christian kings" (153).

28. "Heroism is the theme, and Henry the hero:" *Henry V* (ed.) (Cambridge: Cambridge University Press, 1947), "Introduction," p. xxxii.

29. *Characters of Shakespeare's Plays* (London, 1818), included in J. R. Brown (ed.), *Henry V*, pp. 211–16, 213.

30. *The Meaning of Shakespeare*, pp. 235, 228.

31. *Shakespeare's History Plays*, p. 305.

32. *Shakespeare* (New York: Henry Holt, 1939), p. 176.

33. "Ambivalence: The Dialectic of the Histories," in *Angel with Horns* (London: Longman, 1961), p. 58.

34. *Characters of Shakespeare's Plays*, p. 212.

35. *Shakespeare: A Survey* (1925; repr. Harmondsworth: Penguin Books, 1964), p. 113.

36. Max Meredith Reese, *The Cease of Majesty: A Study of Shakespeare's History Plays* (London: E. Arnold, 1961), comments on how *Henry V*, "proof against the perversity of directors," unites the audience when it is performed in the theater (319). William Tydeman, *William Shakespeare,* Henry V (Harmondsworth: Penguin, 1987), also finds that Henry can seem "a mass of contradictions and yet galvanize us in the theatre" (107).

37. "The King Disguised," p. 101.

38. In *Shakespeare and the Problem of Meaning*, pp. 33–62.

39. Ibid., p. 61.

40. This, and other points that undermine the speech, are argued in more detail by Goddard, *The Meaning of Shakespeare,* pp. 220–22, and Gordon Ross Smith, "Shakespeare's *Henry V*: Another Part of the Critical Forest," *JHI,* 37.1 (1976), 3–26, 11–12. Karl P. Wentersdorf, "The Conspiracy of Silence in *Henry V*," *SQ,* 26 (1976), 264–87, considers that the shadow of Mortimer's claim to the English Crown (pursued by Cambridge but seemingly effaced in the Southampton scene) hangs over the play and calls into question Henry's pursuit of the French throne.

41. That kings served their realms better by staying at home and not pursuing war is argued by Erasmus in *Institutio Principis Christiani*. Roy Battenhouse makes this point in *"Henry V* in the Light of Erasmus," *ShStud,* 17 (1985), 77–88.

42. A. R. Humphreys (ed.), *Henry V*, "Introduction," p. 24.

43. Trans. Peter Whitehorne (1550), in the Tudor Translations (London, 1905), p. 197, cited in Jorgensen, *Shakespeare's Military World*, p. 98.

44. *Chronicles*, in J. R. Brown (ed.), *Henry V*, p. 198.

45. In *The Union of the Two Noble and Illustre Famelies of Lancastre & Yorke* (London, 1550; repr. Menston: Scholar Press, 1970), fol. 49, verso.

46. See also John Wilders, *The Lost Garden: A View of Shakespeare's English and Roman History Plays* (Totowa, N.J.: Rowman and Littlefield, 1978), p. 63; and Zdeněk Stříbrný, *"Henry V* and History," in Arnold Kettle (ed.), *Shakespeare in a Changing World* (New York: International Publishers, 1964), pp. 84–101, 94.

47. Pointed out by Goddard, *The Meaning of Shakespeare*, p. 232.

48. Samuel Johnson (ed.), *Works of Shakespeare* (1765), included in Michael Quinn (ed.), *Shakespeare, Henry V: A Casebook* (London: Macmillan, 1969), p. 33.

49. In *Henry V* (ed.), p. 29.

50. *A Kingdom for a Stage*, p. 175. John Palmer, *Political Characters of Shakespeare* (London: Macmillan, 1945), also finds *Henry V* at once "the glorification of a patriot king and an exposure of the wicked futility of [his] enterprise" (228).

51. *Shakespeare's Political Plays* (New York: Random House, 1967), p. 186.

52. "The *Henriad*: Shakespeare's Major History Plays," in J. Leeds Barroll, Alexander Leggatt, Richard Hosley, and Alvin Kernan (eds.), *The Revels History of Drama in English* (London: Methuen, 1975), vol. 3, pp. 292–93. In "*Henry V* and the Paradox of the Body Politic," *SQ*, 45 (1994), 33–56, Claire McEachern offers a challenge to the assumption that "the exercise of state power stands in an unequivocally negative relation to human bonds" (37).

53. *Shakespeare and the Frontiers of Drama* (London: Methuen, 1945; repr. 1964), pp. 44, 47.

54. *Ideas of Good and Evil*, in *Essays and Introductions* (New York and London: Macmillan, 1967), included in Brown (ed.), *Henry V*, pp. 220, 222.

55. Peter Philias, "Shakespeare's *Henry V* and the Second Tetralogy," *SP*, 62 (1965), 155–75, finds that Shakespeare's political plays dramatize how "success in public life depends on the ability to reconcile the demands of the public function with the claims of the individual life" (159); he concludes that Henry V achieves this balance.

56. E.M.W. Tillyard, *Shakespeare's History Plays*, p. 312. Tillyard is right in pointing out the "unevenness of the verse," but he underrates the energy of much of it. Mark Van Doren also finds an "astounding inflation in the style" (*Shakespeare*, p. 172).

57. Gary Taylor perceptively points out how the "repetitiveness, understatement, incoherence, and menace" of Nym's style anticipate that of the characters of the modern playwright Harold Pinter (*Henry V* [ed.], p. 63).

58. P. K. Ayers is more skeptical. In " 'Fellows of Infinite Tongue': Henry V and the King's English," *SEL*, 34 (1994), 253–77, he finds that Henry's "insistence upon the plainness of his speech" is "an amusingly ironic linguistic conceit at the expense of the French" (254).

59. Ralph Berry, *The Shakespearean Metaphor: Studies in Language and Form* (Totowa, N.J.: Rowman and Littlefield, 1978), points out that there are seventy-eight occurrences of "therefore" in the play, half of them spoken by Henry; he deduces that Henry is "the master of the fallacious argument" (150).

60. This is Gurr's verdict, discussing "Language and Structure" in *Henry V* (ed.), p. 36. Conversely, Joseph A. Porter, *The Drama of Speech Acts: Shakespeare's Lancastrian Tetralogy* (Berkeley; Los Angeles; London: University of California Press, 1979), decides that *Henry V* embodies an "order that involves and recognizes the variety of tongues" (124).

61. See Taylor (ed.), *Henry V.*

62. Brian Vickers, *The Artistry of Shakespeare's Prose* (London: Methuen, 1968), p. 156.

63. *The Drama of Speech Acts*, p. 138.

64. See Caroline Spurgeon, "Flight Images in *Henry V*," in *Shakespeare's Imagery and What It Tells Us* (Cambridge: Cambridge University Press, 1935), pp. 243–45.

65. For further comments on this, see S. S. Hussey, *The Literary Language of Shakespeare* (London and New York: Longman, 1982), pp. 168–69.

66. See Gurr (ed.), *Henry V*, pp. 14–15.

67. In "Imagery and Irony in *Henry V*," *ShS*, 21 (1968), 107–13, C. H. Hobday thinks that the succession of imagery associated not only with death but with cruelty and murder, as in Henry's oration at Harfleur, points to Shakespeare's revulsion from the King and his war.

68. Wilders interprets the garden image more pessimistically: "Henry, whatever the Archbishop may have thought, was not the New Adam nor did he recover the lost garden" (*The Lost Garden*, p. 143).

4

THEMES

Image patterns are often a clue to a play's underlying concerns. In *Henry V* the garden metaphor sets ordered fertility against disorderly chaos; images of blood (symbolizing both familial ties and violent destruction) project a multifaceted concept of war; and the extended personification of "ceremony" in the King's troubled soliloquy before Agincourt expands on the key issue of kingship. These three central themes—the importance of order in the nation, the ambivalence of war, and the challenging nature of kingship—emerge from the play's development of plot and character as well as its language.

As might be predicted in a play that Shakespeare wrote only a year or two before *Hamlet*, the treatment of these themes is complex; *Henry V* offers no straightforward celebration of the King and his military mission. The play raises questions rather than providing clear answers. Is it possible to achieve lasting unity in the state of England, or do currents of disorder inevitably destabilize this society? Can war against another nation ever be justified, and is it always a mixture of the vile and the heroic? What is the nature of kingship? Must the successful monarch combine the expediency of a Machiavel with the virtues of a Christian? These issues develop in dialectical fashion.

ORDER AND DISORDER

While the key dramatic topics are clear enough—order, war, and kingship—readers or directors of the play may differ in their interpretation of how these topics are handled in the drama, and thus how they build into fully articulated themes. "Order" is a case in point. The topic is introduced very deliberately in I. ii, where Exeter first develops a musical analogy to evoke the harmony of a well-ordered kingdom:

> For government, though high, and low, and lower,
> Put into parts, doth keep in one consent;
> Congreeing in a full and natural close,
> Like music. (I. ii. 180–84)

Then the Archbishop of Canterbury elaborates a parable on how the honeybees "by a rule in nature teach / The act of order to a peopled kingdom." The speech, a rehearsing of a fable that had classical and Renaissance precedents,[1] is often cited by earlier critics as a key to the play's central theme; J. H. Walter terms it a "reflection of Shakespeare's concern with unity of action in the structure of the play,"[2] and A. R. Humphreys thinks it "is meant as a genuine celebration of national harmony."[3] Deconstructive critics, discussed in Chapter 5, have been more skeptical, discovering in the speech a propaganda pitch for the dominant Elizabethan ideology of social order through submission to authority. In its context it is certainly a piece of special pleading by the clergymen—a reminder to Henry that he can achieve the throne of France if his subjects who are left at home cooperate obediently. Social harmony is thus promoted a little too stridently. Canterbury expounds the parallel between the beehive's "rule in nature" and the well-ordered kingdom, where all levels of society (magistrates, merchants, and soldiers) work for the good of the ruler. Yet the bees' monarch, described as "busied in his majesty," is strangely passive, content merely to survey the labors of his underlings—the pillaging soldiers and the toiling porters. The progression of the imagery suggests that order at home is easily achieved. Canterbury buttresses the concept of unity in diversity—"That many things, having full reference / To one consent, may work contrariously"—with a series of images from nature (fresh streams meeting in one salt ocean) and human culture (arrows flying to one mark, lines converging in the dial's center). This takes him smoothly to the main point at issue, the military campaign:

> So may a thousand actions, once afoot,
> End in one purpose, and be all well borne
> Without defeat. . . . (211–13)

Yet beneath this ideal of harmonious order in the state lurk rebellious segments, barely kept in check; the Scots are threatening to pour into England "like the tide into a breach" and suck the "princely eggs" of "eagle"

England (149, 169–71). In a sense, too, Canterbury's speech deconstructs the premise of order, since its powerful rhetoric is finally in the service of a divided rather than a strongly unified kingdom. The prelate is urging Henry to partition England in four and to trust that the commonwealth will continue to run smoothly in his absence, so that he can deploy one-quarter of the male population in his war against France. Ironically it turns out that Canterbury's paradigm of a unified state, all parts interlocking, is at odds with much of what we see in the play: the conspiracy of Cambridge, Scroop, and Grey; the fraternity of thieves (Pistol, Bardolph, and Nym) defying Henry's decree that nothing be stolen from France; and Williams' muted threat of insubordination when he challenges the King's "cause." There is even the slight possibility, up to the very end of the play, that Princess Katherine might sabotage Henry's plans for unifying the two kingdoms by failing to exercise her womanly duty and conform to his grand design.

Do we interpret the theme here as the necessity for order in the commonwealth, or the difficulty of maintaining it?[4] The specious way in which Canterbury's speech sets up the "act of order" as an assured achievement, masking disorder, may undercut its viability. It is clear that the play presents social unity under a strong monarchy as preferable to anarchy (or the cut-throat rivalry of the so-called brotherhood of Eastcheap), but this theme is not presented simplistically. The stability and order of the kingdom partly depend on Henry's proving his qualities as a strong leader (unified in himself),[5] so that the theme of order and disorder is linked to that of kingship. Moreover, war may temporarily unite England, but it creates havoc and disorder in France; the images of the wasted garden do more to convince the audience of the importance of a unified kingdom than does Canterbury's complacent speech. In particular, Burgundy's dignified exposition of what happens to civilization in wartime, when "hateful docks" and "rough thistles" stamp out the "cowslip, burnet, and green clover" (V. ii. 49–52), drives home in realistic detail the disorderly "savagery" in a society where peace is "mangled."

WAR

Henry V has been described as the "anatomy of a war."[6] Anatomy is an appropriate term: The play presents different aspects of warfare for our inspection, and we are left to decide whether war is a heroic enterprise or one that brings out the worst in its participants. If the theme can be summed up at all, it is that war has many faces. Filmgoers conditioned by Olivier's movie may think that *Henry V* glorifies war. But the text provides no stirring

battle after the call to arms at Agincourt, only a scene in which the
mercenary-minded Pistol captures the cowardly Le Fer. We simply do not
see much of the "pride, pomp, and circumstance of glorious war" (*Othello*,
III. iii. 354); the heroism of York and Suffolk, for instance, is reported, not
shown.⁷ War in this play is frankly the means to an end—a way of unifying
the country and extending England's boundaries—but the means is often
sordid and always costly.

Because Henry revives an old, somewhat tenuous claim to the throne of
France, the war is not strictly necessary. Only by sleight of hand can he turn
the French into the initiators; the campaign is more a political opportunity
for him to prove his prowess as a leader and a conqueror. Nevertheless,
Henry is not depicted as an aggressive warmonger. It is Canterbury who,
for pragmatic reasons, urges Henry to "unwind your bloody flag" while
Exeter reminds him to emulate his ancestors, the "lions" of his "blood."
Acknowledging both the "waste" and the responsibility incurred, Henry's
vision of war is sober:

> For never two such kingdoms did contend
> Without much fall of blood, whose guiltless drops
> Are every one a woe, a sore complaint
> 'Gainst him whose wrongs gives edge unto the swords
> That makes such waste in brief mortality. (I. ii. 24–28)

The King's speech personifies drops of blood as bitter complainants, but
Williams goes further in imagining how the dismembered body parts of
those killed in war will rise up in protest on the Day of Judgment:

> all those legs and arms and heads, chopped off in a battle, shall join
> together at the latter day and cry all, "We died at such a place," some
> swearing, some crying for a surgeon, some upon their wives left poor
> behind them, some upon the debts they owe, some upon their children
> rawly left. (IV. i. 137–43)

The speech is a graphic reminder of the cost of war in terms of human lives
and relationships. Williams also illuminates the corrupting nature of war,
the inevitable clash between moral sensibilities and concentration on killing, when he ponders, "I am afeard there are few die well that die in a battle;
for how can they charitably dispose of anything when blood is their
argument?" Blood, as the Eastcheap Boy remarks, is "unwholesome food"
(II. iii. 58). This theme of moral coarsening through an obsession with blood
(as murder) is echoed in Burgundy's description of how France is affected

by the war. Even the children, suffering from the devastating aftereffects of Henry's military campaign, "grow like savages—as soldiers will / That nothing do but meditate on blood" (V. ii. 59–60).

It is at Harfleur that the "savagery" of war is delineated most clearly. In a passage that again focuses on blood and extends into rape, Henry envisages how, if the town refuses to surrender, "the fleshed soldier, rough and hard of heart, / In liberty of bloody hand shall range / With conscience wide as hell" (III. iii. 11–13). Despite this human ferocity, the vision of war becomes curiously impersonal, for the images that follow show abstractions, rather than people, taking the initiative: "Impious war" is personified and compared to the "prince of fiends," Satan himself; "licentious wickedness" races downhill; and "murder, spoil, and villainy" are envisaged as natural phenomena, "filthy and contagious clouds." Once the war machine grinds into gear, it generates its own horrors, so that the "enraged" warriors are somehow not held morally accountable. Indeed, to be a soldier at all means cultivating a tough impersonality, as Henry makes clear when he backs up his exhortations at the breach—"Disguise fair nature with hard-favor'd rage" (III. i. 8)—with images of the eye as a brass cannon and the brow as a rock lashed by the sea. In contrast to the Roman warrior Coriolanus, depicted in battle as a "thing of blood, whose every motion / Was tim'd with dying cries" (*Coriolanus*, II. ii. 109–10), Henry never becomes an inhuman war machine. Nor does he indulge in the mindless fury parodied in Macmorris's "so Chrish save me, I will cut off your head!" (III. ii. 135). He can, nevertheless, be ruthless in military strategy, prepared to use "bloody constraint" in fighting for the French Crown (II. iv. 97) and to kill the prisoners when his dominance on the battlefield is threatened.

The apparent contradictions in Henry's response to war—compunction coupled with sublime indifference or even callous acceptance—point to a central ambivalence in the way that war is presented. The question of the King's responsibility for lives lost in war, introduced in Act I, resurfaces in Act IV. Henry cannot completely argue away his nagging sense of shedding "guiltless drops" of blood by separating the state of the individual's soul from his "duty" to go to war for his king, as he attempts to do in his conversation with Williams. And the idea that death in battle can serve as the scourge of God—"War is his beadle, war is his vengeance" (IV. i. 173–74)—may come across as a convenient rationalization too. On the other hand, the King at Harfleur accurately points out the inexorable momentum of war, where the "blind and bloody soldier," swept up in battle fury, acts like an automaton. Such momentum, Henry argues, is out of his control and therefore beyond his jurisdiction. These perspectives on war in the play remain antithetical; they cannot be reconciled.

There is a tension, too, between the creative energy of being transformed into an effective soldier ("bend up every spirit / To his full height!" is phallic, as are other images connected with storming the breach) and the repulsive acts of destruction engendered by this ferocity: rape, carnage, and mortal combat leading to the stench of corpses on the battlefield. Exhilaration is counterbalanced by grotesque detail in the exhortation at the breach, which A. R. Humphreys defines as "desperate, appalling, and inspiring at once."[8] War in *Henry V* is envisaged as a test of manhood, ranging from the images of virility at Harfleur ("Stiffen the sinews, conjure up the blood" [III. i. 7]) to the Dauphin's lament that French "mettle is bred out" (III. v. 29). To be on the losing side of the war game is to experience impotence or sexual dishonor, as when Bourbon feels an overwhelming "shame" at seeing the broken ranks of the French. Refusing to return to the fray, says Bourbon, is equivalent to being a "base pander" who watches his daughter being raped by a "slave" (IV. v. 15–17). And war lust is always yoked to death, as suggested in the erotic image of York and Suffolk embracing as they die on the battlefield (IV. vi).

The theme of war in *Henry V* encompasses more than heroic excitement and violent bloodshed. Hard work and drudgery are also required in any military campaign. With his consternation that the mines at Harfleur are not "according to the disciplines of the war" and his pride at the "excellent discipline" of his compatriot Exeter at the bridge, Fluellen represents the military man's meticulous attention to detail. War is exhausting, too. Branagh's movie adds to the text by showing the slog through mud and rain as part of the campaign's horrors; but a simple stage direction in Shakespeare's play, "Enter the King and his poor Soldiers" (III. vi. 90), is enough to convey the total enervation of the army as they march toward Calais. Exhaustion, as well as resolve, emerges from the halting rhythms and monosyllabic weight of the speech in which Henry addresses Montjoy at the end of this scene. What at first glance appears to be flat, even repetitive verse gives a clue to Henry's underlying emotions: He is bracing himself, presenting a bold front to the French despite being terribly weary. He admits that "My people are with sickness much enfeebled, / My numbers lessened" but continues:

> If we may pass, we will; if we be hind'red,
> We shall your tawny ground with your red blood
> Discolor; and so, Montjoy, fare you well.
> The sum of all our answer is but this:
> We would not seek a battle as we are,
> Nor, as we are, we say we will not shun it. (168–73)

In *Henry V* the different dimensions of war—its exhilaration and opportunities for courage, juxtaposed with its horrors, grinding weariness, and inhumanity—build into a complex vision, a questioning of whether war can ever be fully justified. King Henry does harness the military venture to his advantage and to the glory of England, for the war effort makes possible not only national unity in the abstract sense but the strongly forged brotherhood felt in the Crispin's Day speech. What is more, the speed with which Shakespeare turns from this heroic speech to Pistol's capture of Le Fer, and from Montjoy's somber request to collect the French corpses to the comic interlude between Fluellen and Williams (IV. viii), may discourage too prolonged a questioning of war's bleakness. Darker nuances remain, however, in the unheroic thievery of the Eastcheap men, sucking the blood of France, and the vision of atrocities that the "blind and bloody" soldier may at any moment perpetrate. And although the English are granted a relatively bloodless victory (few of their men are killed), the war, as Burgundy points out, is disastrous for the fertile garden of France. While a performance of *Henry V* with a totally anti-war message would be a distortion of the text (and run counter to the energy Henry inspires as a military leader), stage productions in the second half of the twentieth century have taken up hints from the play script and delivered some critique of the war. The Royal Shakespeare Company's 1984–85 version, for instance, did not allow the audience to forget the cost of the French campaign. Even as the marriage between Henry and Katherine was being sealed, "the battlefield, with candles glimmering beside corpses, was seen through a gauzy traverse curtain behind the tableau of Henry's triumphant diplomatic wedding."9 Branagh's film (discussed in detail in Chapter 6) reveals more of the contradictions of war than does Olivier's, with its firmer emphasis on the pageantry and patriotism of the military endeavor. As *Henry V* itself continues to insist, war is both terrible *and* energizing.

KINGSHIP: THE PLAY AS THE TESTING OF A MONARCH

The central theme of *Henry V* is kingship; in terms of both plot and character, the play unfolds as the testing of a monarch. Henry cannot rely on the sacred "name" of king that Richard II invoked, since divine right has been cancelled by his father's act of usurping the throne. As a de facto rather than a de jure ruler, Henry IV struggles to maintain his authority throughout the *Henry IV* plays, and Henry V, once he is King of England, must also prove his fitness to rule through appropriate choices and actions. A long list of "king-becoming graces," helpful in defining the ideal monarch, appears in *Macbeth* when Malcolm is addressing Macduff. The future king specifies

> . . . justice, verity, temp'rance, stableness,
> Bounty, perseverance, mercy, lowliness,
> Devotion, patience, courage, fortitude . . . (IV. iii. 92–94)

Arguably Henry exemplifies most of these Christian qualities during the course of the play; yet, like Malcolm disguising his true nature from Macduff in order to test him, he is also capable of deviousness, even machiavellianism. As Robert Egan comments, there is an inevitable "dichotomy between conqueror and Christian"[10] in *Henry V*. Strong leadership, Shakespeare implies, requires cunning as well as open "courage"—the combination that Machiavelli outlines when he advises the prince to be both "fox" and "lion."[11] And far from being a straightforward demonstration of kingship, with Henry displaying various facets of the royal persona in a fairly static way,[12] the play allows for undercurrents of uneasiness or doubt, moments of possible failure as Henry refines his roles as monarch.

Before we see him, Henry is projected as a kingly paragon; Canterbury expresses wonder at this new king's attributes in the opening scene. As well as being a great orator, Henry excels in four areas: he can "reason in divinity," he is an expert in "commonwealth affairs," his "discourse of war" is highly impressive, and he can expound on "any cause of policy" (i.e., argue about politics). What is more, Henry goes beyond the rhetorician who theorizes on abstract propositions, for he has put into practice an active rather than a contemplative virtue:

> . . . the art and practic part of life
> Must be the mistress to this theoric. (I. i. 51–52)

King Henry has much to live up to. Can he establish himself as an accomplished orator, a pious man of God, a statesman-politician, and a military leader? All of these roles are manifested, to some degree, as the play progresses, and most of them are touched on in Henry's opening scene.

When Henry first appears on stage, in I. ii, he is very much on trial. Not only is this the first time that the theater audience sees him, but he is still a relatively new king—and a young one, historically only twenty-five—who needs to make a strong initial impression on the inner circle of noblemen. As a decisive ruler he must take command of the situation and display his control publicly. The key term here is "resolved." Almost Henry's first words, referring to the legitimacy of his title in France, are "We would be resolved," and once Canterbury's explanations are complete and the King is ready to call in the Dauphin's ambassadors, he closes the debate with "Now are we well resolved" (I. ii. 222). Not only has the issue been clarified, enabling him to proceed, but he is fully determined ("resolved") to go ahead with his military campaign. In addition, Henry projects himself as both responsible and pious before he allows Canterbury to launch into his discussion of Salic law. Concerned with the "truth" of his claim, he urges the Archbishop to expound the case "justly and religiously." In effect the King adopts the role of spiritual authority (the "prelate" who can "reason in divinity") when he warns Canterbury

> Under this conjuration, speak my lord:
> For we will hear, note, and believe in heart
> That what you speak is in your conscience washed
> As pure as sin with baptism. (29–32)

At the end of the Archbishop's speech Henry checks again, in front of witnesses, that his own "conscience" will not be sullied by pursuing a title that is specious:

> May I with right and conscience make this claim? (96)

Showing his skill in "commonwealth affairs," he cuts through Canterbury's rousing talk of heroic royal ancestors to discuss instead practical steps to "defend / Against the Scot" while the English troops are away in France. Shrewdly Henry recalls how the Scots invaded England while Edward III was away campaigning in France, but Canterbury, also a politician, caps this by reminding Henry how England under Edward III not only defended itself adequately against the Scots but also captured the Scottish King. The King listens carefully to his counselors; he is persuaded by their pragmatic arguments that one-quarter of the English forces can win the war in France while the rest defend their own country.

Once Henry is "resolved," he is ready to act decisively: "France being ours, we'll bend it to our awe, / Or break it all to pieces" (224–25). Whatever Henry's other possible motives (desire for a heroic enterprise to unify England or the need to busy "giddy minds with foreign wars" as his father advised), it is clear that winning France is also a personal quest for him—a means of proving his prowess as king. The sentiment that he expresses more openly at the end of II. ii, "No king of England, if not King of France!", is registered here in his extremist attitude to the enterprise. Either he will succeed magnificently and rule France "in large and ample empery," or he will die in obscurity with no memorial tomb, his deeds uncelebrated.

Achieving France will be, as Robert Ornstein comments, "an ultimate proof"
of his "kingliness."[13]

The arrival of the French ambassador and his entourage presents Henry
with another opportunity to demonstrate his royal command of the situation.
In assuring them that they may deliver their message from the Dauphin
"freely," Henry contends

> We are no tyrant, but a Christian king,
> Unto whose grace our passion is as subject
> As is our wretches fett'red in our prisons. . . . (241–43)

Henry is promising to behave temperately; because he is gracious (Canterbury respects him as "full of grace" [I. i. 22]), he is not prey to outbursts of
anger or tyrannical behavior. Although highly provoked by the Dauphin's
references to his earlier frivolity ("galliard" and "revel") and by the demean-
ing present of tennis balls, the King keeps his promise. The English court,
as shown in Branagh's movie, may be watching keenly. How exactly *will*
Henry react? He keeps his temper under control, converting anger into irony
and rousing rhetoric:

> And tell the pleasant prince this mock of his
> Hath turned his balls to gunstones. . . . (281–82)

Again, he is aware that the campaign will test him, enabling him to display
to both nations the "practic part of life":

> But tell the Dauphin I will keep my state,
> Be like a king, and show my sail of greatness,
> When I do rouse me in my throne of France. (273–75)

"Be like a king" is significant. The opening Chorus regrets that the stage
lacks resources to show "the warlike Harry, like himself," but here Henry
goes one better; he promises to "dazzle all the eyes of France" with his
intrinsic "greatness." Although this is kingship in quest of national glory,
his heroic impulse is always tempered by rational control. In planning the
French campaign Henry judiciously recommends an "expedition" (punning
on military invasion and speed) that will progress with "reasonable swiftness" rather than reckless haste.

In Act II Henry faces a more probing test: how to deal with the traitors in
a way that proves he understands when "mercy" must give place to just
punishment. His related dilemma—can a king be powerful *and* popular?—is

pointed up by Cambridge's hypocritical tribute, "Never was monarch better feared and loved / Than is your Majesty" (II. ii. 25–26). As Machiavelli comments in *The Prince*,[14] it is difficult to inspire both emotions equally, and more important for the strong leader to be respected than adored. In an ideal society, the king could rely on "hearts create of duty, and of zeal" (31). But Henry learns by hard experience that his "bedfellow" Scroop appeared to love him only to take advantage of his friendship. Holinshed captures some of the precarious balance between being "loved" and "feared" when he describes Henry as "so severe a justicer" that "his people both loved and obeyed him"; he left "no offence unpunished nor friendship unrewarded" and proved a "terror to rebels, and suppressor of sedition."[15] In the Southampton scene Henry does not hand out rewards for friendship (although he promises "quittance of desert and merit / According to the weight and worthiness" [34–35]), but we do see him firmly administering punishment, acting the part of "severe . . . justicer" so that he can effectively crush sedition.

The scene opens with Bedford's reassurance that "the king hath note" of all that the traitors "intend." This ensures that the audience can savor the dramatic irony, knowing that Henry is orchestrating the situation toward disclosure and that what appears to be naive overconfidence in his subjects ("We carry not a heart with us from hence / That grows not in a fair consent with ours" [21–22]) is actually a tactic for unmasking his enemies. Admittedly the King's strategy is machiavellian. But he is using deception (the pointed irony of referring to the traitors' "too much love and care" of him [52–53]) to expose hypocrisy; one might view him, in John F. Danby's terms, as the "machiavel of goodness,"[16] doing what the cunning leader must do to establish his authority. He shows magnanimity in pardoning a drunken man for verbal abuse, even when Grey, damning himself in advance, urges the "taste of much correction." (In a parallel sequence in IV. viii, Fluellen advocates "martial law" for Williams, whereas Henry pardons him because, as Williams explains, "All offenses . . . come from the heart" and his heart has remained loyal to the King.) For the traitors, however, there can be no mercy. Henry perhaps speaks as a man in his long speech where he deeply regrets the perfidy of Scroop, who has "infected / The sweetness of affiance" (126–27). But his voice is that of a responsible monarch who puts the safety of his kingdom first when he declares:

> Touching our person, seek we no revenge,
> But we our kingdom's safety must so tender,
> Whose ruin you have sought, that to her laws
> We do deliver you. (174–77)

Since the three traitors, like Shylock in *The Merchant of Venice*, have shunned mercy, Henry pursues justice rigorously through the letter of the law. Only God's "mercy" (twice repeated) remains, to which Henry piously commits them. Shakespeare suggests here that kingship entails a firm administering of justice that cannot always be tempered with mercy; moreover, the monarch's show of authority may sometimes depend on the machiavellian technique of entrapment.

At Harfleur the King's challenge is to prove himself a military giant, displaying the qualities of "courage" and "fortitude" as a warrior-king. Strong leadership, Shakespeare suggests, is a matter of playing the role convincingly and encouraging others to do the same—to become what they act:

> In peace there's nothing so becomes a man
> As modest stillness and humility;
> But when the blast of war blows in our ears,
> Then imitate the action of the tiger. (III. i. 3–6)

The aggressive soldier must "Disguise fair nature with hard-favor'd rage" and assume the properties of a war machine or a predatory animal. By the time he speaks to the Governor (III. iii), Henry has completely appropriated the persona of the soldier, calling it "A name that in my thoughts becomes me best" (6). His threatening speech is thus predicated on a total divorce between the sensitive mortal who is bound to feel "pity" for violated women and butchered babies and the hardened military leader who would fatalistically let his soldiers run amok. If Henry actually allowed this brutality to take place, could he remain a respected ruler, full of "king-becoming graces"? Again there is a tenuous balance between the monarch's ruthlessness[17] (a kind of "justice," if Harfleur breaks the rules of war that Henry outlines here) and "mercy." It is possible, though not certain, that the blood-chilling threats are merely a clever tactic to coerce surrender, so that once the Governor has capitulated Henry can "Use mercy to them all" (54). There is a similar conflict between the King's "lenity" and "cruelty" toward an individual when Henry, while insisting on treating the French with respect and not stealing from their land because "the gentler gamester is the soonest winner," nevertheless approves Bardolph's execution (III. vi. 112). He reveals no regret over the death of an old comrade for theft. The expedient military leader clearly cannot afford to be sentimental.

Michael Goldman comments astutely on how *Henry V* reveals "the effort of greatness" and "the demands on the self that being a king involves."[18] In Act IV Henry as king faces several challenges: keeping up the morale of his soldiers before and during battle, and justifying his cause (while in disguise) to his men. The Chorus paints a glowing picture of Henry as the "royal captain" who rallies his troops the night before battle with his resilience and "sweet majesty." Indeed when we first see him at the beginning of IV. i, he is succeeding admirably in cheering up his comrades. He makes the best of a bad situation, "gathering honey out of the weed" by turning adversity to advantage:

> For our bad neighbor makes us early stirrers,
> Which is both healthful, and good husbandry. (IV. i. 6–7)

Even the mind, he argues, is "quick'ned" by harsh conditions. It is quite possible, judged by his later "I and my bosom must debate a while" (31), that the King is experiencing anxiety on a deeper level; yet he projects a "cheerful semblance"—the king-becoming grace of "stableness"—so convincingly that we believe in his fundamental optimism and, most important, in his ability to transmit a positive outlook to his subordinates.

The sequence where the King is in disguise points up the ultimate irony: Henry is unable to shed the royal persona and its responsibilities. The price of kingship is isolation from other people, even though Henry is eager to present himself to the commoners (Bates, Court, and Williams) as an ordinary human being: "I think the King is but a man, as I am. . . . His ceremonies laid by, in his nakedness he appears but a man; and though his affections are higher mounted than ours, yet when they stoop, they stoop with the like wing" (103–10). He does not appear to convince them. Indeed, whatever emotions he may be feeling, Henry must remain committed to the public role of "outward courage" in order to rally his subjects; as he goes on to explain, "no man should possess [the king] with any appearance of fear, lest he, by showing it, should dishearten his army" (112–14). For a king, the appearance of strength is paramount. Yet Henry continues to defend the King's private self and his "conscience," maintaining that the King's cause is "just" and his quarrel "honorable." Whereas Bates expresses unquestioning loyalty, Williams probes the implications, the "heavy reckoning" at the Day of Judgment, if the cause is not "good." Sensitive on the issue of the King's responsibility for so many lives lost in battle, Henry concentrates on separating the "duty" of the subject, which belongs to the King, from the "soul" of the subject, which is that person's own concern, regardless of whether or not he has been sent to war on a valid pretext. The long speech (150–90) is perhaps a Pyrrhic victory for the King's position. It convinces Williams that "the king is not to answer" for the sins of individual subjects but leaves him suspicious of the King's "word," his promise that he will never be ransomed: "Ay, he said so, to make us fight cheerfully; but when our throats are cut, he may be ransomed, and we ne'er the wiser" (197–99). Henry's defense of kingship, so coherent on one level, has confirmed the wide chasm—the lack of complete trust, the sense of operating by different standards, the inability to communicate frankly—between the monarch and his subjects.

Henry's meditation on "ceremony" bitterly explodes the mystique of kingship: its dependence on empty forms, which calls into question its genuine substance. Suddenly the emperor is admitting that he has no clothes. Whatever authority the King possesses he must forge for himself, since "place, degree, and form" have no creative or healing powers. No wonder that Henry deeply resents the "ceremony" that both insulates him from his subjects and traps him in a web of anxieties and public responsibilities. Inevitably he romanticizes the lives of the private man (as "infinite heart's-ease") and the peasant (who "Sleeps in Elysium"), just as he exaggerates the "hard condition" of being a king. On a deeper level, though, he faces up to the implications of his title. When he prays that God will take from his men the "sense of reck'ning" he refers literally to the soldiers' ability to count the huge number of the French enemy, but he also touches on the somber meaning that Williams has introduced just before: a "reckoning" on the Day of Judgment.

The two soliloquies crystallize the King's dilemma; he must accept the penalties of his role if he is to play it successfully on the following day. Acknowledging and coming to terms with his solitary burden (that he alone must "bear all") releases fresh confidence in his public persona. His oratory before Agincourt demonstrates the positive side of kingship, for it is not only a superb display of his own "courage" and "fortitude" but of the king-becoming grace of "perseverance" in building the same confidence in his followers. To Westmoreland, desperate for ten thousand more fighting men, Henry responds, "What's he that wishes so?" Again turning adversity to advantage, he stresses, "The fewer men, the greater share of honor" and projects a Hotspur-like persona who thirsts for glory in battle when he describes himself as "the most offending soul alive" in coveting "honor." But whereas Hotspur wanted no "corrival" in the honor stakes (*Henry IV, Part i*, I. iii. 207), Henry inspires others to join him in a fellowship of heroic feats. The Crispin's Day speech is the ultimate proof of Henry's strength as a leader. Gone is the defensiveness that made communication with the three commoners difficult; paradoxically, in his public address to the army he can reach out to his men on personal terms, abandoning the royal "we" for the "we" of shared enterprise as he forges English brotherhood on French soil:

> We few, we happy few, we band of brothers (IV. iii. 60)

The apocalyptic overtones of "The day, my friends, and all things stay for me" (IV. i. 315) have dissolved into the absolute conviction that he and his men together have the necessary mental fortitude: "All things are ready, if our minds be so" (IV. iii. 71). No longer fearing the infamy or silence of a failed campaign, Henry proudly tells Montjoy that even those Englishmen who die this day will "draw their honors reeking up to heaven" and be remembered for the terrible plague they bred in France. Valiant as ever, the King again swears that the French will never ransom his living body. Moreover, Henry projects confidence without appearing boastful; he takes pride in his "warriors for the working day," but his fundamental humility, his submission to the will of God, is underlined in the proviso that they will win the battle only "if God please" (120). This humility (the "lowliness" outlined by Malcolm in *Macbeth*) is most fully revealed in his conclusion, after he reads the brief list of English dead at Agincourt, that "O God, thy arm was here!" (IV. viii. 108). Regardless of the underlying reasons for Henry's piety, what matters is that he manifests it appropriately, and, by making it a capital offense to "boast" of victory, he deflects his army from the kind of arrogance that has undermined the French.

This is a superb display of practical kingship. The scenes that follow, presenting the King in action at Agincourt, are less clear in their intention—in particular, Henry's order to kill the French prisoners followed by a second threat to cut the throats of all those captured by his soldiers is confusing.[19] Shakespeare may be trying to encompass too much here—presenting Henry as a shrewd leader who is coldly ruthless when he foresees danger for his army but also as a furious, spontaneous avenger of the slaughter of the boys in the camp, to the point where he is no longer required to be temperate or magnanimous: "And not a man of them that we shall take / Shall taste our mercy" (IV. vii. 66–67). At any rate, Henry's royal magnanimity is again tested when he has the chance to punish Williams for his "bitter terms" the previous night. Instead of doing so, he graciously accepts Williams' entreaty to "take it for your own fault, and not mine" and rewards the man for his honest heart: "Here uncle Exeter, fill this glove with crowns, / And give it to this fellow" (IV. viii. 58–59). This gesture may serve as an example of Henry's generosity (or the King rewarding his loyal friends); yet it has the effect of patronizing Williams, who is now addressed as "fellow" and not as the "brother" of the Crispin's Day speech. And it is ironic that Henry thinks it appropriate to reward Williams—possibly to buy his loyalty—by giving him gold, even though he himself has spurned wealth in favor of "honor."

The ambivalence here points to the complexity of Shakespeare's treatment of the theme of kingship. On one level the sequence illustrates Henry's "bounty" as one of the king-becoming graces, just as Henry has displayed "temperance" to the Dauphin's messengers, "justice" to the traitors, "devotion" to God, and "courage" and "fortitude" in battle. But the King's justice is sometimes akin to ruthlessness and his honesty undercut by deviousness or cunning, although these too (the play suggests) may be necessary attributes of kingship. *Henry V* reflects what Michael Manheim terms the Renaissance "acceptance of deception and intrigue and violence as legitimate instuments of political behavior."[20] And for Henry the dark side of royalty is its utter isolation—the king, vulnerable to betrayal, can have no close friends—as well as its deceptive appearance of glory. Since the "ceremony" of monarchy is merely symbolic, the king must work on his own initiative, with talents honed through trial and risk, to win solid achievements for his country.

NOTES

1. The fable of the bees was developed by both Virgil (*Georgics*, Book IV) and Pliny (*Natural History*, Book XI). Shakespeare might have found it in the Renaissance authors Erasmus (*Institutio Principis Christiani*) and Lyly (*Euphues*); see Andrew Gurr, "*Henry V* and the Bees' Commonwealth," *ShS*, 30 (1977), 61–72.

2. *Henry V* (ed.), *The Arden Shakespeare* (1954), p. xvi.

3. *Henry V* (ed.), *The New Penguin Shakespeare*, p. 11.

4. Derek Traversi, *Shakespeare: From* Richard II *to* Henry V (Stanford, Calif.: Stanford University Press, 1957), decides that "the principal theme of *Henry V* . . . is the establishment in England of an order based on consecrated authority and crowned successfully by action against France" (166). Conversely, Jonathan Dollimore and Alan Sinfield, "History and Ideology: The Instance of *Henry V*," in John Drakakis (ed.), *Alternative Shakespeares* (London and New York: Methuen, 1985), single out "insurrection" as the play's "obsessive preoccupation" (216).

5. Rose A. Zimbardo, "The Formalism of *Henry V*" (1964), in Michael Quinn (ed.), *Shakespeare,* Henry V: *A Casebook* (London: Macmillan, 1969), pp. 163–70, pushes this idea to its ultimate conclusion, arguing that the play is a formal

celebration of how "the ideal king embodies in himself and projects upon his state the ideal metaphysical order" (164).

6. Alexander Leggatt, *Shakespeare's Political Drama: The History Plays and the Roman Plays* (London and New York: Routledge, 1988), p. 114.

7. See Anthony Brennan, " 'Mangling by Starts the Full Course of That Glory': The Legend and the Reality of War in *Henry V*," in *Onstage and Offstage Worlds in Shakespeare's Plays* (London and New York: Routledge, 1989), p. 196.

8. *Henry V* (ed.), p. 34.

9. Russell Jackson and Robert Smallwood (eds.), *Players of Shakespeare 2* (Cambridge: Cambridge University Press, 1988), p. 5.

10. "A Muse of Fire: *Henry V* in the Light of *Tamburlaine*," *MLQ*, 29 (1965), 15–28, 26.

11. *The Prince*, trans. George Bull (Harmondsworth: Penguin Books, 1961), Chapter 18, pp. 99–100.

12. As Moody E. Prior concludes in *The Drama of Power: Studies in Shakespeare's History Plays* (Evanston, Ill.: Northwestern University Press, 1973), p. 323.

13. *A Kingdom for a Stage* (Cambridge, Mass.: Harvard University Press, 1972), p. 185.

14. Chapter 17, p. 96.

15. *Chronicles*, in J. R. Brown (ed.), *Henry V, The Signet Classic Shakespeare* (1965; 1988), p. 208.

16. This is the term he uses for Prince Hal, in *Shakespeare's Doctrine of Nature* (London: Faber and Faber, 1949), p. 91.

17. Ronald S. Berman, "Shakespeare's Alexander: Henry V," *CE*, 23 (1962), 532–39, explores the "dark side of Henry's majestic purposefulness" (537).

18. "*Henry V*: The Strain of Rule," in *Shakespeare and the Energies of Drama* (Princeton: Princeton University Press), p. 73.

19. John Arden, *To Present the Pretence* (London: Eyre Methuen, 1977), calls it a "part-justified, part unmotivated moment of horror" (206).

20. *The Weak King Dilemma in the Shakespearean History Play* (Syracuse, N.Y.: Syracuse University Press, 1973), p. 13.

5

CRITICAL APPROACHES

TRADITIONAL CRITICAL APPROACHES TO *HENRY V* (1900–1980)

Critical movements often develop in strong reaction to those that precede them. Deconstructionist and new historicist critics now reject older historical models—patterns of cosmic and social order proposed by scholars such as E.M.W. Tillyard in *Shakespeare's History Plays* (1944) and Lily B. Campbell in *Shakespeare's "Histories": Mirrors of Elizabethan Policy* (1947)—as a useful way of interpreting Shakespeare's *Henry V* and other Renaissance history plays. Likewise, formalist critics from the 1940s on reacted against a tendency to read the plays as part of the history of ideas or as studies of complex, realistically conceived characters.

Character and Psychoanalysis

A. C. Bradley was not the first critic to offer a sustained analysis of Shakespeare's characters. In 1777, Maurice Morgann drew attention to the "roundness" and "integrity" of these creations in his *Essay on the Dramatic Character of Sir John Falstaff*;[1] but it was Bradley's *Shakespearean Tragedy* (1904) that proved most influential in sanctioning a realist-psychological approach to the dramatic characters in Shakespeare's plays. Even though he wrote perceptively about other aspects of the drama (rhythm, imagery, and mood), Bradley is most remembered—praised and reviled—for his detailed character analyses. One example of Bradley treating a dramatis personae as a real person (with a past and a future beyond the context of the play) is his speculation, in the *Oxford Lectures on Poetry*, on the way in which the new Henry V rejects Falstaff: "We may imagine that, after he had left Falstaff and was no longer influenced by the face of his old companion, he gave way to anger at the indecent familiarity which had provoked a compromising scene on the most ceremonial of occasions . . . and that he sent the Chief Justice back to take vengeance."[2] Bradley's essentially romantic"[3]

An interest in the psychology of the individual dramatic character has sometimes extended into psychoanalytic methods of interpretation, usually on Freudian lines, which Norman N. Holland covers in his *Psychoanalysis and Shakespeare* (1964). In conjunction with an archetypal approach,[4] this has proved especially illuminating for Shakespeare's *Henriad*. Hal's rebellion against Henry IV can be viewed as an oedipal one (although he must ultimately assimilate and internalize his father), and his choice of Falstaff, who is associated with fertility rituals and the pleasure principle, represents a temporary release from the parental and social demands of the superego. The fat knight "serves as the projection of those wishes of Hal which are inconsistent with the ego ideal of the hero king, Henry V."[5] More recent studies of the patriarchal bias in Shakespeare's plays (mentioned below in the section on feminist approaches) have also drawn on the Freudian model of psychoanalysis. Bernard J. Paris uses "Third Force psychology"—in particular, Karen Horney's view of the "evolutionary constructive force"[6] within the human personality—to analyze Henry V's constant effort "to justify his aggression in such a way as to bring it into harmony with the demands of his perfectionistic and self-effacing tendencies."[7] This helps make sense of Henry's sudden and often perplexing rushes of piety after he has behaved aggressively, as in the tennis balls sequence (I. ii. 289–90), in the traitors scene (II. ii. 185–86), and after the victory at Agincourt (IV. viii. 108–10).

For *Henry V* the most fruitful kind of character analysis has usually been combined with a historical perspective. Several critics have examined how far Henry conforms or fails to conform to the image of the ideal Renaissance prince (displayed, for example, in Erasmus's *Institutio Principis Christiani*)[8] or whether he comes closer to Machiavelli's pragmatic guidelines, in *The Prince*, on how the national leader should behave.[9] Other commentators (such as Una Ellis-Fermor[10] and Derek Traversi[11]) have discussed the character of Henry V within the play's political context, finding a conflict between the man and the role of prince at the heart of the drama.

Formalist and New Critical

Such analyses are helpful reminders that the study of character, as long as it does not exclude other elements in the play, need not be discounted as outmoded or irrelevant. Yet for a while this was the case. An inevitable reaction to the work of Bradley came from L. C. Knights, one of the *Scrutiny* critics of the 1930s, the title of whose essay "How Many Children Had Lady Macbeth?" parodies Bradley's approach. Knights asserts instead that "a Shakespeare play is a dramatic poem" and that "to stress in the conventional way character or plot or any of the other abstractions that can be made is to impoverish the total response."[12] Attention to Shakespeare's language is crucial, for only by penetrating the subtleties of the poetic language in a "total response" can the sensitive, imaginative reader discern the "living whole" of the play. In this vein, Knights praises Burgundy's concrete, detailed speech on the "uncultivated" garden of France (*Henry V*, V. ii), where Shakespeare "envisages a fully human way of life as closely related to the wider setting of organic growth," as "an imaginative vision that transcends the simple sequence of the argument."[13]

This concentration on the language of the playwright and the reader's response to it also sprang from the "practical criticism" movement in Cambridge, England, in the late 1920s. I. A. Richards, in a famous experiment, asked his students to write about poems divorced from their authors and historical contexts, so that they could respond more freshly to the words and poetic techniques.[14] In the United States the parallel movement that became known as new criticism blossomed in the 1930s, 1940s, and 1950s. It also encouraged close readings of poetry (and treated plays, to some extent, as dramatic poems), since the new critics wanted to free literature from its historical trappings, or from the intention of the author, in order to concentrate exclusively on its aesthetic form and analyze what made it a unique, self-contained discourse. The titles of two of these critics' books— *The Verbal Icon*, by W. K. Wimsatt (1954), and *The Well-Wrought Urn*, by Cleanth Brooks (1947)—illustrate the method: Controlling metaphors and dominant symbols constitute the organic unity of the poem or play and are a key to its meaning. G. Wilson Knight also perceived metaphors and symbols as helping create the "spatial" unity of a Shakespearean tragedy.[15] This formalist approach, with some modifications to include analysis of characters and their interactions, was developed by Cleanth Brooks and Robert Heilman in *Understanding Drama* (1945). The authors aimed to treat drama as a "special form" and not merely as "the history of ideas or the expression of the author's personality." Time has shown that anything that encourages close analysis, or "the richest and fullest definition of *reading*,"[16] is unlikely to fall out of favor completely.

Genre

Plays are crucially different from lyric poems, however, and one way of interpreting *Henry V* has been to decide which dramatic genre best fits the play. Quite possibly the category "history play" was not clear-cut for the Elizabethans; they might have responded to such drama as chronicle material developed in a comic or tragic fashion. Whether or not Shakespeare thought of himself as pioneering a new genre, by 1599 he had nevertheless covered England's history from the reign of Richard II to the accession of Henry Tudor in eight plays that share a concern with political issues. Twentieth-century critics therefore appear justified in assessing *Henry V* as part of the history play genre and relating it to the other plays in Shakespeare's second tetralogy.[17] The play is epic in its celebration of a hero who embodies his nation's triumphant destiny, and, despite the somber overtones of its Epilogue, *Henry V* ends in the comic renewal of marriage. In *Shakespeare's Festive Comedy* (1959), C. L. Barber traces connections between the *Henry IV* plays and folk rituals that generate a saturnalian release. There is less festive comedy in *Henry V*, where Falstaff dies. But the dramatic action, with its patriotic quest, miraculous victory at Agincourt, and love interest for the hero, is clearly indebted to the romance tradition— what Northrop Frye, in *The Anatomy of Criticism* (1957), terms the "mythos of summer."[18]

Theatrical

Just as genre criticism explores the play's rootedness in much broader social and anthropological contexts than does new criticism, so the theatrical approach to *Henry V* also refuses to abstract the play to a "spatial unity," examining instead its changing temporal sequence as it unfolds in performance. This dimension has never been ignored completely, of course. Interest in the original conditions of Shakespeare's theater (initiated by William Poel in the early twentieth century) continued through studies such as M. C. Bradbrook's *Themes and Conventions of Elizabethan Tragedy* (1935) and Harley Granville Barker's *Prefaces to Shakespeare* (1927–47), which drew on his experiences as a director of the plays. In *Shakespeare's Stagecraft* (1967), J. L. Styan points out how the shape of the stage in the Elizabethan theater helps determine dramatic significance; at the end of

Henry V "the nature of civil war is symbolically emphasized by the symmetry of the entrances,"[19] with the French leaders coming in through one of the large doors at the back of the stage and the English through the other. But it is Styan's *Elements of Drama* (1960) that is most significant in abandoning a formalist approach to dramatic literature and examining the play as a musical score, a kinetic form carried by actors and changing from moment to moment. Reacting against both Aristotle's structural categories (plot, action, character, thought, spectacle) and the new critics' notion of organic unity created by verbal images, Styan recommends analyzing the play as a dynamic process, a shifting "sequence of impressions" that ultimately coheres in the minds of the audience.[20] Privileging the dynamics of the play and the audience's perception of them has paved the way for a variety of performance criticism that examines in detail various productions, including filmed and televised Shakespeare, to assess how they make significant choices in interpreting the script.

Metadramatic

Attention to the ways in which drama works on stage sparked interest, too, in how Shakespeare's plays use theatrical motifs self-reflexively, so that instead of presenting action in a purely mimetic way, the plays also explore the medium of dramatic art—its possibilities and limitations—on a metadramatic or metatheatrical level. Ann Righter's *Shakespeare and the Idea of the Play* (1962) was one of the earliest of these types of study, which proliferated in the 1970s. James L. Calderwood's seminal *Shakespearean Metadrama* (1971) defines "dramatic art itself—its materials, its media of language and theater, its generic forms and conventions"—as Shakespeare's "most abiding subject."[21] His *Metadrama in Shakespeare's "Henriad"* (1979) *extends this study to three of Shakespeare's history plays, culminating in Henry V.* Calderwood draws a compelling parallel between Henry V's dilemma within the action—having to earn his victory at Agincourt through self-questioning and effort—and the playwright's need to redeem himself from the "charge of artistic despotism";[22] that is, from having imposed a simplistic design of unity at the beginning of the play and loaded the dice too heavily in favor of victory for the King. Thomas F. Van Laan also considers the histrionic dimension of *Henry V* —though more in relation to the main character than through Shakespeare's self-conscious use of his materials—in *Role-Playing in Shakespeare* (1979). He concludes that the character of Henry is a "nexus" of interrelated roles displaying kingship. Shakespeare "takes on the difficult task of dramatizing the positive account"[23] of monarchy by showing Henry (in contrast with the other kings of the history plays) performing these roles effectively. Metadramatics, an often ingenious mode of criticism, provides a good counterbalance to concentrating too exclusively on the realistic presentation of plot and character.

These approaches to drama, offering different insights into Shakespeare's plays, can all be seen as part of the "humanist" tradition; they are concerned with dramatic literature as a unique type of discourse that embodies human values. Thus F. R. Leavis, the most famous of the *Scrutiny* critics, finds the business of understanding and evaluating literature an intensely humanist (and moral) endeavor: "The study of it is, or should be, an intimate study of the complexities, potentialities and essential conditions of human nature."[24] J. L. Styan, too, maintains that "playgoing expects us to make the contibution of what ultimate qualities of fine feelings and intellectual honesty we possess."[25] It is the idea of an "essential" human nature, or the analysis of literature as a cultivation of individual sensibility, to which most recent critical movements object.

Structuralist

Structuralist critics, precursors of the deconstructive and political movements of the 1980s, also veer away from humanist concerns or the study of the individual in literature. Following the theories of De Saussure, they concentrate on language as a system of signs, or on culture as a system of codes, as theorized by Levi-Strauss. Their emphasis is on the *system*, for it is the relationship between the items, or the difference between the signifiers, that creates meaning, since what is signified, the thing itself, perpetually eludes "presence"(as explained by the French theorist Derrida, in *Of Grammatology* [1976]). A structuralist approach to dramatic character, for instance, examines the differences between characters as a clue to their meaning and, like new criticism, declines to look outside the text to interpret this meaning. To be sure, analyzing how a character such as Fluellen functions in relation to Henry as well as to the other British soldiers is more conducive to dramatic appreciation than is speculating on whether he is modeled on the historical character Sir Roger Williams.[26] But deducing semiotic and dramatic codes[27] may not be an integral part of watching the play in the theater. Whereas structuralists take the focus away from the individual, or human agency, and place it on the system of which the subject is part, the audience immersed in a play performed by flesh-and-blood actors will tend to do the opposite: become caught up in the particularities of human conflict and crisis.

RECENT CRITICAL APPROACHES
TO *HENRY V* (1980–   )

Cultural Materialist

Canterbury's speech on the "honeybees" (I. ii. 183–204) is a good place to begin discussion of the cultural materialist approach to *Henry V.* By way of expounding on Exeter's comparison between music and government (a "congreeing" and harmony on different social levels), and to convince Henry that it is safe for him to leave England and pursue his war in France, Canterbury develops a second emblem of a well-ordered society:

> . . . Therefore doth heaven divide
> The state of man in divers functions,
> Setting endeavor in continual motion;
> To which is fixed, as an aim or butt,
> Obedience; for so work the honeybees,
> Creatures that by a rule in nature teach
> The act of order to a peopled kingdom. (183–89)

The analogy between the beehive and the state is not original; it derives from Plato, Virgil, and Pliny. In his *Book Named The Governor* (1531), Thomas Elyot also discusses how the honeybee, which chooses one "principal bee" for the hive, was "left to man by nature" as "a perpetual figure of a just governance or rule."[28] Shakespeare appears to have been elaborating a commonplace here, and indeed the passage does not do much to further plot or character interests (it disappears from the streamlined versions of the play in Olivier's and Branagh's films). Just what is the significance of this speech?

In *The Elizabethan World Picture* (1943), E.M.W. Tillyard finds such a hierarchical vision, within the microcosm and the macrocosm, central to that era: "It is what everyone believed in Elizabeth's days."[29] Canterbury's speech on the honeybees begins by acknowledging the role of "heaven" in human government. The "rule in nature" is the intermediary between divine law and human society, enabling bees, programmed to follow the laws of Nature, to model the hierarchical "act of order" for human citizens. Whereas Tillyard finds such a vision entirely reasonable and commendable—he asserts that the Elizabethan belief in the "ideal order animating earthly order" was what made their age a "great one"[30]—critics since 1980 have refused to take Shakespeare's disquisitions on order at face value. The cultural materialist Jonathan Dollimore finds such speeches a form of special pleading to ensure the continuation of the Elizabethan power structure. In his reading, the speech on honeybees is not a celebration of empirical reality but an "assertion that such power [the government's] derives from an inherent natural and human order encoded by God."[31] The "obedience" of subjects (a key word emphasized by its position at the beginning of the verse line) is the linchpin of the enterprise, guaranteeing the functioning of the well-ordered government.

In other words, the "conception of order" is not "part of the collective mind of the people" (Tillyard's conclusion)[32] but an imposition of the dominant ideology of the time—at its crudest, a form of propaganda on behalf of the ruling elite in an age when the gap between social classes was huge. Cultural materialism, like Marxism, defines ideology not only as a neutral set of shared beliefs but as "those beliefs, practices, and institutions which work to legitimate the social order."[33] In an explanation that could be applied to Canterbury's speech, Dollimore states that "the principal strategy of ideology is to legitimate inequality and exploitation by representing the social order which perpetuates these things as immutable and unalterable—as decreed by God or simply natural."[34] Once we endorse this coercion theory it is difficult to read eulogies on degree in Shakespeare's plays in an unproblematic way, or to interpret the Archbishop's words as part of a straightforward network of images affirming organic unity.[35]

Cultural materialism, which assimilates Marxist theory, is a strong reaction against earlier conservative criticism of Shakespeare, whether it is Tillyard promulgating the "notion of degree," humanist critics who stress the transcendent, ahistorical values of the plays, or new critics who set literature apart as a formally constructed, autonomous discourse. The 1980s movement decenters the "essential self" (the focus of humanist criticism), and instead concentrates on the power relations operating in the texts, where the self is an "object and effect of power."[36] The term "cultural materialist" (attached to this mainly British group of critics) originates with Raymond Williams, who worked hard to integrate literature with sociology. The movement is also inspired by the work of Althusser, a Marxist anti-humanist, and especially by the French theorist Foucault. Foucault analyzed discourse as an agency of power; and both new historicist and cultural materialist critics emphasize how literature functions in this way—not as a discourse separate from history but as an ongoing part of the culture, which reproduces or contests the dominant ideology of the time. In this way they repoliticize Renaissance texts. Moreover, they admit frankly that readers' political concerns and interests in the present shape what they discover in the texts of the past. With their left-wing bias, cultural materialists are committed to exposing how patterns of the dominant ideology function both in the past and at this moment in history, and thus how the current status quo—in Shakespeare studies as in conservative Britain—might actively be changed.

In "History and Ideology: The Instance of *Henry V*," Jonathan Dollimore and Alan Sinfield find that the play espouses the theory of ultimate power— the Elizabethan idea that a strong monarch can unify his country through foreign war. The theory is strongly contested, however, through threats from other quarters in the play: the churchmen, who must be appeased before Henry can go to war; the aristocratic conspirators; the squabbling Irish, Welsh, and Scots; and the basely motivated lower classes (the Eastcheap crew). According to Dollimore and Sinfield, the play is actually preoccupied with the underside of unity: insurrection. There is even a threat from within, when Henry demystifies his own kingly authority in the "ceremony" speech (IV. i). Analyzing this speech, the authors conclude that "the fantasy of establishing ideological unity in the sole figure of the monarch arrives at an impasse which it can handle only with difficulty."[37] In the England of the 1590s, this "fantasy" of a "single source of power in the state"[38] was seriously threatened when the Essex crisis came to a head. But in *Henry V*, ultimately, "antagonism is reworked as subordination or supportive alignment."[39] The King appropriates the power of the clergy, the traitors repent publicly, and the Celtic trio are united in the cause of war. Meanwhile the Eastcheap crew are either killed off or (like Pistol) excluded from the play's final harmony.

New Historicist

American new historicism is so closely aligned with British cultural materialism that in many ways it is misleading to speak of two separate movements. Stephen Greenblatt gave currency to the term "new historicism" in the early 1980s, with his seminal *Renaissance Self-Fashioning* (1980), which deconstructs the notion of the autonomous individual and emphasizes instead those cultural institutions and political contexts that fashion the human subject. Following Foucault, new historicism stresses the function of discourse as an agency of power and refuses to privilege literature as a special category. Literary works are read in the context of social and political history, and the marginalized in these areas receive special attention. Accordingly, new historicists cast the net wider than traditional historians do, connecting obscure or little-known texts with the well-known ones; in "Invisible Bullets: Renaissance Authority and Its Subversions, *Henry IV* and *Henry V*," Greenblatt begins by analyzing the strategy of Thomas Harriot's *A Brief and True Report of the New Found*

Land of Virginia (1588) to show, by analogy, how the dominant Elizabethan ideology is tested and then reasserted in three of Shakespeare's history plays. Greenblatt's thesis is that "Shakespeare's plays are centrally and repeatedly concerned with the production and containment of subversion and disorder."[40] The dominant power structure, as part of legitimating itself, produces subversions of its "ideal image" but then almost always succeeds in containing (including and subordinating) these subversions. This process is a clever form of vaccination against disruption, one that serves ultimately to strengthen the power base. Inevitably new historicists are fatalistic, even cynical, about the possibilities for radical subversion —any movement that will seriously undermine or actually change the status quo—since all resistance is ultimately contained within the totalizing image of power. Greenblatt concludes that in *Henry V* "the subversive doubts the play continually awakens serve paradoxically to intensify the power of the king and his war, even while they cast shadows upon this power."[41]

How exactly does the power-subversion-containment paradigm operate in the play? Members of the lower classes—such as Pistol with his quest to "suck" blood in France or Williams with his challenge to the King's conscience on the eve of battle—cast doubts on the official line about war. But they are either marginalized (like Pistol, who does not share in the victory of Agincourt) or appropriated by the monarch (Henry defuses Williams' challenge in IV. viii). And those aspects of Henry himself that are most troubling, such as his machiavellian pact with the churchmen and his ruthlessness at Harfleur, are all subsumed within the image of the victorious warrior who unites his British subjects. As Greenblatt puts it, *Henry V* "registers every nuance of royal hypocrisy, ruthlessness, and bad faith, but it does so in the context of a celebration, a collective panegyric to 'This star of England', the charismatic leader who purges the commonwealth of its incorrigibles and forges the martial national state."[42]

One significant difference between Greenblatt's new historicist approach and that of the cultural materialists is this stress on final containment. Dollimore and Sinfield admit that resistance is contained in Henry V, but they emphasize "not only the strategies of power but also the anxieties [italics mine] informing both them and their ideological representation."[43] David J. Baker criticizes Greenblatt more openly for hearing only the "monological" voice of English authority in this play, and not attending sufficiently to the muted voice of the "Other"—the words of the displaced Irishman Macmorris, for instance.[44] If more weight is given to these dissonances the door is ajar, at least, for a more progressive reading of Shakespeare, whereas the new historicists tend to view Shakespeare's drama as a "primary expression of Renaissance power"[45] that never fully challenges the source of that power.

To some extent their criticism can serve as a springboard to further analysis of the play. Students might fruitfully discuss the degree to which the subversive elements *are* given a voice in the play, and how strongly characters such as Pistol and the Hostess challenge the status quo. But both cultural materialism and new historicism have been attacked for imposing a predetermined pattern on the plays—Charles Forker complains that "power and aggression become exclusively and reductively the theme of this criticism,"[46] while Graham Bradshaw lambastes "politicized readings that short-circuit the genuinely exploratory process of Shakespeare's dramatic thinking"[47]—and for refusing to see anything positive about the notion of "order" or anything *un*problematic about the dominant ideology inscribed in Shakespeare's plays. It is inevitable, too, and consistent with their strategy, that these critics subordinate close attention to the play's poetic language and dramaturgy to an examination of power relations in the drama, so that their analysis of particular passages is often sketchy or skewed to the political theme. Jarrold Plotnick has pointed out how Dollimore and Sinfield, in their analysis of Henry's soliloquy on ceremony, ignore the speech's central focus on the emptiness of royal forms and the heavy responsibilities of kingship when they erroneously conclude that the King is "*really*" tormented by his "inability to ensure obedience."[48] Students of *Henry V* may still want to discuss Henry's character as a major component of the play and to analyze it in terms of the conflict between political or kingly attributes and human qualities, not only as part of the abstract "paradoxes, ambiguities, and tensions of authority."[49] The choice of critical approach should always be based on what helps the reader or viewer engage with the play and understand it most fully. An eclectic approach, one that accommodates older methodologies or ways of viewing the play as well as newer ones, is probably the most productive for studying *Henry V*.

Appropriations

Cultural materialists such as Graham Holderness are particularly interested in how Shakespeare has been appropriated in various ways by different eras. As we can never uncover the original Shakespeare, it makes sense, they argue, to analyze the ways in which Shakespeare and his plays have been taken over by, or subtly assimilated to, modern society: "For every particular present, Shakespeare is here, now, always, what is currently being made of him."[50] This penetrating analysis of Shakespeare's role in both the past and the present is an effort to demystify the Bard. In *The Shakespeare Myth* (1988), Holderness and others set out to show how in this century Shakespeare has been turned into a cultural institution in both society and schools in Britain: a form of myth that supports the conservative establishment (a bourgeois-democratic society) and the "high culture"[51] of the early and mid-twentieth century. They provide several examples of how Shakespeare has been appropriated by the dominant culture. David Margolies concludes that the traditional reading of the *Henry* plays, which marginalizes the misgivings of the commoners and stresses instead the transformation of the "wayward prince" into a "wise and popular king," interprets the plays "in terms of what is relevant to ruling-class interests—order and authority."[52] And according to Holderness, the BBC/Time Life televised series of The Shakespeare Plays (1978–85) could not escape the iron hand of the British Broadcasting Corporation—"a classic monument of national culture, an oppressive agency of cultural hegemony."[53]

Earlier in this study I touched on the way that a critic's own political views or values inform his or her reading of *Henry V*; we find the anti-royalist Hazlitt deploring Henry as a tyrant in the nineteenth century, while Dover Wilson, editing the play during World War II, praised the monarch as a great war leader. The history of performance also shows how productions of *Henry V* are never free from ideological presuppositions or from the political climate of the time. Alan Howard chose to present the progress of the king through the play as a personal odyssey; yet this production (Royal Shakespeare Company, 1975) balanced the individual quest with an emphasis on the closeness between the "band of brothers"—a pulling together that reflected the RSC's difficult economic times following the international oil crisis. The play has sometimes clashed with the current zeitgeist—*Henry V* was booed off the London stage in 1938, the final year of attempting to appease Hitler—or it may try consciously to exploit it. Olivier's 1944 film of *Henry V* was promoted by the Ministry of Information as a rallying cry for the Allies, a prelude to D-Day. Branagh aimed to be apolitical in his version of the play, but of course that is never really possible; his film may have absorbed some of the anti-military sentiment following the Falklands war (1982) that many critics thought fueled the 1984–85 RSC production in which Branagh played the title role. Holderness interprets the film, with its emphasis on rugged individualism, as more in line with the "characteristic emotions of patriotism"[54] in the late twentieth century. On a deeper level, he thinks that Branagh is projecting into the film some of his own cultural anxiety about being an Irishman now absorbed into conventional English society.[55] In this interpretation, Henry's surprisingly tearful outburst to Fluellen, "for I am Welsh, you know," displaces Branagh's animus about national identity onto another, less rebellious, outsider from the British mainstream: the Welshman. Certainly this approach and others like it enable us to perceive the play as less monolithic; it changes every time a critic, director, or actor reinvents it in a new historical context, and in doing so either reconfirms or actively interrogates the traditional discourse on Shakespeare and the norms of the dominant culture.

Feminist

What scope does *Henry V* offer for a feminist analysis? Although women play important roles in Shakespeare's tragedies (sometimes as the demonized "other"[56]) and in his comedies, where the heroine often breaks through gender barriers by disguising herself as a man and proving instrumental in the action, women have less impact in the world of the histories. As Coppelia Kahn notes, "the patriarchal world of Shakespeare's plays is emphatically masculine."[57] Phyllis Rackin echoes this sentiment in her study of the history plays: "Renaissance historiography constituted a masculine tradition," and "In the central scene of historical representation, women have no place."[58] With the exception of Joan of Arc (demonized in *Henry VI, Part i*), women in the late Middle Ages did not fight in wars or influence the course of national history significantly. In *Henry IV, Part i*, Kate Percy provides a strong voice of opposition; she complains about, and implicitly satirizes, Hotspur's war games—the "palisadoes, frontiers, parapets" (II. iii. 52) that bubble up in his dreams—but she cannot, as his wife, prevent him from going to fight at Shrewsbury, where he is killed by the future Henry V.

The women of *Henry V* are clearly circumscribed within a male-dominated society. But despite the play's fairly relentless focus on Henry and his war, four female characters are given speaking parts: the Hostess, who appears in two scenes; Princess Katherine and her attendant Alice, also in two scenes; and Queen Isabella, who appears in the final scene only. Act IV, centering on Agincourt, not surprisingly contains no appearances by women; yet III. iv is given over exclusively to two French women, who converse in their own language without any male intervention. It is important to assess how far, if at all, the women in the play offer a challenge to the values of Henry and his male associates.

The most searching kind of feminist criticism of the Renaissance adopts a materialist approach, exploring ways in which the concept of woman, in sixteenth- and early-seventeenth-century texts, is determined by changing social and economic conditions of the time. What was the status of women within the family structure? Did they have any property rights? How were they represented in medical and legal documents, or conduct books of the time? The notion of the female is culturally constructed, dependent on the shifting ideology of the age. To fully assess the meaning of "woman" in *Henry V* we would need to look at other Renaissance discourses (to "over-read text with history," as Carol Thomas Neely advises[59]) in order to understand how women, aristocrats as well as working-class women, are represented in the various social documents and records of the time. Students approaching *Henry V* can reap the benefits of this historical perspective, ably provided by feminist (and cultural materialist) critics such as Catherine Belsey[60] and Linda Woodbridge.[61]

At the other extreme from this is the more accessible "essentialist" approach (adopted by Marilyn French in *Shakespeare's Division of Experience* and currently out of critical favor), which examines the idea of femaleness, as represented in Shakespeare's plays, in terms of universal, mythic categories. While the masculine principle is associated with "assertiveness" and "power-in-the-world," the feminine principle is identified with nature, both generative (the nurturing side) and destructive.[62] Most desirable, though rare in Shakespeare's plays, French thinks, is a balance between the two principles. Certainly the Hostess in *Henry V* can be viewed as embodying the positive side of the feminine principle; she offers the nurturing qualities of affection and sympathy in a play where the hero is shown submerging those characteristics in the interests of strong masculine leadership. In a phrase that stands out in this male-centered play (and that comments obliquely on Henry's claim to the throne of France through the female), the Hostess calls out to the three Eastcheap comrades, when Falstaff is dying, "As ever you come of women, come in quickly to Sir John" (II. i. 120–21). She readily diagnoses Falstaff's terminal condition as the result of a devastating emotional loss (to her he is a "poor heart" because "the king has kill'd his heart"), and she shows compassion by defending his death as a "finer end" than that of any "christom child" (II. iii. 11–12).

Queen Isabella, at the top of the social scale, can also be seen as an important counterbalance to the acquisitive concerns of the male enclaves, both English and French, at the end of the play. It is she who looks into Henry's eyes and is relieved that they have lost their "venom" against the French. It is she who accompanies the negotiators, offering a "woman's voice" should the bargaining reach a sticking point ("When articles too nicely urged be stood on"), and who gives her daughter "leave" to stay with Henry. Finally, after the match between Henry and Katherine is sealed, it is Isabella who envisages political stability in terms of a strong personal relationship when she prays that "God, the best maker of all marriages, / Combine your hearts in one, your realms in one!"(371–72). To leave her out of the last scene, as Branagh's movie does (by giving her speeches to the men), is to silence the woman's voice for peace and amelioration at the end of this war-driven play.

A feminist approach that gives full weight to the female voices in the play, even to the point of amplifying them in a "compensatory" way,[63] should be tempered by one that honestly examines the ways in which the play in general marginalizes women's roles. They are limited not only by what we understand, in general terms, to be the patriarchal conditions operating in fifteenth- and sixteenth-century European society, but by the actual dramaturgy of the play—what Kathleen McLuskie calls the "narrative, poetic and theatrical strategies which construct the plays' meanings and position the audience to understand their events from a particular point of view."[64] The Hostess is a case in point. Although she acquires a certain independence when she is narrating Falstaff's death—she takes the theatrical spotlight, and her poignant speech, culminating in "and all was as cold as any stone" (II. iii. 26–27), contains some of the most moving language in the play—she is overshadowed, within the dramatic structure of the Eastcheap scenes, by the men around her. Pistol's parting words put her firmly in her wifely place, associating her with his "chattels" and "movables" (II. iii. 49) and warning her not to take liberties while he is gone:

Let housewifery appear; keep close, I thee command. (62)

The Hostess fails to break up the fight between Nym and Pistol (II. i), nor can she prevent the men from leaving for war (II. iii). If Pistol's laconic "my Doll is dead"(recounted in V. i. 84) actually refers to Nell Quickly rather than to Doll Tearsheet of *Henry IV, Part ii*, then he is informing us that his wife has succumbed to venereal disease. Whichever character the lines refer to, the female here is appropriated to the needs of the male, less envisaged as an independent human being than objectified as Pistol's "rendezvous" (86).

Similarly, Queen Isabella's importance in the final scene is not negated but is displaced somewhat by the male pact between her husband and Henry. When Henry claims Katherine he bypasses Isabella and asks permission from the French King. King Charles then sets his patriarchal seal on the match, hoping to perpetuate his own stock through this union:

Take her, fair son, and from her blood raise up
Issue to me. (V. ii. 360–61)

Women are necessary in the line of succession, but only as vehicles to guarantee men's eventual inheritance and the continuation of male prowess. Canterbury had to prove the irrelevance of the Salic law's decree that "No woman shall succeed" so that Henry could claim France through his great-great-grandmother, also named Isabella. It was this female who produced the famous warrior-king Edward III; and Henry trusts that Katherine, too, will prove a "good soldier-breeder."[65]

Princess Katherine is the most important female character in the play, but even she is marginalized. While she does exert some influence in the wooing scene and establishes her independence before acceding to Henry's wishes, the way she is positioned in the play, both narratively and theatrically, subordinates her to male strategy. She is first mentioned as a bargaining chip, a pawn in the war game. The Chorus to Act III reports that the French ambassador

> Tells Harry that the King doth offer him
> Katherine his daughter, and with her to dowry
> Some petty and unprofitable dukedoms.
> The offer likes not. . . . (29–32)

Henry presumably wants Katherine only if he can get all of France as well. The Princess's first appearance on stage (III. iv) is strong theatrically—an all-female scene in startling contrast to the exclusively male scenes at Harfleur—but Alice qualifies the impression of Katherine's independence somewhat by playing the role of her guardian and language instructor. What is more, Henry's cruel threats to the Governor to let his soldiers mow down the "fresh fair virgins" of Harfleur, still ringing in our ears from the previous scene, inevitably cast a shadow over Katherine's ebullient naming of body parts. Her frank enjoyment of the double entendre on "foot" and "count" is a breath of fresh air after Henry's vision of rape; but it is difficult not to see her, too, as an unwitting victim, a spoil of war like the "shrill-shrieking" daughters of Harfleur in Henry's brutal imagination.[66] (To have a woman play the role of the Governor of Harfleur, a totally unhistorical touch used in the RSC's 1994 production, is to make much more prominent the plight of women in France and thus strengthen the case against Henry.) Katherine's implication in the war is further foregrounded in Branagh's film, where, after her exuberant antics with Alice, she opens the door of her chamber to encounter the somber presence of her father and brother on their way to discuss Henry's progress to Calais, and her face clouds over too.

In the wooing scene (V. ii), Katherine again is presented as a combination of appropriated property (the marriage is a foregone conclusion to secure Henry's position in France) and an individual who is expected to give her personal assent. The framing of the scene makes us see the marriage as part of Henry's game plan; at the opening Henry tells the French court that Katherine is his "capital demand," while near the end the male badinage that Burgundy initiates with Henry unpleasantly dehumanizes Katherine, subordinating her to the men's sexual jests.[67] She is discussed both as a sex object (one who will "endure handling") and as part of a package deal, a maid whose sexual initiation is contingent on the handing over of "maiden cities" in France to the English King. It is true, to a significant extent, that "heterosexual relations are here assimilated to the martial masculine culture."[68]

Although Katherine is never truly assertive with Henry, she does win an equivocal victory by at least making him treat her as a human being. There is no disputing that Henry takes the initiative in the encounter, while Katherine's role is reactive. He expects to conduct the conversation in his native tongue, and the Princess follows his lead, even though she fears he will "mock" her because she is not fluent in English. Her responses to him are usually laconic (she has twenty-nine lines to his two hundred or so), and many of them are evasive: "I cannot speak your England,""I cannot tell wat is 'like me,' " "I cannot tell what is dat," "I cannot tell," and "I do not know dat." Her longest speech is one of shocked concern, beginning "Laissez, mon seigneur, laissez, laissez!"(263), when she explains (in French, as she is under the pressure of emotion) why it is improper for him to kiss her hand. Her evasions can be interpreted as natural defensiveness; although she knows that the match must go on, she does not want to give herself until she has drawn him out. Indeed she *does* draw him out. Her line "les langues des hommes sont pleines de tromperies"(117–18) encourages him to cut the nonsense of flattery and engage with her more frankly, like the "plain" person he is. Her "Sauf votre honneur, me understand well" (134) is a put-down after his overly blunt approach ("clap hands, and a bargain. How say you, lady?"), and her penetrating question "Is it possible dat I sould love de ennemie of France?" (174–75) is a further incitement to honesty; it makes Henry admit his great love for the country he has just conquered as well as for its princess. And her claim not to understand his explanation that "when France is mine and I am yours, then yours is France, and you are mine" (180–82) leads into his attempt to speak French with her. This is an important breaking of the ice. Not only can they laugh together, but their roles are briefly reversed in that now he becomes vulnerable, a possible object of her mirth. So Katherine, while she cannot openly defy her lord or "seigneur," has asserted her will through tactful but firm resistance, precipitating in him an honesty that in turn leads him to treat her as more of an equal. Finally, though, she cannot escape her traditional role as a female subservient to the male authority figures in this patriarchal society, for she can take Henry only if "it shall please de Roi mon père" (257). She also submits to Henry's kiss, accepting the logic that "nice customs cursy to great kings" (281–82).

Any feminist analysis of the wooing scene will be fuller if it takes into account, too, the different ways it has been performed in our own age. As Kathleen McLuskie makes clear, "meaning is constructed every time the text is reproduced in the changing ideological dynamic between text and audience."[69] It is instructive to compare the scene in Laurence Olivier's film version (1944), produced some time before the women's movement surfaced fully in the 1960s and 1970s, with that in Kenneth Branagh's postfeminist film made at the end of the 1980s. The position of the two characters within the film set, the choice of camera shots to focus on one or the other, and the style and interpretation of the actors playing the King and Princess all combine to reveal a more compliant Katherine and a more confidently assertive Henry in Olivier's version than in Branagh's.

In Olivier's *Henry V* the wooing scene is choreographed as a conquest of Katherine's personal space. The King, often separated from Katherine by pillars or the small columns within the window frames of the stylized French court, must circumnavigate these barriers and gradually close the gap between them. As the sequence begins, each is leaning against a pillar facing the other. When Henry moves forward to address Katherine the camera pulls back to show Alice, her guardian, in the left of the frame; there is to be no real privacy for the couple. During much of their dialogue the window columns stand between them, so that when Henry attempts to converse with Katherine in French, for instance, they symbolize the language barrier. At the very moment he succeeds in moving around Katherine's column, into her space, to draw from her the concession that their marriage will "content" her, he throws away the advantage by attempting to kiss her hand. Katherine rushes away from him to the protective Alice and then barricades herself in an alcove on a higher level, where she gazes at him through another set of protective bars. Henry follows her there as he explains how "nice customs cur[t]sy to great kings"; he then takes her hand to lead her firmly around, out of the alcove and into a neutral, open space (free from pillars) where they kiss.

Olivier's Henry, whose gestures and tone of voice are firm and confident, never loses control of the encounter. It is true that Katherine, played by Renée Asherson, is not presented totally as a pawn. She moves away from the King when he asks, "What say'st thou then to my love?" and the camera focuses on her gazing out of a window, contemplating the consequences for her country as she questions the rightness of her loving the "ennemie of France." The camera also lingers on Katherine, in reaction shot, during Henry's long disclaimer of his own attractiveness. But here she is sitting in the window seat, very much the object of Henry's male gaze as he circles around her. When he moves back into the frame he places his hand proprietorially on her arm to explain the merits of a "good heart"; this means that when she rises in consternation at his admission that he will not die of love for her, Henry is able gently but firmly to push her down again.[70] What is more, Henry's hearty laughter at several of her remarks—as when she complains about the "deceits" of men's tongues—is positively grating. It signifies the satisfied chuckle of a wooer confident of eventual success.

Indeed, apart from her alarm at Henry's one social blunder, Katherine's willingness to concede to him is never really in doubt. Asherson plays the Princess as gracious and composed, always ready to respond to her suitor with a sparkling smile. She is unfazed when he bluntly requests "clap hands, and a bargain"; her only discomposure is produced by his attempt to kiss her hand.

In Branagh's film of *Henry V*, Emma Thompson projects a much less compliant Katherine. This is the key difference between the two interpretations of the Princess's role: Much more than Asherson's Katherine, Thompson's exerts a measure of control in the arena of personal relationships—limited though it must be in this patriarchal society—so that she induces Henry to play the wooing game on her terms. Even before she lifts her veil for their interview we are given a quick glimpse of her anxious, perplexed features. At the beginning of their conversation she refuses to look at him directly (delivering "Your Majesty shall mock at me" out front, with quiet dignity), and she is positively cold when he clumsily offers to "clap hands, and a bargain." Still grave and unsmiling as he entreats her to "take a soldier, take a king," she finally holds his gaze to ask the key question: "Is it possible dat I sould love de ennemie of France?" What breaks down her defenses is his imperfect speaking of French; suddenly, in his confusion and potential humiliation, he is on her level (literally, too, as their faces are shown together in profile) so that they can genuinely laugh together. As he continues to woo her she gradually warms to his apology for his "stubborn outside," and although there is more consternation when he moves to kiss her hand, she is again won over by his gently mocking "O Kate" and his firm invitation for them jointly to become the bold "makers of manners." By her quiet resistance throughout the scene, Thompson conveys an impression of the Princess as a strong personality. She amplifies what are only possibilities in the text, but in doing so—by withholding eye contact and only gradually allowing a true interaction to take place—she exerts a much stronger pressure against Branagh's Henry than Linda Bamber allows in her dismissal of Katherine as a "negligible presence in the scene."[71] Initially bewildered and saddened by the invidious position she is placed in as the King's "capital demand," Katherine is unwilling to concede to Henry until they have established some common ground. She must capitulate eventually, but need not do so graciously. By withholding her affection she can expose the coercion for what it is—and stymie the progress of a workable relationship. Therefore she makes Henry work hard to gain her confidence, contradicting Bamber's text-based conclusion that "Henry's power and desire" are "wholly unopposed by Katherine."[72]

Branagh's Henry, for his part, is a risk taker, much less self-assured and commanding than Olivier's kingly lover. He appears, at least, to believe in the possibility of Katherine's remaining hostile, whereas Olivier's buccaneering laughter suggests no doubt that his lady will eventually be won. In Branagh's production, too, there is a literal as well as a metaphorical gap to be closed—the protagonists begin at opposite ends of the huge council table—but his Henry is uneasy at first, improvising various strategies (first flattery, then bluntness) as he moves closer to Katherine. He briefly takes her hand to explain his deficiencies in wooing, and a series of close-ups of each face sets his expression of earnest candor against her skeptical concern. The intimacy and spontaneity of their strenuous encounter is pointed up both through these close-ups (we see the look in their eyes, as we never do in Olivier's middle-range shots) and in the way that Henry's words, such as "yet I love thee too" (156), are often spoken quietly. Olivier's Henry has to move with dexterity to conquer Katherine's space, but his vocal delivery remains fairly constant in pitch and tone. Branagh's handling of the scene continually exploits the intimate medium of film to accentuate the personal nuances and gender conflicts that late-twentieth-century audiences are attuned to; this ensures that the wooing comes across in modern terms rather than being presented as a relatively public display, as would most likely have been the case in the Elizabethan theater.

As Branagh's Henry stumbles through his French and provokes Katherine's mirth, their faces are close (in profile), with Alice's face discreetly behind and between them. After his comic outburst of frustration, "Can any of your neighbors tell, Kate?" (203), Henry moves round behind Katherine's chair and bends down to talk to her, still almost on the same level with her. He is also prepared to communicate with her as an equal by refusing to treat their union as a fait accompli, since he emphasizes the conditional in his proposition: "Thou hast me, *if* thou hast me, at the worst; and thou shalt wear me, *if* thou wear me, better and better" (240–2). (Significantly, the crudeness of his imagining Kate as a "good soldier-breeder" shortly before this is cut in both productions—in Olivier's in the interests of gentility, in Branagh's to avoid anything that might alienate the Princess at this stage of increasing intimacy.) Branagh's delicate gesture of turning Katherine's face toward him to assure her that their marriage "shall please" the King of France is much less controlling than Olivier's firm leading of Katherine out of her shelter and into a neutral space. Branagh's gesture signals the couple's established closeness, which is only briefly interrupted by the King's social gaffe in trying to kiss Katherine's hand. Their full kiss, shown in close-up, is a solemn pact and a moment of wonder, in which Henry's "You have witchcraft in your lips, Kate" (288–89) rings with absolute sincerity. Its effect is quite different from that of the stylized kiss between Asherson and Olivier, where the camera moves down quickly to focus on their clasped hands displaying rings that unite in one shot the English lions with the French fleur de lys. This is as much the sealing of a political pact as a moment of intimacy.

Feminist criticism of *Henry V* should not ignore the fact that in the Elizabethan theater female characters were played by boy actors. Since cross-dressing violated the decree of Deuteronomy (22:5) that a woman should not wear a man's clothing, "neither shall a man put on a woman's garment," sixteenth-century Puritans excoriated it as both unnatural and blasphemous.[73] Actually, this theatrical convention challenged the notion of gender as "natural": The idea of womanhood, constructed by a male playwright, was being mediated on stage by a male actor who could at any time remind the audience of this artificiality. It is in Shakespeare's comedies that the convention is used most self-consciously, as when the actor of Rosalind steps out of role to deliver the Epilogue to *As You Like It*. The results might well have been subversive. Catherine Belsey, for instance, finds that the transvestism in these plays—the plot device of a girl (played by a boy) who then disguises herself as a boy—unsettles gender categories, providing an opportunity for the character to "speak from a position which is not that of a full, unified, gendered subject."[74] Other feminist commentators have argued that this doubleness results in a creative androgyny,[75] in which the characters of Rosalind-Ganymede (*As You Like It*) or Viola-Caesario (*Twelfth Night*) combine male and female qualities—boldness with compassion, physical aggressiveness with patient restraint—to both solve and ride out plot complications. There is no such temporary synthesis in *Henry V*, but the convention of the cross-dressed male actor must surely have affected the dynamics of the wooing scene. Whether or not we agree with Lisa Jardine, who believes that a level of homoerotic attraction was part of the appeal for Elizabethan theatergoers,[76] we can speculate that the scene played between two male actors might provide some give and take (the kind of honest rapprochement between Henry and Katherine allowed for in the text) with less stereotyping along the lines of dominant male/ passive female. It is just as possible, though, that the boy representing Katherine concentrated on the traditional function of the aristocratic lady— courtly and gracious but subservient to her mate—and did not, consciously at least, inform the role with his own maleness.

The cross-dressing convention is explored in Olivier's film version of *Henry V*. As Peter S. Donaldson points out,[77] Olivier contrasts the probable limitations of boys playing the roles of women in the Globe Theatre—their stylized, simplified versions of the female—with the more complex, subtle performances of actresses in the twentieth-century film. By means of a hidden cut in the final wedding sequence at the French court, the film converts the radiant actress Renée Asherson into a boy actor at the Globe: a stark contrast between the realism of the twentieth-century film medium and the conventional representations afforded by the theater 350 years earlier. What happens in the center of the film, where Princess Katherine is played by a skilled actress, is Olivier's way of making good what he perceives as a "deficiency"of the Elizabethan stage.[78] Olivier fails to use the cross-dressing convention consistently, however. Mistress Quickly's opening scene at the Globe is not, Donaldson to the contrary,[79] played by a boy actor; the facial makeup is crude and the gestural mode of acting projects a stylized vulgarity, but it is still the actress Freda Jackson playing the role. Once off the Globe stage she delivers her account of Falstaff's death with compassion and sorrow—a much deeper portrayal of the female character than in her first scene. But the change here is in locales and styles of acting, not in a physical switch from boy actor to mature actress.

Finally, a feminist analysis of *Henry V* can turn from an exploration of how female characters function in the play to a psychoanalytical interpretation of the hero—specifically, of the ways in which the female, or the mother figure, is excluded from his psychic development. The historical Henry's mother died when he was a young boy, and there is no mention of her in the *Henry IV* plays. It has been argued, by Coppelia Kahn,[80] that Falstaff, with his huge belly, his associations with fertility, and his warmth toward Hal, represents not just a surrogate father but a maternal presence; but even Falstaff is firmly excised from the world of *Henry V*. There will be no threat of "engulfment"[81] by the mother as Henry concentrates on establishing his male identity as a king. Emphatically Henry defines himself through his relationships with men, exhibiting what Kahn terms "aggression" (here in the cause of war) as "the means of masculine self-definition."[82] His uncle and his brothers support his war enterprise in the play, and the exploits of his great-grandfather Edward III and his great-uncle the Black Prince serve as a constant standard of military glory for him. On a deeper level, too, Henry is striving to assimilate and outmatch his dead father. Indeed, the battle of Agincourt, where God grants victory to the King instead of punishing him for Henry IV's "fault" in usurping the throne, seems to vindicate the son's rightful inheritance of the crown from his father.

Peter Erickson points out that male bonding is central to *Henry V*: the "idealised male comradeship"[83] that is portrayed, in sentimental language, in the sketch of the mortally wounded York embracing his dying cousin Suffolk on the battlefield ("A testament of noble-ending love" [IV. vi. 27]). Yet it is surely an overstatement to contend, with Erickson, that in *Henry V* "all emotional depth is concentrated in male relations."[84] Whether or not we agree depends largely on our interpretation of Henry's relationship with Katherine; and I have argued that while Katherine is certainly subordinated to male designs in both plot and dramaturgy, she is more than an "unresponsive straw woman"[85] in the wooing scene. For much of the action Henry is engaged in the heroics of war, a glorious blood brotherhood that accentuates aggression[86] and dominance at the expense of emotional sensitivity. As a result, the female sensibility that the Hostess invokes when she entreats the Eastcheap men, "As ever you come of women," to attend to the dying Falstaff, is definitely missing from most of the play. But the fact that the wooing scene is more than perfunctory (the actor Alan Howard, who played Henry V in the Royal Shakespeare Company's 1975 production, found it central to the play) suggests that Henry, through the benign "witchcraft" of Katherine, may finally be discovering more of the female within himself. That is to go beyond the boundaries of the play, of course, which stops short of the actual marriage. As Phyllis Rackin comments astutely about Shakespeare's history plays, "the incorporation of the feminine can only take place at the point where history stops."[87]

NOTES

1. In Daniel A. Fineman (ed.), *Maurice Morgann: Shakespearean Criticism* (Oxford: Clarendon Press, 1972), p. 167.

2. "The Rejection of Falstaff," in *Oxford Lectures on Poetry* (1909; London: Macmillan, 1965), pp. 258–59.

3. Ibid., p. 273.

4. As in Northrop Frye, *The Anatomy of Criticism* (Princeton: Princeton University Press, 1957), and C. L. Barber, *Shakespeare's Festive Comedy* (Princeton: Princeton University Press, 1959).

5. *Psychoanalysis and Shakespeare* (New York; Toronto; London: McGraw Hill, 1964), p. 210.

6. Karen Horney, *Neurosis and Human Growth: The Struggle towards Self-Realization* (New York: Norton, 1950), quoted in Bernard J. Paris, *Character as a Subversive Force in Shakespeare: The History and the Roman Plays* (Rutherford, N.J.: Fairleigh Dickinson University Press, 1991), p. 23.

7. *Character as a Subversive Force*, p. 91.

8. See J. H. Walter (ed.), *Henry V, The Arden Shakespeare* (1954), pp. xiv–xvii.

9. As argued in Harold C. Goddard, *The Meaning of Shakespeare* (Chicago and London: University of Chicago Press, 1951), pp. 215–68.

10. *The Frontiers of Drama* (1945; London: Methuen, 1964), pp. 34–55.

11. *Shakespeare: From* Richard II *to* Henry V (Stanford, Calif.: Stanford University Press, 1957), pp. 166–98.

12. *Scrutiny* (1933), repr. in *Explorations* (1947; New York: New York University Press, 1964), pp. 15–54, 18–19.

13. *Some Shakespearean Themes* (1959; Harmondsworth: Peregrine Books, 1966), p. 108.

14. *Practical Criticism* (1929; London: Routledge, 1964).

15. *The Wheel of Fire: Essays in Interpretation of Shakespeare's Sombre Tragedies* (London: H. Milford, 1930), p. 4.

16. *Understanding Drama* (New York: H. Holt, 1945), p. lx.

17. "Bibliographic Essay," covers some examples of this criticism.

18. Pp. 186–206. See also Joanne Altieri, "Romance in *Henry V*," *SEL*, 21 (1981), 223–40, who finds a lack of cohesion in the play's mixture of realistic and romantic elements.

19. *Shakespeare's Stagecraft* (Cambridge: Cambridge University Press, 1967), p. 20.

20. *Elements of Drama* (Cambridge: Cambridge University Press, 1960), Chapter 4, pp. 64–85.

21. *Shakespearean Metadrama* (Minneapolis: University of Minnesota Press, 1971), p. 5.

22. *Metadrama in Shakespeare's "Henriad"* (Berkeley; Los Angeles; London: University of California Press, 1979), p. 156.

23. *Role-Playing in Shakespeare* (Toronto; Bufffalo; London: University of Toronto Press, 1978), pp. 33, 35.

24. "Literature and Society," in *The Common Pursuit* (1952; Harmondsworth: Peregrine Books, 1962), p. 184.

25. *Elements of Drama*, p. 288.

26. See J. Dover Wilson (ed.), *Henry V* (Cambridge: Cambridge University Press, 1947), "Introduction."

27. As in Keir Elam, *The Semiotics of Theatre and Drama* (London and New York: Methuen, 1980).

28. Ed. S. E. Lehmberg (London: Dent, 1962), p. 7.

29. *The Elizabethan World Picture* (London: Chatto and Windus, 1943), pp. 9–10.

30. Ibid., pp. 13, 100.

31. Jonathan Dollimore and Alan Sinfield, "History and Ideology: The Instance of *Henry V*," in John Drakakis (ed.), *Alternative Shakespeares* (London and New York: Methuen, 1985), p. 213.

32. *The Elizabethan World Picture*, p. 7.

33. "History and Ideology," pp. 210–11.

34. Ibid., pp. 211–12.

35. See J. H. Walter (ed.), *Henry V*, p. xvi.

36. Jonathan Dollimore, *Radical Tragedy* (Brighton: Harvester Press, 1984), p. 179.

37. "History and Ideology," p. 225.

38. Ibid., p. 220.

39. Ibid., p. 217.

40. "Invisible Bullets," in Jonathan Dollimore and Alan Sinfield (eds.), *Political Shakespeare* (Ithaca and London: Cornell University Press, 1985), pp. 18–47, 29. A slightly expanded version of this essay appears in *Shakespearean Negotiations* (Berkeley and Los Angeles: University of California Press, 1988), pp. 21–65.

41. "Invisible Bullets," p. 43. Richard Helgerson, "Staging Exclusion," in *Forms of Nationhood* (Chicago and London: University of Chicago Press, 1992), also finds that the potentially "subversive" elements do little to disrupt the play's "fixation on monarchic power" (245, 335); Derek Cohen discusses the play's strategies against subversion in "Monopolizing Violence: *Henry V*," in *Shakespeare's Culture of Violence* (New York: St. Martin's Press, 1993), pp. 62–78.

42. "Invisible Bullets," p. 42.

43. "History and Ideology," p. 226.

44. " 'Wildehirissheman': Colonialist Representation in Shakespeare's *Henry V*," *ELR*, 22.1 (1994), 37–61, 55, 51.

45. "Invisible Bullets," p. 45.

46. *Medieval and Renaissance Drama in England* (New York: AMS Press, 1986), vol. 3, p. 315.

47. "Being Oneself: New Historicists, Cultural Materialists, and *Henry V*," in *Misrepresentations: Shakespeare and the Materialists* (Ithaca and London: Cornell University Press, 1993), pp. 34–124, 38.

48. " 'Imaginary Puissance': The New Historicism and *Henry V*," *ESC*, 17.3 (1991), 249–67, 252–53.

49. "Invisible Bullets," p. 45.

50. Graham Holderness, *The Shakespeare Myth* (Manchester: Manchester University Press, 1988), p. xvi.

51. See John Drakakis (ed.), *Alternative Shakespeares*, "Introduction," pp. 1–25, 4.

52. "Teaching the Handsaw to Fly: Shakespeare as a Hegemonic Instrument," in *The Shakespeare Myth*, pp. 42–53, 45.

53. Graham Holderness, "Boxing the Bard: Shakespeare and Television," in *The Shakespeare Myth*, pp. 173–89, 181.

54. "Reproductions: *Henry V*," in *Shakespeare Recycled* (London: Barnes and Noble, 1992), p. 201.

55. Ibid., pp. 206–7.

56. See Linda Bamber, *Comic Women, Tragic Men: A Study of Gender and Genre in Shakespeare* (Stanford, Calif.: Stanford University Press, 1982), for an analysis of the feminine in Shakespeare's plays as "a principle of Otherness" (4).

57. *Man's Estate: Masculine Identity in Shakespeare* (Berkeley and Los Angeles: University of California Press, 1981), p. 47.

58. *Stages of History: Shakespeare's English Chronicles* (Ithaca, N.Y.: Cornell University Press, 1990), p. 147.

59. "Constructing the Subject: Feminist Practice and the New Renaissance Discourses," *ELR*, 18.1 (1988), 5–18, 15.

60. *The Subject of Tragedy: Identity and Difference in Renaissance Drama* (London and New York: Methuen, 1986). See also Margaret W. Ferguson, Maureen Quilligan, and Nancy J. Vickers (eds.), *Rewriting the Renaissance: The Discourses of Sexual Difference in Early Modern Europe* (Chicago and London: University of Chicago Press, 1986).

61. *Women and the English Renaissance: Literature and the Nature of Womankind, 1540–1620* (Urbana: University of Illinois Press, 1984).

62. *Shakespeare's Division of Experience* (New York: Summit Books, 1981), pp. 21–22.

63. The term is used by Carol Thomas Neely in "Feminist Modes of Shakespearean Criticism: Compensatory, Justificatory, Transformational," *WS*, 9 (1981), 3–15, 6.

64. "The Patriarchal Bard: Feminist Criticism and Shakespeare: *King Lear* and *Measure for Measure,*" in *Political Shakespeare*, pp. 88–108, 92.

65. Katherine Eggert, "Nostalgia and the Not Yet Late Queen: Refusing Female Rule in *Henry V*," *ELH*, 61 (1994), 523–50, points out that by failing to mention Katherine's later marriage to Owen Tudor (through which she became the grandmother of Henry VII), the play "effectively cancels the woman's part in English succession, and instead hails Henry V as the sole shaper of kingship" (542).

66. Lance Wilcox, "Katherine of France as Victim and Bride," *ShStud*, 17 (1985), 61–76, argues this point but thinks that the wooing scene goes some way

toward metamorphosing "this relationship from one of predator and prey to that between two mutually romantic partners" (73).

67. It is worth noting that the French often displace their military fears onto sexual anxieties in images that degrade the female. The Dauphin is convinced that unless they oppose Henry's army, the French women "will give / Their bodies to the lust of English youth" (III. v. 29–30), while Bourbon envisages the "shame" of not returning to battle as equivalent to acting as a pander while one's daughter is raped by a "slave" (IV. v. 16–17).

68. Robert Lane, " 'When Blood Is Their Argument': Class, Character, and Historymaking in Shakespeare's and Branagh's *Henry V,*" *ELH,* 61 (1994), 27–52, 44.

69. "The Patriarchal Bard," p. 93.

70. Peter S. Donaldson, "Taking on Shakespeare: Kenneth Branagh's *Henry V,*" *SQ,* 42.1 (1991), 60–71, also points out how Olivier often holds "Asherson in place . . . with a firmly controlling index finger" (69).

71. *Comic Women, Tragic Men,* p. 146.

72. Ibid. In contrast, Karen Newman, "Englishing the Other: 'le tiers exclu' and Shakespeare's *Henry V,*" in *Fashioning Femininity* (Chicago and London: University of Chicago Press, 1991), pp. 97–108, concedes that Katherine's "linguistic disadvantage" in the wooing scene becomes a "strategy of equivocation and deflection" (107).

73. See Jonas Barish, "Puritans and Proteans," in *The Antitheatrical Prejudice* (Berkeley and Los Angeles: University of California Press, 1981), pp. 80–131.

74. "Disrupting Sexual Difference: Meaning and Gender in the Comedies," in John Drakakis (ed.), *Alternative Shakespeares,* pp. 166–90, 180.

75. See Phyllis Rackin, "Androgyny, Mimesis, and the Marriage of the Boy Heroine on the English Renaissance Stage," *PMLA,* 102 (January 1987), 29–41. Like Belsey, Rackin concludes that transvestite heroines "give us a glimpse of a liminal moment when gender definitions were open to play" (38).

76. *Still Harping on Daughters: Women and Drama in the Age of Shakespeare* (Brighton: Harvester, 1983), Chapter 1, pp. 9–36.

77. " 'Claiming from the Female': Gender and Representation in Laurence Olivier's *Henry V,*" in *Shakespearean Films/Shakespearean Directors* (Boston, Mass.: Unwin Hyman, 1990), pp. 6–14.

78. Ibid., p. 13.

79. Ibid., p. 8.

80. *Man's Estate,* p. 72.

81. Ibid., p. 11.

82. Ibid., p. 49.

83. *Patriarchal Structures in Shakespeare's Drama* (Berkeley and Los Angeles: University of California Press, 1985), p. 54.

84. Ibid., p. 62.

85. Ibid., p. 59.

86. C. L. Barber and Richard P. Wheeler, "From Mixed History to Heroic Drama," in *The Whole Journey: Shakespeare's Power of Development* (Berkeley and Los Angeles: University of California, 1986), point out how "primary male bonds" in *Henry V* are validated through aggression, as when Henry quickly turns from "mistful eyes" over the deaths of York and Suffolk to ordering the slaughter of the French prisoners (227).

87. *Stages of History*, p. 176.

6

THE PLAY IN PERFORMANCE

HENRY V ON STAGE: THE ROYAL SHAKESPEARE COMPANY'S PRODUCTION (1975)

We study *Henry V* as literature because Shakespeare's plays are so rich in meaning. Yet this play, like others, is primarily a script for performance, and when a director with a team of actors and technical assistants decides to present it, the aesthetic possibilities are almost infinite. Shakespeare wrote for a stage within a particular type of theater—the Elizabethan "wooden O," a compact, hexagonal structure where an audience of two thousand or more stood in the pit or sat in tiers around the large thrust stage. But stage designs have altered drastically over the centuries, and with them productions of *Henry V*. In the eighteenth and nineteenth centuries[1] the play was performed as a pageant, a magnificent spectacle using the resources of a representational stage. The elaborate scenery for Macready's staging (Covent Garden, 1839) included a huge diorama of the English fleet setting off for France, as well as the castle of Agincourt. The 1872–79 production starring Henry Rignold delighted many audiences (though not the novelist Henry James) by having King Henry ride on stage on a white horse called Crispin—an idea carried through, more appropriately, in Laurence Olivier's 1944 film. Then in the mid-twentieth century, Peter Brook's influential ideas on "rough" theater,[2] using minimal or symbolic sets, resulted in a fresh approach to *Henry V*.

Why pick the production of *Henry V* performed by the Royal Shakespeare Company in 1975 to consider in detail? Certainly there have been other successful and thought-provoking performances of the play in the last thirty years. Peter Hall directed it at Stratford-upon-Avon in 1964 as part of the history cycle (with Ian Holm playing Henry),[3] and Adrian Noble's 1984–85 production for the RSC, starring Kenneth Branagh, was a forerunner of Branagh's 1989 movie version of *Henry V*. The play also formed part of Michael Bognadov's untraditional "The Wars of the Roses" cycle, with Michael Pennington in the lead role.[4] But the production mounted in the RSC's centenary year, with Alan Howard playing Henry, invites particular study: It contained some innovative concepts that illuminated the play; it was well received by both the critics and the theatergoing public; and a book, compiled by Sally Beauman and published in 1976, helps record the production's essential features.

The art of performing a play is a transitory one. The ephemeral nature of the enterprise, and the sense of its being a special occasion, is nevertheless part of the power of the stage; when we go to the theater we dress up to attend a collective experience that is quite different from the private act of watching television in our living rooms.[5] Theater is a decidedly two-way street. An indifferent audience or an enthusiastically responsive one affects the actors, so that although the script may remain the same, no two performances are quite identical. Reviews are written with a sense of the occasion, too, and are usually forgotten more quickly than the production, which itself is new only until the next mounting of the play. It seems a contradiction in terms, then, to write a book recording such a transient event. But Sally Beauman's compilation, in addition to providing a performance text, does much to capture the spirit of that moment: the circumstances in which the production took root, the director's conception of the play, the actors' responses to their roles, and the critics' enthusiastic reception of the final product. All these are preserved with remarkable freshness. Commentary by Terry Hands (the director) and Farrah (the designer) captures the energy of the initial project, which gradually evolved, in the spirit of RSC ensemble enterprise, from a long exploratory process ("there was no 'blocking' until the last week of rehearsals"[6]) to a polished production.

As luck had it, I was able to see this production in April 1975. But because I did not take notes my recollection of individual sequences in detail is very hazy; twenty years later, Sally Beauman's book furnishes an invaluable record. One thing that I do recall, in addition to the satisfying coherence of the theatrical experience, is the unusual opening. Most of the first two scenes of the play were performed in the spirit of a rehearsal. The actors, who were warming up on stage while the audience took their seats, were dressed in jeans or track suits, and when they were not performing they sat at the side of the stage observing those who were. Only Montjoy entered in period costume for contrast. Henry, perhaps to suggest that he was hiding behind a role, was wearing dark glasses. The term "Brechtian" came to mind (although it is not used once in Beauman's book): a deliberate strategy to cut through the expected, a way of foregrounding the actors and their roles and encouraging a critical response to the action rather than immersing the audience in the comforting illusion of costumed characters in a realistic setting. Certainly the idea came from the urgent reminder of the Chorus (who remained in modern dress throughout the performance) that the audience should "Piece out . . . imperfections" with their "thoughts." It was both a response to Shakespeare's nonnaturalistic theater and a determined "back to basics" approach in a time of fiscal exigency. The critics, though, seemed puzzled by this opening, often regarding it as gimmicky instead of a genuine response to the message of the Chorus;[7] they were relieved when the costumes and props did appear. This happened when the Chorus opened Act II and a huge, colorful canopy billowed open over the stage while the actors began to retrieve their costumes from the gun carriage pushed onto stage. Even after the traditional, naturalistic style of theater took over, the audience was still not allowed to remain passive. In the scene where Henry challenges the Governor of Harfleur (III. iii), Alan Howard faced the audience and boomed out his words to the Governor in the upper circle, so that the audience "[became] Harfleur."[8]

The stage design and set also took their cue from the Chorus's opening words—an awareness of the constraints of the "wooden O" and the "cockpit"—as well as rising to the challenge of stringent budget restrictions at the RSC in 1975.[9] It was essential to come up with a minimalist set, with just a few stunning devices, to create the appropriate environment and tone for the play. Accordingly, the back walls of the stage were stripped down and painted white, and a large, slightly raked stage was built, one designed to "launch the actors into the audience."[10] The designer, Farrah, was proud that someone compared it to the huge deck of an aircraft carrier. When the Chorus to Act III encouraged the audience to "work your thoughts and therein see a siege" (Harfleur), an enormous ramp rose up from the stage to the musical accompaniment of percussion; this was the breach, with scaling ladders and ropes attached, over which soldiers came crashing. An incredibly versatile prop (actually reminiscent of the canopy, known as the Heavens, which covered part of the Globe Theatre's stage) was the suspended canopy or giant umbrella. At first it was a "heraldic, glorious roof"[11] over the heads of the actors (matched by a gold canopy that hung over the French court for the final scene). Then it descended onto the stage for the march through Picardy (III. vi) to do duty as a muddy battlefield, a "mass of brown bulges and peaks"[12] on which the English army huddled. The formal French looked immaculate in comparison. Usually dressed in blue, at Agincourt they glittered in gold armor.

This production of *Henry V* also broke from tradition in its overall concept of the play and its presentation of the King. Neither the director nor the lead actor perceived the play as a chauvinistic pageant, a confident march forward to assured success in war. Rather, they saw it as a pattern of resolution followed by delays, high points, and lows; as Terry Hands put it, the play "runs hot and cold."[13] The RSC's decision to put on *Henry V* before the *Henry IV* plays (which were also part of the season) was a bold one. It meant that instead of revealing Henry as mature monarch, fully formed after his explorations as Prince Hal, the action of *Henry V* became an odyssey in which Henry had to find himself as king and man.

Alan Howard's Henry was neither confident nor effortlessly heroic, much less a warmonger. Like the production, he built from the ground up, engaging in a painful process of self-realization that did not end until his final challenge, the wooing of Katherine. There was anguish in his early question "May I with right and conscience make this claim?", passionate anger and terrible loss of confidence in the traitors' scene at Southampton, and horror at the sick brutality of war when he threatens the Governor of Harfleur, followed by immense relief when the town capitulates. Two reviewers used the word "queasy" to describe Henry's sensibilities at these moments.[14] Henry also registered pain at the death of Bardolph, since he had to give the order, by raising his sword and finally lowering it in assent, for the offstage execution.[15] The King reached his emotional nadir in the soliloquy in Act IV. (The two adjacent soliloquies were presented as one, with no interruption from Sir Thomas Erpingham.) Howard describes it as an "angry, bitter speech."[16] Nonetheless it served as a turning point; the subsequent recognition that "The day, my friends, and all things stay for me," with the stress on "me," was a catalyst for Henry's full emergence into confident leadership. This Henry believes that self-reliance and partnership will lead to victory—"All things are ready, if our minds be so"—rather than piety or capitulation to the will of God.

And indeed he did forge a shared confidence, a renewed partnership, through the Crispin's Day speech that follows the anguished soliloquy. This production, in keeping with the spirit of cooperation between director and actors and Terry Hands' apparent willingness to let the cast make decisions for themselves, emphasized the building of brotherhood within the English army. "Improvisation, inter-dependence, and unity"[17] were the keynotes for the action on stage as well as for the theater company. Various rehearsal exercises—the soldiers kitting up a camp each day and an energetic rugby scrum to prepare for the assault on the breach—helped get the army "welded together."[18] Their camaraderie was by no means assured at the beginning of the campaign in France. In dismal retreat following Harfleur, the army was almost mutinous by the end of III. vi, after Henry gave the order for Bardolph's execution and imposed strict military discipline. Henry virtually had to force the soldiers to sing their marching song as they exited, just before the interval. Small touches then demonstrated the army's regrouping into stronger identity by the battle of Agincourt. Fluellen's challenge to Williams (IV. viii) turned into a brawl from which the King's two brothers, Gloucester and Clarence (Bedford is cut in this production), were pushed unceremoniously away; Agincourt's "band of brothers" overrode any class distinctions now.

The ensemble approach worked to create a unified, dynamic production. *Henry V* was a financial success as well, turning a profit for the RSC in difficult times; the Duke of Edinburgh's comment on the "success of the tiny, hungry, ill clad band of troops"[19] in *Henry V* proved true on more than one level. Beauman's book also reveals a remarkable consensus among the director, the lead actor, and the critics about how this Henry V develops. Terry Hands emphasized the "personal redefinition" of Henry; Alan Howard found tentativeness and "self-discovery" in the role; and the reviewer from *The Times*, Charles Lewsen, perceived in Alan Howard's "intelligent" performance "a man's attempt to forge himself in the painful fires of authority and battle."[20]

Beauman's study is an eye-opener for those students not well acquainted with theater, who may have little knowledge of how a production of Shakespeare is mounted. It will sharpen their awareness, too, of how the critic's intellectual analysis of the play is often quite different from the director's apprehension of the subtle rhythms of dramatic movement and from the way that actors respond to the characters they must play. Each actor has to build a role, not necessarily through total identification with the imagined emotions of the character (the Stanislavsky approach) but with some empathetic understanding of the persona. It is amusing to find Trevor Peacock convinced that his character, the sentimental Fluellen, would be "weeping into the dawn" during the Crispin's Day speech.[21] And Richard Derrington's thespian account of why the soldier Court has only one line is enlightening: "Court is clearly so numb with terror he can hardly speak."[22] Alan Howard makes an excellent point about how the critic, unaware of the choices an actor must make, sometimes interprets a line one-sidedly, when he explains that Henry's comment "None else of name" after he reads the list of English dead at Agincourt need not brand him as a "callous snob."[23]

The words might be delivered as full of irony and sadness; and indeed the photograph of Howard's Henry, surrounded by his troops as he reads the line, manages to convey just these emotions.

SHAKESPEARE ON FILM

Filmed versions of Shakespeare's plays offer a permanent record of performance. Before the 1980s, however, analysis of Shakespeare on film was often somewhat impressionistic.[24] At best, a critic could sit through the movie several times and write notes feverishly, hoping to come up with a fairly complete description of a multilayered experience in which, as Jack J. Jorgens puts it, "the way lines, shapes, colors and textures are arranged affects our responses, as do music and nonverbal sounds, montage, and the structuring of the action beat by beat, scene by scene."[25] The advent of the videocassette has made commentary much more precise. True, when the silver screen is scaled down to the box in the living room the viewer must exercise some compensatory filmic imagination. It is also not as easy to scrutinize a frame as it is to linger over a word in reading, and you destroy the rhythm of the sequence if you keep stopping the tape. Nevertheless, repeated viewings not only settle disagreements over detail but can significantly modify initial impressions; I saw much more to praise in Olivier's and Branagh's battle scenes after watching them several times than I did on first viewing.

The crucial differences between stage and screen productions are spatial. The camera, unlike the spectator in a theater, is not restricted to an architecturally defined space (facing a stage that is usually box-shaped, with scenery that may be realistic or nonrepresentational) or to a fixed angle and distance within that space. Film, where the work of the camera is enhanced through the subsequent editing and arrangement of shots, thus affords great variety of viewpoint and image. The key distinctions between cinema and television are level of involvement—we are simply not as immersed in the spectacle on the "box" as we are when watching a huge screen in a darkened movie theater—and scale. Whereas most televised Shakespeare is produced on a studio set, film producers of Shakespeare can go much further in using large-scale, actual locations to depict places only sketched in through the words of the play text. Zeffirelli's *Romeo and Juliet* (1969) and *Hamlet* (1990) are particularly adept at utilizing actual towns and landscapes to give depth to the action. Or the film producer may go beyond photographic realism to create a setting that heightens the symbolism of Shakespeare's plays, as with the icy Jutland landscape in Peter Brook's *King Lear* (mirroring the "hard hearts" of many of the play's younger characters) or the claustrophobic castle in Olivier's *Hamlet* as an extension of the main protagonist's state of mind. In these cases the expressionistic visual imagery counterpoints the play's verbal imagery; but there is always the possibility that excessive detail or superimposed patterns in a film will distract from Shakespeare's poetry, or that dialogue will be displaced by images.[26]

Laurence Olivier would disagree, convinced that the camera can open up Shakespeare's plays—capture their different levels of illusion—without sacrificing the words. Yet, notwithstanding film's penchant for a musical score to highlight mood and emotion, the tyranny of the visual is more pronounced on the silver screen than on the television, where the intimacy of the tube restricts bolder visual effects but encourages more attention to the words. One reason why the greatest films of Shakespeare are more properly called adaptations than straightforward presentations of the plays is their tendency to shift from the aural to the visual, to transform what the Russian director Kozintsev calls "poetic texture" into the "dynamic organization of film imagery,"[27] which may also require substantial rearranging of the play's action. Kozintsev's own *Hamlet* and *King Lear* are classic examples of film adaptations, as are the Japanese Kurosowa's *Throne of Blood* (based on *Macbeth*), and, to some extent, Olivier's *Hamlet* and *Henry V.*

Laurence Olivier's *Henry V* (1944)

If the iconoclastic Kenneth Branagh had not come along, students would be less inclined to treat Olivier's film version of *Henry V* merely as an interesting museum piece. It is certainly a great movie, clearly an interpretation of the play rather than a faithful transcript of the text. Students of the 1990s, alas, tend to compare it invidiously with Branagh's moving, up-to-the-minute version, dismissing Olivier's as pageant-like and overstylized, a glorified version of King Henry that beefs up the chauvinism at the expense of the play's ambiguities. Or they may find it pictorially pleasing but simply old-fashioned. These are hasty judgments that underestimate the strengths of the movie: its energy, form, and fluidity, and especially its inventiveness in presenting Shakespeare's *Henry V* through the medium of film. By beginning the action in the Globe Theatre and gradually moving it to less stylized settings, Olivier bridges the gap between Elizabethan theatrical artifice and the relative realism afforded by the cinema of the 1940s. But Olivier's production does not invite the viewers to become immersed uncritically in the illusion of reality as they watch *Henry V.* In fact the self-conscious exploitation of artifice continues on several levels.

The film reveals how cinematic techniques can do full justice to Shakespeare's play, but also makes a point, through its layers of style, about how any transmission of the past and its characters is artfully constructed; and it requires the audience's energetic collaboration.

Certainly this *Henry V*, released close to the end of World War II (1944), triumphed as a splendid patriotic celebration. Olivier was invited to make the film by the Ministry of Information as part of the war effort, and although there is no direct correlation between the Nazis and the fifteenth-century French (since France was Britain's ally in World War II), the film was enormously popular as a tribute to the "band of brothers" who fought off Hitler. It was dedicated to the RAF, "the Commandos and Airborne Troops of Great Britain."

Olivier's main interest as director, however, lay in the potential of the medium itself. He seized the opportunity to "take Shakespeare from the 'wooden O' and place him on the silver screen,"[28] to translate the play into movie terms that would be accessible to a wider audience than Shakespeare usually enjoys. He describes his mission as though he were possessed by the spirit of the dramatist himself: "I felt Shakespeare within me, I felt the cinema within him. I knew what I wanted to do, what he would have done."[29] Convinced that the Agincourt sequences, in particular, were "frustrated cinema" (and Shakespeare a would-be movie director!), he decided to exploit the filmic techniques of cross-cutting and montage, superimposing one image on the next to convey the quick changes and full panoply of battle. To build to this climax he made some careful artistic choices. Sensitive to how the Chorus sets the tone of the drama by drawing attention to the limitations of the Elizabethan theater and encouraging audience collaboration with the spectacle, Olivier decided to modulate gradually from the frank artifice of the Elizabethan stage to the fuller illusion of reality made possible by film technology. Thus the audience remains aware throughout of the distance between art and life, even while helping close the gap. The film presents us with three levels of simulated reality: first the representation of the Globe, a frankly anti-illusionist theater with mannered acting and stage conventions; then the stylized pictorial settings for scenes after Act I, especially the French court; and finally the fuller verisimilitude of the Agincourt scenes, filmed within an actual landscape.

The Globe Theatre, or rather an imagined reconstruction of it, is the frame that encloses the play. Partly this affords the fascination of a documentary, as the film assumes the privilege of recording and bringing to life the Globe (May 1, 1600) as it might have been when the play was new. The camera begins with a crane shot high over a convincing model of Elizabethan

London, hovers over the exterior of the circular auditorium of the Globe, and then moves from its upper levels (where a man hoists a flag and summons the public with a trumpet fanfare) to inside the theater. There spectators are noisily taking their seats, some on the large thrust stage itself. We watch a boy introduce the play with a placard and the Chorus pull aside the curtain from the inner stage after delivering his Prologue. Thanks to what Olivier calls the "prying" camera,[30] we are also taken backstage and shown what happens behind the tiring house wall: the boy actors trying on wigs, Ely getting drunk, and, most important, the actor who plays Henry, heavily made up for the role, waiting to make his entrance. This is Laurence Olivier transformed into Richard Burbage (Shakespeare's star actor, who played Hamlet, King Lear, and, we assume, Henry V). He enters the frame suddenly, from screen left, and clears his throat nervously before the camera, now positioned behind, shows him striding onto the stage to receive tumultuous applause from the pit and the galleries.

The acting style has already been established as gestic and oratorical, and fully cognizant of those who surround the stage. The Chorus amplifies his exposition with large gestures, while Canterbury and Ely must try to placate the theatergoers when they explain Henry's reformation and his banishment of Falstaff (at that point the audience's disparaging murmurs grow louder). Henry, too, is a performer. Kneeling down and handing the Archbishop one of the crucial documents, he plays straight man to Canterbury's farcical delivery of the Salic law speech, and then rises to a powerful crescendo as he reacts to the Dauphin's gift of tennis balls. In a flamboyant, self-assured gesture after the messengers have left he tosses his crown so that it hooks onto the back of the throne. We are encouraged to see the character of Henry V as a construct by an experienced actor;[31] on a deeper level, these metadramatics may suggest that the King's whole enterprise is a piece of theatrical chicanery, a series of heroics dependent on skillful role-playing and therefore easily deconstructed. For the most part the acting becomes more naturalistic once we leave the Globe Theatre, although Pistol's flamboyant style (with actor Robert Newton playing to the gallery and the groundlings) remains unchanged when he travels to France, and thus provides some continuity. The return to the Globe at the end of the film further stresses the fictive nature of what we have seen. In a stunning transition, the camera cuts from Katherine and Henry, resplendent in white wedding robes at the French court, to Henry as the actor Burbage in the playhouse. Lips rouged, he smiles at the Princess who becomes, in long shot, the boy actor from Shakespeare's company.[32] Reversing the initial sequence, the camera now takes us back outside the Globe

Theatre and tracks into an aerial view of Elizabethan London, until a playbill
floats out of the clouds to provide the credits for the film.

Olivier explains that he used the Globe frame partly as a technique to
foreground the action that followed. He wanted to acclimatize the audience
to a heavily theatrical style and then, just as they might be getting bored
with the wooden O, provide relief with a plunge into greater naturalism.[33]
But the Chorus, spokesman for the Elizabethan theater, does not disappear
as the action progresses; in fact his speeches are divided up so that he is
seen on five separate occasions (at one point suspended in the clouds as the
fleet sails for France) and heard five other times. With some exasperation,
Olivier acknowledges that the Chorus dictated the mode of the entire
enterprise: "The goddamn play was telling me the style of the film."[34]
Indeed the early advice of the Chorus on how the audience should supple-
ment the visual spectacle with their "imaginary forces" is crucial; that is the
one point in the opening scene where the Chorus stares directly into the
camera, underlining the significance of his words for twentieth-century
moviegoers as well as for the Globe clientele.

To signal departure from the Globe Theatre the Chorus points to the
curtain over the inner stage, which now depicts the town of Southampton
and its cliffs. The camera then tracks through this transparency into a
backdrop that we might expect to be real buildings in front of actual cliffs
and ocean. In fact it is a painted canvas using a deliberately shallow
perspective (the "narrow seas" are ridged waves), and when the camera pans
left to show the religious ceremony taking place, the harbor is arranged as
a perfect medieval pictorial composition, with ship's rigging on the right
and stylized, crenellated castle walls in the center. The film's designers
modeled this and the scenes in France on the illuminations in the fifteenth-
century manuscript *Les Très Riches Heures du Duc de Berri*. Our first
glimpse of the French palace, with its ornate pillars, arches, and staircases,
confirms this style, as does the fairy-tale castle at Harfleur and the stylized
backdrop when the Princess walks around the battlements of the Louvre to
reach her walled garden. Moreover the winter scene at the village of
Agincourt, where Fluellen makes Pistol eat a leek, is patterned closely on
the illustration for the month of February in the *Très Riches Heures*. Olivier,
determined that Shakespeare's poetry should not present a formidable
obstacle to a twentieth-century audience, wanted to make the language
appear more "real" by placing it against an "unreal" background; he was
convinced that the characters would gain credibility if they could "spring
out from the beautiful, stylized, almost cutout scenery."[35] Whether the
surroundings propel the characters into extra authenticity is open to ques-

tion. The effect may partly be to suggest that the French court—where King Charles is played as a sad-eyed depressive and the Dauphin as effete in voice and manner—is locked into a static medieval formality.[36] But the formalized, pictorial settings do serve as an inspired transition from the nonrepresentational stage at the Globe. They continue to remind the spectators that the reality of *Henry V* is being constructed artfully, encouraging the eye of the viewer to perceive formal patterns in the action as well as in the composition of the settings.

The siege of Harfleur, set on a dirt beach with mounds of rock on each side, is another move toward realism of setting. But it is in the Agincourt battle scenes, where Olivier adapts most freely from Shakespeare's text, that the film exploits deep focus[37] and panoramic breadth to create the illusion of verisimilitude. This part of the film was made on location in the rolling green hills of Ireland (Lord Powerscourt's estate in Enniskerry); it took about eight weeks to capture the crucial fifteen minutes or so of Agincourt footage. Olivier was able to use 150 Irish horsemen and about 500 infantrymen to swell Henry's troops. In the meantime Irish nuns had improvised medieval costumes, creating suits of armor by crocheting heavy wrapping twine which was then sprayed with aluminum paint. Some of the filming required extra technology. To get the sweeping shot of the French cavalry galloping toward the field of battle, for instance, the film crew had to construct a railroad a mile long so that the camera could travel alongside the horsemen. There are so many short sequences, such complex cross-cutting at this point in the film, that it is difficult on one viewing to appreciate everything that is going on. One memorable image is the Dauphin, in full armor, being winched up by a derrick and lowered onto his horse; but we may miss the brief balancing shot of Henry donning his chain mail. We are not quite sure which of the French aristocrats sets fire to the English camp and kills the boys (groups belonging to Orleans and Bourbon, who separate from the others in long shot and turn toward the camp, seem to be responsible).[38] The joust between Henry and the Constable, invented by Olivier, also relies on a number of quick close-ups to reveal the narrative sequence. Both men are disarmed of their swords but Henry strikes the Constable on the side of the head with his mailed fist (the coup de grace) just as the Frenchman is raising his mace to smite the King.

As well as making the audience strain to assimilate and interpret all the images, many of the Agincourt sequences are choreographed as formal patterns that point up vital contrasts between the English and French armies. To evoke preparations for battle, the camera cuts between shots of the long row of English archers hard at work sharpening or knocking their staves into the ground and shots of the more leisurely activities of the French: a line of drummers and then the smiling Dauphin at the center of his aristocratic group, toasting his companions. The musical score by William Walton, with its brass, woodwind, and drum rolls, helps build the suspense. As the charge into battle begins, the action becomes a series of waves[39]—French infantrymen and cavalrymen advancing in turn from screen right to left, more intercutting between the armies, and then a rain of black arrows released by the English longbowmen. When the two sides encounter we are given close-ups of the melee (horses rearing, men falling) and finally a powerful image of stasis in a long shot of soldiers stymied in the mud, still waving their pikes but no longer moving. This patterning, which avoids appearing too contrived and static because of the fluidity within shots, reflects Olivier's meticulous planning in advance; as he explains, "I couldn't afford to reshoot, so I designed every angle in advance, knew every move, every cut."[40] While he obviously enjoyed the opportunity to shoot on location, to push the play out into a wider setting with thrilling panoramic perspectives, Olivier admitted that to stay in line with the film's overall stylization the battle should have been fought not on real grass but on "green velvet." Certainly this director avoids anything too gory—there are no "bloody gashes"[41] in combat and the only blood we see is on the mouth of the dead boy in the ravaged camp—but Olivier provides at least a hint of the mud that plays such a crucial role in Branagh's movie. A reflection of the French horseman and their banners in marshy water as they cross to the field of battle prepares us for that in-depth image of the muddy arena, clogged with soldiers, which closes the first stage of the fighting.

How does all this patterning affect the presentation of King Henry? At Agincourt he is not the dominant figure, for we concentrate on the formal composition of several groups. The film gives prominence to the English archers—arguably the true heroes of Agincourt, though not even mentioned in Shakespeare's play—and counterpoints their industry with the more trivial occupations and tournament flourishes in the French camp. Just before the director adds the medieval trial by combat between the King and the Constable, which turns Henry, preceded by his red-cross banner, into a veritable Saint George figure, the camera lingers over the retreat of the Dauphin (also not given in the play). As the Dauphin gallops petulantly down the hillside he is watched in consternation by Montjoy.

This part of the movie is not as much Henry's show as is, say, the RSC's 1975 production of *Henry V*. While William Walton's score brilliantly creates moods for different sequences—an up-tempo pseudo-Elizabethan tune for the Globe action, romantic music (an adaptation of the Auvergne folk song "Bailero") to introduce Princess Katherine halfway through the action and for Burgundy's speech near the end, stirring orchestral variations for Agincourt, and choral arrangements for the wedding—there is no distinctively "Henry" music. But when the main protagonist is on screen he is, thanks to Olivier's charisma and vocal delivery, mesmerizing; and Olivier plays him as the epic hero, a confident performer rather than a flawed or doubting monarch. Much of the abbreviated script (about half the lines of the play are cut)[42] enhances this favorable impression of Henry. In the second scene we forget that Henry may have made a deal with the bishops, for any suggestions of machiavellianism are played down as he gets caught up in the farcical delivery of the Salic law speech. His stirring response to the Dauphin's insult also obscures the fact that he is the aggressor in the war with France. Olivier's film excludes the unmasking of the traitors at Southampton, Henry's ruthless threats to the Governor of Harfleur, and his connivance at Bardolph's execution. It also cuts the "Not today, O Lord" part of the King's prayer before Agincourt (where Henry acknowledges his father's guilt in gaining the English throne) as well as the King's command to kill the prisoners after the French appear to rally.

In keeping with the patriotic, even propagandistic motives for making the film, the heroic image of King Henry is prominent; yet it is unfair to describe Olivier's movie as a drastically sanitized version of the play, flattened into a "simple-minded fairy tale."[43] Darker elements do help balance the film's epic portrait of Henry. The death of Falstaff, for instance, is actually shown, not merely narrated as in the play. The camera takes us through a window and into Falstaff's bedchamber, where we can see his horrified, staring eyes and gaping mouth as he recalls being rejected by the new King (whose words, "I know thee not, old man," from *Henry IV, Part ii*, are given in Olivier's steely voice-over). Pistol's function as a mock-heroic parody of Henry's ambitious quest is underlined when he leaves from France quoting lines from Marlowe's *Tamburlaine*: "Is it not passing brave to be a king, / And ride in triumph through Persepolis?" Henry's malevolent stare after he receives the gift of tennis balls—repeated at certain key points in the action, as when he discovers the slaughtered boys—suggests a capacity for ruthlessness. Olivier cuts Williams' challenge to the disguised King and downplays Henry's anger by the campfire; but this has the effect of leaving Henry's underlying doubts and resentment unresolved rather than emphasizing the King's gallant restraint and magnanimity.

Yet these darker elements remain nuances; they do not undercut Olivier's projection of Henry as a strong, relatively uncomplex leader. Predominantly Henry appears as a charismatic warrior, a stirring orator whose confidence is never fundamentally shaken. Even the nighttime soliloquy (IV. i) is a brooding meditation, using voice-over, which carries none of the anguished soul-searching, the extreme shifts of tone that marked Alan Howard's performance (1975) or David Gwillim's for the BBC videotape (1979). The camera, in one sustained shot, focuses on Olivier's stern and unmoving face, where any emotion is carried by his restless, dark eyes. Gazing into the dawn, now in profile shot, he looks and sounds resigned rather than embittered. The camera has moved back to reveal Court sleeping on the ground close to Henry, and Henry's concerned, even tender, observation of the soldier suggests that there is no rift between king and subject.

The soliloquy, filmed in close-up, is an anomaly in the film; Olivier's Henry gives his most compelling performances as the mobile center of a large group. The climaxes of the great battle orations—"Once more unto the breach" and the Crispin's Day speech—are shown not in close-up but through long shot. This means that Olivier's unusually resonant voice and compelling presence are heard and seen to full advantage rather than cramped within the confines of the small screen, as often happens in the medium of television where actors are not encouraged to "play big." Experienced in the differences between performing in the theater and acting for the camera, Olivier explains how he discovered the long shot technique to capture moments of greatest power on the screen: "the film gesture is a closeup; the Shakespearean climax is a fine gesture and a loud voice. . . . For *Henry V* I tried to see how it would work [on film]. . . . As I raised my voice the camera went back . . . and I have done that ever since."[44] Accordingly the speech at Harfleur begins in medium shot, but as Henry's rhetoric builds the camera circles back, up, and around to reveal him at the center of a large group; the top left of the frame even captures two men watching him from high up in the crow's nest of a ship. Henry reaches a vocal climax on "greyhounds in the slips" (the longest shot) before the camera moves in on his rearing white horse, an appropriate visualization of the "England and Saint George" motif with which the speech ends. There is the same sense of Harry as a terrific performer, feeding off the audience, catching the "wave"[45] of the moment, in the Crispin's Day speech. At the opening he appears to be talking to a few followers. But when he steps up onto the cart (screen left) to speculate on how particular warriors will be remembered, the camera pulls back and up so that when Henry reaches a peak at "fought with us upon Saint Crispin's Day" he is greeted by shouts of appreciation and raised arms from the hundreds of soldiers who (as we now see) surround him. This provides a visual echo of Henry in the earlier Globe Theatre scene, where he circles the stage for his energetic retort to the Dauphin's "mock."

There, too, the camera pulls back at the climax to show him surrounded by applauding audience members who are positioned on the stage, in the pit, and in the galleries.

The theatricality of Henry's presentation—the artful construction of himself as strong leader and his rhetorical mastery of the audience—is emphasized throughout the film. Olivier's Henry also performs for Katherine, played by Renée Asherson, in the final scene. He acts out the role of Prince Charming (not as vulnerable as Gwillim in the BBC production or Branagh in his film version) to his sweet princess, and his ultimate success in directing her responses and winning her hand is never in doubt. The immaculate appearance of the pair, Henry dazzling in white tights and red tunic embroidered with gold while virginal Katherine wears a pale blue dress, enhances the fairy-tale nature of the action here.

The more one views the film, the more artful it appears.[46] Visual parallelism deftly links different parts of the action:[47] The flag that flies over the Globe is iterated in the banners advancing on the battlefield in France, while the small curtain drawn across the window of Falstaff's bedchamber indicates the closure of Sir John's life (and that part of Henry's associated with him) in the same way that the curtain across the inner stage of the Globe signals the end of a dramatic sequence. Just as Henry disarms the Constable and then strikes him on the side of the head, so Fluellen knocks Pistol on the pate and takes away his sword when he makes him eat a leek. The Constable's showy black armor, painted with large white stars, is first shown in close-up before the nighttime conversation in the French camp. It finally reappears worn by the scavenger Pistol, who has donned the breastplate and is holding the helmet to make his last entry. One metacinematic touch (self-reflexive commentary on the art of the film) is our quick glimpse of the Duke of Berri scrutinizing his *Très Riches Heures* at the French court—the very book to whose illustrations the movie designs are indebted. Movie buffs note visual parallels between Eisenstein's *Alexander Nefsky* (the lines of horsemen massed on the skyline before the Battle on the Ice)[48] and the French gathering for battle. And the inveterate chameleon Olivier disguises himself to take on a few bit parts in the movie, most notably the lisping messenger who tells the Constable how close the English are to his tent in the night scene. All these details reinforce the art of illusion in the movie.

Occasionally Olivier's craftful picture-making may come across as *too* exquisite. When the camera moves out of the window of the French castle and pans over the parched landscape during Burgundy's speech on postwar France, we are shown two children gazing wistfully over a fence: a perfectly composed but sentimental image that fails to convey any of the savage "wildness" that Burgundy is evoking. Perhaps it is more than a late-twentieth-century passion for realistic detail that makes contemporary viewers welcome the rougher energy of Branagh's *Henry V*. But it is pointless to quarrel with Olivier's stylization, which is endemic to the film's meaning. For the movie achieves a deeper significance beyond its superb visual and narrative coherence by drawing attention to its particular techniques and its own artful creation of reality.

Olivier's *Henry V* demonstrates that cinema can be an ideal medium for opening up Shakespeare's play. The camera becomes a magician. It takes us inside the Globe Theatre, filming it relatively straightforwardly but actually providing multiple perspectives—the high long shot from the gallery, the medium shot from the pit, and the close-up and the behind-the-scenes shots—on what a spectator would normally see only from one fixed position in the theater. It takes us inside the medieval storybook pictures of the French court, and it does what the Chorus regrets that the theater cannot do: opens up the full panorama of battle to show us the "vasty fields" of France. Paradoxically, the camera work becomes more virtuoso, with varied angles and complex patterns through montage, as the setting (the open countryside at Agincourt) becomes more realistic. So what appears, on one level, to be a filmic progression from the stagy and nonnaturalistic to the naturalistic is also a series of Chinese boxes concealing artifice within artifice; the outer layer is the obviously "anti-illusionistic" frame of the Elizabethan theater while the center contains the formal patterning of the "quasi-naturalistic" Agincourt sequences.[49] Thus the movie pays tribute to art as much as to life: to the conventional art of the Globe Theatre in the Renaissance, which gave birth to Shakespeare's *Henry V* in the first place, and to the illuminated manuscripts of the Limbourg brothers, which so brightly depict fifteenth-century France. Both these are subsumed within the artfulness of the film of *Henry V*, created by the twentieth-century director and his cameramen and enhanced by the skillful performance of the lead actor, also Olivier.

This is more than an obsession with art for art's sake, however. In addition to providing formal beauty, so much attention to style and artifice reminds us that what we understand as "reality," whether the events of history or our everyday modes of perception, is always controlled, never unmediated. Olivier may not have intended this kind of philosophical or ideological statement, but the theatrical envelope (the Globe performance enclosing the action) certainly suggests it. Without the Globe frame the movie is a celebration of one of England's great military victories—a tribute to

Henry's heroic resolution (in contrast to the brittle formality of the French) and to the strengths of "discipline, determination, leadership and union in a common cause"[50] in 1944 as well as 1415. But with the frame the emphasis shifts to the way that Henry's kingly persona is constructed through artful role-playing; he must ultimately be seen as a product of the conventions of the Elizabethan theater, which rely heavily on the good will and imaginative cooperation of the audience.

Kenneth Branagh's *Henry* V (1989)

It seems unlikely that Kenneth Branagh set out deliberately to earn the sobriquet of the "new Olivier" by tackling the film territory of *Henry V*. While Branagh has never lacked spunk and initiative, such a venture would have been superfluous, since he had already demonstrated his artistic originality. After performing in Adrian Noble's production of the play in the 1984–85 Stratford season, the actor was eager to explore his conclusions about *Henry V* in movie form. He had decided that the play was much "darker" and "harsher"[51] than Olivier's exuberant pageantry suggested and that the "many paradoxes in [Henry's] character should be explored as fully as possible."[52] These insights go right to the heart of the film; instead of an aesthetic portrayal, Branagh offers a compellingly realistic, inward presentation of King Henry and his fifteenth-century world. We are shown the details that make up the machinery of power surrounding Henry and the graphic horrors of medieval warfare. Above all, a concentration on inner life as well as the outward trappings of kingship emerges from the film's tracing of Henry as a daring young professional who reveals the complexities of his character as he grows in leadership.

The very choice of camera angles helps create a strong sense of interior reality in the movie. Whereas Olivier habitually uses medium and long shots to enhance group dynamics and the formal, pictorial composition of individual scenes, Branagh favors close-ups.[53] This is immediately established in the opening scene (after the Chorus) where the two bishops, their visages half-lit in the darkness, whisper conspiratorially about the impending church bill. The face of each one, in turn, fills the screen. In complete contrast to the comic rendition of this scene in Olivier's movie, which shows Canterbury and Ely conversing on the upper stage of the Globe and adjusting their performance to the demands of a chafing audience, Branagh's camera takes us through the invisible fourth wall to share in the intimacy of this clandestine conversation. Branagh's *Henry V* is much more than a documentary of faces, of course. But shots at each stage of the action focus in detail on the speaker, or on the reaction of those around him, so that we are drawn to the wary, controlled features of Henry in his opening council scene, to Bardolph's grimy, world-weary face in Eastcheap, and later to the lugubrious and haunted expression of the French King. Observing the physiognomy in close-up, we penetrate the emotions that underlie it. Particularly powerful is the terror contorting Sir Thomas Erpingham's features as the French cavalry charge up to the English line at Agincourt, and the naked fear in Henry's eyes just before he gives the command for the archers to shoot.

The Chorus, played by Derek Jacobi, also helps immerse us gradually in the verisimilitude of the action. Initially he is an alienation device, exposing not the sparseness of the "wooden O" but the modern technology of film devices that lies behind the spectacle. In total darkness he strikes a match (a symbol of the "Muse of fire" not available to Shakespeare's contemporaries) and then walks down the iron staircase to flick on a switch that floods the set with electric light—a major "invention" of the twentieth century. We follow this figure, clad in a black overcoat that makes him a recognizably 1980s figure, around the floor of the movie studio, past props (such as the candelabra that we later see in the French court) as well as cameras and sound equipment. This goes one step further in demystifying the medium than Olivier's Chorus does. After apologizing for the restrictions of the Globe Theatre, Olivier's movie revels in the opportunities for realism afforded by the silver screen; Branagh's Chorus, showing less reverence for the magic of the camera forty-five years later, ruefully finds as wide a gap between illusion and reality within the sophisticated movie studio or through the lens of the state-of-the-art camera as on the bare boards of the Renaissance theater. Yet when he leads us up to the heavy wooden doors, which burst open on his thunderous shout of "play," we are immediately drawn into realistic illusion: the opening scene with the clerics.

Olivier's Chorus (Leslie Banks), who introduces us to different levels of illusion, remains a presenter rather than a participant in the action. He takes us through the transparent curtain of the Globe into the stylized harbor at Southampton, wafts us across the ocean to Harfleur, and finally returns us to the nonrepresentational Globe for the Epilogue. The Chorus in Branagh's movie, on the other hand, becomes more fully engaged in the action as it progresses. In this way he enhances the mimesis, helping close the gap between the twentieth-century viewer and the simulated reality of fifteenth-century Europe. When he introduces Act II he is still a detached presenter; his voice-over of "all the youth of England are on fire" is ironically juxtaposed with the image of a very old man passing through the doorway to the Boar's Head, while his reference to the "crowns and coronets" that will reward Henry's followers synchronizes with our glimpse of Bardolph rifling through the pockets of a drunk. The Chorus is later filmed walking along the cliffs (supposedly above Southampton) as he introduces us to the "three corrupted men," the traitors who are seen in long shot on the clifftop before the camera zooms in on each of their faces. By Act III the Chorus is no longer just the master of ceremonies but is thoroughly involved in the action. He crouches by an earthwork at Harfleur, urging us to "see a siege" and cueing in a huge explosion when he excitedly tells us how the "linstock . . . touches" and "down goes all." To introduce the French and English camps (Act IV) he enters the frame beneath the suspended corpse of Bardolph, inviting us to help create the sights and sounds of the night before battle. We then find him sitting by a cart, his eyes following Henry as he offers his deeply admiring speech on the "captain of this ruined band." When he somewhat disingenuously apologizes for lack of verisimilitude at Agincourt (the "ragged foils" representing armed combat), he is actually in the thick of battle preparations. He walks briskly up the archers' line of stakes toward the camera, English soldiers crossing in front and behind him.

The Chorus does not return until the end of Act V, when he neatly closes the spectacle. The camera pulls back to show this modern figure again standing just outside the heavy wooden doors, with the tableau of the Anglo-French union in misty frame behind him. Soberly he reminds us that this moment is transitory, for England will be "lost" under Henry VI. He is clearly affected deeply by this prospect, not detached from it. Olivier's Chorus, in contrast, remains upbeat in his final appearance at the Globe; he omits any reference to England's future and instead jovially invites audience cooperation for one last time before shaking hands with the actors at the close of the play. Even though Jacobi's Epilogue punctures the fairy-tale ending, it comes across not as an obtrusive breaking through the play world or one last chance to foreground the twentieth-century technology that underpins the illusion, but rather as a deep empathizing with the sad realities of historical change.

Having the Chorus appear on the battlefield is a daring touch, but one in keeping with the kind of mimesis Branagh is aiming at: a highly credible imitation of reality that breaks down the barriers between the past and the present. It is in the battle scenes that we are taken most fully into medieval warfare and reminded that war in any age is foul. There is no blinking at the slogging through mud, the unleashing of bloodlust, the mutilation and death. Already the film has given us a feeling for the grim realities of fifteenth-century life, with the huge fire burning in Henry's dark council chamber to ward off the chill, the sequence where Bardolph at the Boar's Head protects his cold leftovers from a scavenging cat, and candid shots of the Hostess's tearful, unwashed face. What is more, Branagh emphasizes not the masterful performance and ceremonial display of kingship (as Olivier does) but the material agents of power in a feudal era, such as the heavy wooden bolt that shoots into place to keep the traitors from escaping at Southampton,[54] while burly Uncle Exeter (whose hand goes instinctively to his sword whenever the situation spells danger) acts as Henry's chief bodyguard.

The immediate occasion for Olivier's film of *Henry V* was World War II and Britain's role in helping liberate Europe from Hitler. Branagh's movie was not fueled by this patriotic impulse, but neither is it a fervently anti-war statement. Both Branagh and producer Adrian Noble wanted to avoid the "post-Falklands" label for the 1984–85 Stratford version of the play, unwilling (as some critics of course did) to categorize that production as a liberal backlash of antiwar sentiment after the decisive victory of Britain over the Falkland Islands in 1982.[55] Nevertheless, the film four years later was made in a climate of skepticism about, and distaste for, war in general. In the intervening years since World War II there had been a sober reexamination of the "Great War" (World War I, 1914–18) and, in the 1980s, a spate of movies on the American nightmare of the Vietnam War. No wonder, then, that Branagh's movie to some extent reflects the mud and carnage of the Somme and the mutilations of Vietnam. In contrast to Olivier's deliberate omission of "bloody gashes," this is no glorious pageant or pristine spectacle of war; in technique it is closer to the realistic battle scenes, shot at close range, in Orson Welles' *Chimes at Midnight*.

Most of the cuts in Shakespeare's script (Act IV of the play) are made here. To ensure narrative and tonal coherence, Branagh leaves out the mock-heroic encounter of Pistol and Monsieur le Fer (IV. iv). Henry's command to kill the prisoners is also cut—not to mitigate the impression of Henry's ruthlessness (which is shown elsewhere), but to avoid deflecting attention away from the crisis of the slaughtered boys. The glove episode, which takes up nearly two hundred lines in Shakespeare, is streamlined into one gesture. Just before the "Non nobis" chant begins, Henry slaps the glove onto Williams' chest and silently passes on, leaving the soldier to register a quick double take.

The one scene that Shakespeare does *not* supply—the full-scale battle of Agincourt—thus becomes the most powerful episode in Branagh's realistic presentation.[56] Admittedly there are stylized elements to offset the relentless shots of horses falling, mud spattering, men grappling in the quagmire.

One pattern, unobtrusive but subtly cohesive, is the repeated image of a dying man surrounded by others in the heat of battle. York, attacked on all sides like a baited animal, spews blood and black bile in his death throes; the Dauphin and Orleans drag the mortally wounded Constable from a pool and support him as he dies in a more dignified manner; Pistol cradles the dead face of Nym, who has been stabbed in the back while ransacking the corpse of a French soldier. Shots recorded in slow motion and accompanied by the "Non nobis" theme, which begins soon after Henry's anguished discovery of York's body, also have the effect of making the horrible (men and horses writhing in mud, Exeter as a grimacing war machine) aesthetic.

This, though, is a coda to the montage of battle images in close-up and the sound of mace clanging on shield, the roar of the wounded, and the scream of the slaughtered boys. Even the slow-motion technique works, on at least two occasions, as a psychological device to evoke the nightmare of clogged movement; it suggests the helpless dismay of the Dauphin and Orleans running to rescue the fallen Constable, and the hopelessness of Fluellen, Henry, and the English nobles when they try to race toward their camp to save the boys. Everything in this battle is magnified. While Olivier's film offers a single shot of the black swarm of arrows traveling to the line of French cavalry, Branagh's shows Gower commanding the archers to fire no less than seven times, with six frames of arrows whizzing through the air. What is more, the arrows find their mark; the camera cuts to French soldiers being felled by them. Later, in the English camp, we see not just one dead boy with blood on his mouth but what appear to be dozens.

On the battlefield Olivier's Henry V is energetic but unruffled, a crusading hero whose bright armor remains immaculate. Branagh's Henry is involved in so much unprotected hand-to-hand combat and so many encounters on horseback that the wonder is he survives at all. A close-up of a horse's eye, wide with terror, is juxtaposed with Henry's face contorted with fury and battlelust. This king is truly a warrior for the working day, dogged and roundshouldered, a Dirty Harry whose tunic—never as colorful as Olivier's—is drenched in mud. (Whereas the sky behind Olivier's king stays blue or at worst cloudy, Branagh's hero must slop through a fresh downpour of rain after the death of York.) When he staggers off the field, cheeks mud-spattered and nose caked in blood, he looks utterly uncharismatic.

Lack of charisma, or a hard look beneath the magic aura of kingship, is crucial to Branagh's interpretation of Henry V.[57] We are shown the human side of Henry and the conflicting strains in his character rather than the unified, relatively straightforward hero that Olivier projects.[58] It is true that our first glimpse of Henry is an imposing silhouette in the doorway of the council chamber (backlit and shot from a low angle so that as he approaches he seems huge); but the myth is quickly punctured when we switch from reaction shots of reverential, bowing courtiers to our first long look at the King. Sitting on the throne he appears incredibly boyish. His not particularly handsome face is expressionless; on public display, he does not intend to reveal any cracks in this tough, opaque facade, and we cannot be sure (from the close-up shot of Henry's face flanked by the profiles of the churchmen, as Canterbury whispers his offer of funds for the war) whether he has already colluded with the bishops in a politic deal or is now being manipulated by them.[59] His response to the gift of tennis balls begins very precisely and coolly. Then his clipped tones (on "play a se*t*") segue into controlled anger as he rises from the throne, eyes flashing, to expound bitingly on what the Dauphin's "mock" will entail. Henry has passed an initial test by showing self-control, leadership, and resolution.

The King's more responsive, emotional self is revealed in flashbacks to the old days with Falstaff (the lost world of *Henry IV, Part i*). At first these memories are Pistol's and Bardolph's, prompted by the news of Falstaff's terminal condition, but they climax in Hal's encounter with his former companion. The two are shown warmly embracing, Hal bathed in golden light and smiling beatifically at Falstaff. But his smile freezes as soon as Falstaff begins his wheedling "banish plump Jack, and banish all the world," and we hear Hal's unspoken resolve "I do, I will" in voice-over.[60] Henry's warmer side, repressed in the interests of strong leadership, also surfaces when Bardolph is executed. What Shakespeare leaves unresolved—Henry's demeanor when he hears about Bardolph's imminent hanging and declares, "We would have all such offenders so cut off"—is clarified in Branagh's production, which shows both the actual execution and Henry's response to it. When Bardolph, nose slit and with a rope around his neck, gazes despairingly at the King, we move back in time to a drinking contest between Bardolph and Falstaff, with Hal jovially egging them on. Taking over words that belong in Shakespeare's script to Falstaff, Bardolph, proleptically shown with the arms of Nym and Falstaff encircling his neck like a hangman's noose, jokes with Hal about how he should not "hang a thief" when he is king. As Hal, almost with a premonition of the future, slowly replies "No—thou shalt," plaintive flute music returns us to the present; then Henry gives a faint nod to Exeter, who kicks Bardolph off the cart and into his death throes. When the camera moves in on Henry he has tears on his cheeks and must struggle for control as he delivers his speech on "all offenders" in a broken voice. Branagh describes the similar sequence from the 1984–85 RSC production (where the company first discovered the rightness of staging Bardolph's death) as one of

The Royal Shakespeare Company's production of *Henry V* (1975): King Henry (Alan Howard) and his troops after Agincourt. Courtesy of Shakespeare Centre Library: Joe Cocks Studio Collection

Laurence Olivier's production of *Henry V* (1944): King Henry addressing his troops before Agincourt. Courtesy of the Museum of Modern Art/Film Stills Archive

Laurence Olivier's production of *Henry V* (1944): The wedding sequence in the Globe Theatre. Courtesy of the Museum of Modern Art/Film Stills Archive

Kenneth Branagh's production of *Henry V* (1989): King Henry addressing his troops before Agincourt. Courtesy of Renaissance Films PLC, copyright ©1989. All rights reserved

Kenneth Branagh's production of *Henry V* (1989): King Henry and Princess Katherine. Courtesy of Renaissance Films PLC, copyright ©1989.

The BBC/Time Life production of *Henry V* (1979): King Henry (David Gwillim) addresses Montjoy (Garrick Hagon) with Bedford (Rob Edwards) to the right of Henry. Courtesy of BBC Picture Archives

The BBC/Time Life production of *Henry V* (1979): The King of France (Thorley Walters) gives Princess Katherine (Jocelyne Boisseau) to King Henry (David Gwillim). Courtesy of BBC Picture Archives

"intense personal cost"[61] to Henry; certainly the movie's flashback to the tavern camaraderie further accentuates the gap between the tough leader who enforces military discipline and the vulnerable man. One other flashback occurs when Henry is listening to Burgundy's speech on the devastations of postwar France and his mind drifts into successive images of the Constable, York, the Boy, the Hostess, Nym, Bardolph, Scroop, and Falstaff. The significance of these characters is that they are now all dead. But Henry's psyche has not forgotten them.

Henry's hurt and anger over Scroop, also a revelation of his underlying self, is heightened by the choreography of this scene in Branagh's movie. Henry's affection for his trusted companion is suggested in his quick caress of Scroop's cheek before the unmasking of "capital crimes" and also at one point during the terrible showdown. For this tirade he hurls Scroop onto a table and leans over him (their faces almost touching) in what must surely be a reminder of the "bedfellow" relationship, especially since it it visually echoes the earlier shot of the Hostess bending over Falstaff on his deathbed. (Exeter, to some extent Henry's reflector and rougher surrogate, registers the deeply personal slight to the King by hitting Scroop across the face in addition to ripping away his chain of office.) Henry clearly feels betrayed both as a man and as a monarch; his anger at how the traitors have jeopardized the safety of England is pronounced in his bitter emphasis on the threatened "desolation" to the kingdom (mainly addressed to Scroop) when he sternly announces the punishment that all three will suffer. The same kind of pain—being knocked for a loop emotionally—breaks through in Branagh's delivery of the "God of battles" soliloquy before Agincourt. The immediately preceding one, where he ponders "ceremony," is more a wry confirmation of what Henry has discovered already; he modulates into a whisper at the end (caressing the sibilants "*s*leeps in Ely*s*ium") to avoid waking the sleeping soldier who serves as an inspiration for the King's whole meditation on the carefree "slave." "Not today, O Lord," in contrast, is delivered at a much quicker, even frenzied pace. The speech is both an appalled recognition of what is at stake and a sudden release of guilt over his father's "fault," as Henry pleads with God to remember all his acts of penance. Tears well up in the King's eyes as he reaches the somber, visionary close: "The day [pause], my friends [pause] and all things [rising pitch] wait for me."

Branagh's Henry is a great performer, too, who often discovers his strengths through role-playing; yet we are always given glimpses of the inner self that lies beneath the bravado. At Harfleur Henry bursts through the flames like the horseman of the Apocalypse, but he is quickly caught up in a more personal interaction with his soldiers as he creates for them mimetically the kind of military toughness required to return to the breach. He becomes fierce on "tiger," exultant at "stretch the nostril wide"; and the success of his inspired speech is confirmed by the reaction shots of Exeter grinning appreciatively at the "brass cannon" simile and Williams drawing his sword with an excited flourish as Henry addresses the "good yeomen." In his speech to the Governor, Branagh's King is much more desperate. His voice strained, he appears genuinely possessed with warlust and fury as he describes the "*shrill-shr*ieking daughters" and "*m*ad *m*others," pointing up the alliteration to give full emphasis to the obscene vision of "murder, spoil, and villainy." Reaction shots of decent English soldiers show none of them, apart from the ever-ready Exeter, empathizing with what Henry is projecting here. We feel that we are watching a "professional killer of chilling ruthlessness."[62] Yet the quick shot of Henry half closing his eyes, suddenly terribly weary the moment the Governor capitulates, suggests his utter relief at not having to act on this ruthlessness.

Branagh's handling of the Crispin's Day speech provides another instance of the private self surging through the polished public role. This Henry delivers the first part confidently, his voice resonant.[63] Like Olivier he climbs on a cart to build to the rhetorical climax, in long shot, of "the ending of the world." But then there is a sudden modulation at "We few, we happy few"—a close-up of Henry speaking more quietly, his eyes luminescent with the personal vision of what this brotherhood means—until, accompanied by swelling music, he steers his audience (including the renegades Pistol and Nym, who are shown cheering as heartily as the rest) to the second climax of "fought with us upon Saint Crispin's Day."

In battle Henry is again the "professional killer," by no means immune to fear (as witnessed by his horrified expression when he sees the huge numbers of French cavalry approaching off camera) but increasingly consumed by aggression and a ferocious determination to get the job done. We see his silent scream as he discovers York's body, which turns into a furious rallying of his soldiers with "But all's not done" as he plunges back into the heart of the fighting. He releases pent-up emotion when he discovers the murdered boys—his "I was not angry since I came to France" is much fiercer than Olivier's controlled response—and again when the herald Montjoy arrives shortly afterwards. Henry, a bulldog smeared with the mud and gore of battle, savagely pulls Montjoy off his horse to demand if he has come for ransom; when Montjoy assures him that he wants only permission to retrieve the dead from the battlefield Henry, suddenly very vulnerable, admits, "I know not if the day be ours or no." It is an intimate few seconds.

The two are still locked together, and their foreheads in profile almost touch as Henry gasps and bows his head in exhausted relief. Once Montjoy has retreated, it is Fluellen who serves as a catalyst for Henry's emotions. The King half laughs, half weeps as the Captain reminds him of his Welsh ancestry; their warm hug as Henry sobs "For I am Welsh, you know" is a moment of intensity that displaces the real cause for tears of joy—the outcome of Agincourt—which is almost too huge to comprehend.

There is a similar lowering of defenses, a mixture of sadness, tenderness, and celebration, in the wooing scene. Because until now Henry has had to maintain a stern seriousness for so much of the action, we have scarcely seen his gaucheness or his sense of humor, which makes it particularly enjoyable to observe the lighter side of his personality when he is with Katherine. Here Henry, his face finally clean, is wearing a gorgeous red robe and golden crown instead of the usual muted colors that characterize this production; the quiet Princess shines in ivory. Just as he had to improvise in his speech at Harfleur, so the King must try a series of new techniques to win over Katherine. Both Kenneth Branagh and Emma Thompson (as the Princess) are accomplished comic actors. Their laughter together when Henry tries to converse in French is infectious (Katherine can hardly curb her hilarity) while Henry's moment of farcical aplomb mixed with schoolboy embarrassment, as he breaks off their kiss with the laconic observation "Here comes your father," is superb.

Along with capturing the light and shade of Henry's character, this film does not ignore what is often, in reading the play, one of the most difficult aspects of the King to interpret: his piety. Branagh has always maintained that Shakespeare's Henry V is a "genuinely holy man" and that it is "ridiculous to play him as some one-dimensional Machiavell."[64] The King's strong sense of relationship with God is, he feels, a corollary of his intense isolation and his sense of responsibility for his people. (Branagh's conversations with Prince Charles confirmed this side of royalty: that "some kind of belief in God was the only practical way of living from day to day, it was the only way to deal with his position."[65]) Moreover, thinks Branagh, Henry has a "genuine visionary quality"[66] that informs his sense of honor, making his campaign in France much more than shallow opportunism. The King's humble deference to God's will is foregrounded on several occasions in the film. When the rain comes on cue immediately after Henry's assurance "We are in God's hand, brother," he looks up ruefully as if to acknowledge divine control of the elements. He then accents "God" in a direct address to the deity before the battle of Agincourt: "And how thou pleasest, God, dispose the day!" Most pointed is his wondering acknowledgment of supernatural protection after he reads the remarkably short list of English dead; his face is transfigured when he confirms that "God [pause] fought [longer pause] for us." In the prolonged tracking shot as Henry carries the dead Boy across the battlefield to the strains of "Non nobis, Domine, Domine," we register his sense of awe at the fulfilment of God's purpose, despite the tableaux of destruction that surround him. At the climax of the choral-orchestral arrangement the King lays the Boy down on a cart and solemnly bows his head in silent recognition of God's power—a gesture that recalls his bowing his head in prayer at the end of his prebattle soliloquy, after his apocalyptic vision "all things stay for me."

Just as Branagh retains Henry's strong piety along with his fierce battlelust and does not try to iron out or explain contradictions in the character, so the mixture of emotions generated by that tracking shot points to a central ambivalence in Branagh's presentation of Henry's war.[67] On one hand, we are invited to share in the majesty and glory of a victory sanctioned by God; Henry's arduous but dignified progess along the field and the moving music ensure that.[68] Nevertheless, the dead Boy carried by Henry is a potent symbol of the sacrifices that war entails. And the images of stiff corpses, frantic Frenchwomen barely restrained from attacking the King, and the grieving pietà of the Dauphin and Orleans holding the Constable all work to imply that the "God of battles" is a fierce warlord indeed and that the sickening carnage of war cannot be smoothed over by a heartwarming war requiem.

Does Branagh try to have it both ways in the film here? It has been argued that his production begins as an ironic assessment of the King—an exposure of the political games underlying power—but that just as the Chorus becomes less detached from the film medium and more immersed in the action, so the movie ends up whitewashing Henry and glorifying "cruel heroism."[69] Or, from the viewpoint of the cultural materialists, Branagh starts by demystifying monarchy but is ultimately coopted by it. (Not for nothing, suggest these critics, was Prince Charles invited to be patron of Branagh's Renaissance Company.) Other commentators have enjoyed analyzing the subtext of the film: the actor-producer's personal odyssey. Determined to conquer the territory previously owned by the great Sir Laurence ("A Brilliant Upstart Takes on the Ghost of Olivier"[70]), Branagh is like Henry V, a bold leader fighting against terrible odds. In this quest to dethrone his theatrical father, the plucky Irish kid from working-class Belfast also challenges the capitalistic movie moguls by making an independent film that cost only around $7 million, but in doing so ends up supporting the conservative, entrepreneurial initiatives of Thatcherite Britain.[71]

This materialist analysis of the film, if carried too far, tends to undercut Branagh's substantial achievement. It sounds suspiciously like sour grapes to complain that Branagh's work is less of an artistic triumph because it is not genuinely subversive or critical enough of Establishment values.[72] In any case, containment within the dominant ideology is probably inevitable unless the movie had chosen to depart radically from Shakespeare's text; as the new historicist Stephen Greenblatt comments, "it is not at all clear that *Henry V* can be successfully performed as subversive. . . . The very doubts that Shakespeare raises serve not to rob the king of his charisma but to heighten it."[73] Rather than placing the movie in an ideological trap, it seems more fruitful to return to Branagh's interest in the complexity of the main character—as a "complicated, doubting, dangerous young professional"[74]—and assess how far his presentation succeeds in creating in the audience ambivalent responses toward the King. The ambiguity is in fact retained, not glossed over, in the movie. Henry's campaign is shown as a horrible waste of human life but also as a marvelous triumph for the gritty working man's hero and his troops. Maintaining power means being ruthless when necessary, but it need not cancel out an individual's capacity for tenderness and humor. Branagh's Henry is both genuinely pious and a shrewd politician.

SHAKESPEARE ON TELEVISION: THE BBC/TIME LIFE PRODUCTION OF *HENRY V* (1979)

Live theater was the Elizabethans' prime source of dramatic entertainment. Now, in the 1990s, many more people visit the cinema to watch films than go to see plays performed, and nearly every household (in the United Kingdom as well as the United States) has at least one television set. Not surprisingly, Shakespeare's plays have been adapted in recent years, with varying degrees of success, to this medium. The BBC/Time Life series (1979–86) made the complete works available on the small screen to students and the general public. It has been estimated that more people have watched a televised version of a Shakespeare play (such as *Hamlet*) than have seen that play in the theater over the past four hundred years.[75] Watching *Henry V* is now as simple as slipping a tape into the VCR.

In critiquing the BBC version of *Henry V*, viewers need to be clear about the particular advantages and disadvantages of the television medium. Only then can they assess how well the production exploits the strengths of the small screen without accentuating its more obvious limitations. It is pointless to castigate television for the passivity it induces in the viewer in contrast to the fuller engagement encouraged by live theater. The box in the living room cannot generate a current between actors and audience, for, as Laurence Olivier points out, "There will never be the smell of the adrenaline on celluloid."[76] You can stop the show by turning off the television set, but your presence in front of the screen will never affect the dynamics of performance on tape. Moreover television, unless the camera stays in one place to film the whole stage area, does not capture the three-dimensional, larger movement of the total action on stage. The camera has the freedom to break up the defined space and vary the angle of vision, but it inevitably selects what the viewer will see. As William Worthen comments, "Watching televison we don't balance several simultaneous performances because the camera relates them to us in a sequence."[77] Nor can the audience expect televised Shakespeare, when it is taped in a studio, to emulate the realism of actual locations that are often captured on film proper, or to provide the panoramic breadth and depth of shot possible on the larger screen. Everything is scaled down and compressed.

But the great strength of television, tied to what has negatively been called "key-hole peeping into a drawing room,"[78] lies in its intimacy; it offers close-up images of faces so that the viewer can be privy to the inner emotions of the dramatic characters. The raising of an eyebrow or a subtle change in the expression of the eyes can be an important psychological pointer, and yet such microgestures are difficult to witness in the theater, even by those sitting in the front row. This opportunity for close-ups does not mean that television must restrict itself to "talking heads." Directors of the BBC series often use three cameras to film each scene. This allows quick cutting between long establishing shots (which provide a fuller sense of mise en scène, or pictorial grouping of characters) and closer shots from different angles that focus on individual actors.

The presentation of sound can also be varied. One important advantage of television over movies is that it does not necessarily relegate Shakespeare's verse, with its rhetorical patterning and poetic images, to second place. It has been pointed out that whereas the roots of cinema lie in silent movies—nothing but images—television has partly evolved from radio broadcasts, so that we expect to pay close attention to the spoken word.[79] We may miss the "range, scale" and "dimension"[80] of acting in the theater, but television compensates for that with vocal as well as visual subtleties. Words really can be spoken conversationally or whispered if appropriate (thanks to boom microphones). They need not always be articulated stridently to reach people in the back rows of the theater.

The BBC/Time Life series has sometimes been criticized as dull and "unadventurous."[81] Indeed Cedric Messina, who conceived the idea for the project (and under whose management *Henry V* was produced in 1979), wanted to provide straightforward Shakespeare without gimmickry[82] or modernist interpretations. Playing it safe, though, risked alienating both Shakespeare specialists and average television viewers, who probably needed something more daring to break down their preconceptions about classic Shakespeare being boring. Because the medium usually calls for detailed naturalism—viewers are used to seeing pictures of real life on the daily news—directors are often wary of using the functional or symbolic sets that work so well on the open stage of the theater. Jane Howell's enterprising decision to direct the three parts of *Henry VI* and *Richard III* in a studio arranged to look like an adventure playground proved that frank stylization can work in the television medium, once the audience adapts to a new convention. Nevertheless directors striving for authenticity, especially early in the series, chose more representational sets, though ones without the absolute realism of on-location sites that full-scale films are able to provide. (In one production that did use the real setting of the woods, *As You Like It*, the foliage and insects were felt to detract from the poetic drama.) The best solution for television seemed to be semirealistic sets. Unfortunately, though, these flat areas and "freshly painted, sharply angled buildings"[83] may look like a failure to conjure up the real thing, an uneasy compromise between naturalism and artifice.

The choice of set is just one aspect of televised Shakespeare that the informed viewer must take into account. In critiquing the BBC *Henry V* we need to ask how those features special to television—choice of studio set, camera angles, shot composition, lighting, and sound effects—enhance or detract from the significance of the play, as well as evaluating the more traditional categories that overlap with theater, such as casting decisions, acting, costume design, and overall production concept.

The BBC/Time Life production of *Henry V* uses relatively stylized sets. David Giles, who also directed the two parts of *Henry IV*, regarded this play as the least naturalistic of the three, partly because of the presence of the Chorus (an obvious illusion breaker) and partly because he conceived of the King as a consummate role-player. In fact the "production's most stylized space"[84] is the French court. A crane shot at the opening of II. iv shows the French grouped in a boxlike set that is draped with blue fabric imprinted with white fleur de lys; the camera quickly moves to the French King, who is sitting on a dais at the left, shouting to make himself heard above the wrangling aristocrats. Just as the set is nonrepresentational, so the style of acting in the

French scenes is more overtly histrionic, establishing a clear contrast between the vaunting, immature French and the sober, controlled English. The final scene at the French court also opens with a long shot on a set that (perhaps echoing Olivier's film) looks as ornate as an illustration from an illuminated manuscript; the cycloramic curtain is lit deep blue and columns are hung with tapestries. There is much formality in the blocking, with the French ranged on the left, the English on the right, and the peacemaker Burgundy in the middle. The groups frequently bow to each other, ceremonial gestures that contrast with the incipient chaos at the French court in earlier scenes. In a tableau that closes the action of the play before the Chorus steps forward, Henry (in gold) and Katherine (in silver) kneel facing each other, hands set in prayer as the Archbishop blesses their union. This static image creates a perfect moment: young, smiling royals captured as figures in a medieval pageant[85] before history moves relentlessly on.

Within this stylized frame the production uses more realistic sets for the war campaign. The pasteboard castle walls at Harfleur, a compromise of "half-realism,"[86] look neither convincingly solid nor symbolic. But the representational sets used for Act IV's outdoor scenes—the campfires and the countryside around Agincourt—are appropriate as more convincing settings in which Henry can converse informally with the commoners and probe his own dilemma as king. In line with the concern for historical authenticity, the costuming follows fifteenth-century designs. At Agincourt the English standards colorfully quarter gold lions on a red background with silver fleur de lys on blue—a combination that dictates the color coding for each nation. Reds, browns, and golds characterize the English court, picked up in the flamboyant Pistol's red and yellow costume and the browns of the Chorus's monkish habit and Mistress Quickly's homespun gown. In the final scene Henry is resplendent in a gold brocade gown with wide sleeves (it suits him better than his armor) while Katherine's silver robe signifies purity. The French are usually dressed in shades of blue or sea green.

Played by Alec McOwen, the Chorus partakes of the production's mix of stylization and realism; he both breaks the dramatic illusion and enters into it. As Prologue, framed against a dark backdrop, he addresses his words directly to the camera, which moves into a close-up of his face on "pardon, gentles all." Exhorting the audience to "let us . . . On your imaginary forces work," the Chorus begins to move forward. Simultaneously the backdrop lightens and, at the mention of the "girdle of these walls," the camera pulls back to reveal framing "walls" (actually columns) on each side, with heraldic banners hung between them. As the camera continues to track the advancing Chorus, two lines of the play's characters slowly appear, one on each edge of the frame, frozen in tableau. This transition from dark emptiness to a populated set suggests a way of opening up the viewer's imagination, creating a depth of vista within the confines of the narrow screen. One might criticize it for making "imaginary forces" too literal, but not, I think, for failing to capture the "sense of the round,"[87] the panoramic sweep of Shakespeare's wooden O theater, which is virtually impossible in the television medium.

The Chorus is presented as a character both inside and outside the play. He nods to the clerics (entering screen right) as he exits after the Prologue, and at the end of Act I, when Henry is genially throwing tennis balls around the court, we cut to a quick shot of the Chorus catching one. The Chorus then delivers his damning exposition on the traitors at Southampton with pace and conviction; at the end he double-takes as he glances screen left and the camera pulls back to show Bardolph nodding to him, apparently reminding him that the Eastcheap scene comes next. The Chorus obligingly explains, "But, till the king come forth, and *not till then*, / Unto Southampton do we shift our scene," thereby making sense of the text's apparent contradiction between elaborately preparing the audience for the traitors' scene and then suddenly moving the action to Eastcheap [emphasis added]. To open Act III the Chorus pops up from a bench in the French court, disguised in a blue cloak, while at the end of III. vii, the prelude to Act IV, he emerges as one of the figures who is captured in long shot outside the French camp. In closing the play he reenacts and partly reverses the sequence of his Prologue. He enters in front of the tableau of King and Princess, and once again the camera pulls back to reveal two lines of characters, French and English, gazing at the kneeling couple. This time they fade to black as the Chorus delivers his somber words on what happens to England during the reign of Henry VI; when he has finished his Epilogue he walks upstage into the darkness. Instead of opening up the illusion the Chorus now decorously closes it, successfully rounding off the play that has enacted the glorious reign of Henry V.

At the start of the play McOwen's Chorus picks up the momentum, delivering his lines with conviction and "suppressed excitement."[88] In general, the acting in this production is strong. There is a real danger, however, that students who first see Branagh's *Henry V* may not judge the televised version on its own merits, not only because the film production is so imaginative and coherent and Branagh so compelling in the title role, but because most of its minor roles are played to perfection. The BBC's Bardolph may look mannered and sound quavery in contrast to the down-to-earth seediness conveyed by Richard Briers in the Branagh movie; Fluellen's praising of the King for his Welshness in the BBC version will seem overblown and melodramatic beside the moving nuances of that master of subtlety, Ian Holm; and, in particular, the BBC's Exeter looks and sounds elderly and effete—more a clergyman than a soldier—when set against the huge physical presence and deep, resonant voice of Brian Blessed, who plays Exeter as an awe-inspiring medieval knight. It must be stressed, though, that the supporting actors in the BBC production nearly all go beyond the competent, and several, such as Brenda Bruce's worldly-wise Hostess and David Pinner's feisty, fresh-faced Williams, give riveting performances. But this is really Henry's show.

Indeed, David Gwillim's version of Henry holds up well on its own terms. This actor plays Henry as a mercurial personality who is wryly ironic and steely by turns: a logical progression from the Prince Hal figure (also played by Gwillim) in the two preceding *Henry IV* plays. Clearly the director perceived a continuity of character through role-playing, as Henry progresses from a prince who is used to hiding his real self under a mask to a young king practicing and mastering a variety of roles—those of politician, soldier, and lover.

Yet the strongest parts of Gwillim's performance, for this viewer, emerge when the mask slips and we see the vulnerable, private self beneath. This is an intelligent, even contemplative Henry rather than an instinctive man of action; he thinks through situations and dilemmas instead of presenting his position as a fait accompli, and his mobile face, with its remarkably "expressive mouth"[89] and twinkling eyes, is shown to advantage in close-up. In his two adjacent soliloquies, we see him in the process of actually discovering what he feels about his role as king. Opening with quiet bitterness ("Upon the king!"), he modulates into irony as he wryly chastises "ceremony" ("Art thou ought else but place, degree, and form?") and expresses deep regret when he contemplates the "flattery" attendant on kingship. Toward the end he registers not contempt for the "wretched slave" who is untroubled by national affairs but rather a mood of wistfulness (on "sleeps in Elysium") and surprised recognition that the labor of the countryman's routines is "profitable"—a new respect for a way of life that he has never understood before. The second soliloquy begins more passionately, and he is almost weeping as he begs God to take the "sense of reck'ning" from his soldiers. In the pause before "Not today, O Lord" Henry suddenly makes the terrifying connection between crime and punishment (we see fear in Gwillim's eyes), followed by an exasperated realization that he can never do enough to atone for the sins of his father: "all that I can do is nothing worth." The television medium, with its carefully positioned microphones as well as its varying camera angles, captures shifts of thought and moments of intense feeling played out through the actor's voice and face.

The same anguish surfaces in Henry's chastisement of Scroop in II. ii. The long speech is not overplayed; he does not harangue his companion but explores his own deep disillusionment. At first Henry is quietly incredulous that a person who knew the "very bottom" of his "soul" could have betrayed him, and then visibly moved to tears (on "my eye will scarcely see it"), which makes sense of his concluding "I will weep for thee." The blocking is informal, with Gwillim standing behind the actor playing Scroop so that we can simultaneously observe the traitor's remorseful reaction. Henry moves down to his level—Scroop is kneeling—for the series of questions that begin "Show men dutiful?", thus making the words intimate rather than stridently rhetorical. To enact spatially the spiritual distance now between them, Henry stands up again on "Another fall of man." This King can be angry too, though not in this sequence. Spontaneous fury, albeit quickly suppressed, flashes out in his response to the Dauphin's gift and to Montjoy's request for ransom just before battle ("Good God, why should they mock poor fellows thus?"). But the high point of his anger—significant loss of control—comes not in his reaction to the slaughter of the boys at camp, which is steely, but when he feels personally insulted by Williams and shouts his promise to challenge him: "I will do it, though I take thee in the King's company."

In public, refining the features of his mask, Henry is usually controlled. In I. ii his performance is careful as he projects the image of a serious monarch, nodding sagely and leaning forward attentively as he listens to the Archbishop. He keeps his passion in check over the tennis balls (his voice rises and tenses when he contemplates the "unborn" French who will suffer as a result); he is able to turn the insult into a splendid theatrical joke at the Dauphin's expense when he closes the scene by tossing the tennis balls around the royal court. At the beginning of the Southampton scene he acts so well that nothing ruffles his jovial exterior (in contrast, Branagh injects heavy irony into his praise of the traitors' "so much care" of him); yet while Gwillim's Henry skillfully maneuvers the traitors to the point where they abase themselves, he does not appear to relish their humiliation.

As a soldier, this Henry has boyish charm but little charisma. Physically he lacks heft. While we cannot expect him to bulk up like Arnold Schwarzenegger for the part, it is regrettable that he has neither the imposing physique of Olivier (at least on film) nor the tough stockiness of Branagh. He moves around awkwardly at the breach of Harfleur, his voice cracking nervously on "Disguise fair nature." This tentativeness, we can assume, is a deliberate choice on the part of the director and actor[90] to suggest that Henry is feeling his way into the role of general, trying to create, mimetically, a warlike exterior as he races from soldier to soldier, exhorting each one to "set the teeth" and "stretch the nostril wide," panting as he enacts the "straining" greyhounds. The problem is that the audience may not appreciate the tactic and will perceive only an unimpressive would-be leader moving jerkily around a small space. Henry's confidence increases in later scenes in France, but subtlety rather than "hectoring rhetoric"[91] remains the keynote of his public performances. The Crispin's Day speech begins in a jokey, even whimsical fashion; working hard to convince his men that he is not anxious, Gwillim's Henry plays for laughs on "most offending soul alive" and chuckles at "Old men forget." But the cultivated heartiness has disappeared by the time he pauses at the word "story" ("This story shall the good man teach his son"), when he suddenly recognizes that his troops are about to create an event of mythic importance. Moreover, he discovers the bond of brotherhood in the act of articulating it—this is not just a ploy to get his army to fight—for he enunciates "Shall be my brother" with quiet intensity. The end of the speech is sober and reflective, with a close-up of Henry's face. Partly because the small screen cannot simulate a huge audience—either the "cast of thousands" that can be shown or implied on the big screen or the impression of larger numbers possible in the "virtual middle distance"[92] of the theater stage—there is no long shot of men cheering. Yet here the BBC director makes a virtue of necessity, deflecting attention away from the speech as a crowd pleaser and concentrating instead on the way that Gwillim builds conviction slowly, shifting the tone of the speech from a humorous beginning to quiet passion at the conclusion.

As a lover (V. ii), Gwillim's Henry is both role-player and young man gingerly picking his way through the minefield of courtship. He begins stiffly, speaking hesitantly and clasping his hands together as he tries to woo Katherine in conventional terms; but he is driven to exasperated bluntness as he discourses on how "plain" a soldier and king he is. As he enlarges his strategy he becomes more confident and purposeful, narrowing the distance between himself and Katherine. He moves close to convince her of the feats their son will perform (taking the Turk by the beard), pursues her around the gazebo after she chides him for "fausse French," and extends his hand decisively on "say . . . 'I am thine.' " Refusing to be daunted by the women's shock when he strides forward to kiss the Princess's hand, he maneuvers Katherine into a solemn kiss on the lips (their heads are in close-up in the frame); by this time we doubt neither his control of the situation nor his sincerity.

Technically the production, completed in only six days, is polished. David Giles, the director, recognizes that the camera can impose a linear tyranny, breaking up the rhythms and spatial patterning of scenes by cutting between individuals and overusing reaction shots. To compensate for this he opens most scenes with an establishing shot, or theatrical perspective, so that we can register how the whole space is being used before moving into medium shots and close-ups. A few scenes, though, do cry out for a wider angle. For example, in the scene between Pistol and Monsieur le Fer (IV. iv), the camera cuts between shots of Pistol's upper body (he is later joined by the Boy) and the prisoner on the ground instead of clarifying the action by pulling back to show the interplay of movement between two or three figures in the frame. The camera work is usually straightforward rather than innovative, but in III. vii, where the French wait restlessly for the morning of battle, a slow fade from one part of the scene to the next helps make the passing of time palpable. The fade comes after the Constable, drinking at the table, exclaims, "Would it were day!" When the scene comes back into focus he is looking outside the tent, relieved that it is finally "time to arm."

Close-up shots enhance Gwillim's mercurial and meditative Henry, not only during his soliloquies and public speeches but for silent reactions—as when Fluellen reveals that Bardolph has been executed (III. vi) and the camera zooms in on Henry's suddenly frozen features. Gwillim's face is often shown in profile. One reason may be that Gwillim, with his basin haircut, bears more than a passing resemblance to the portrait of Henry V, also a profile study, hanging in the National Gallery. But this angle also accentuates moments of resolution and intensity for Henry: his calling in the French messengers, his unmasking of Scroop, and the marriage ceremony at the end. The production uses this shot, too, when Ely and Canterbury are kneeling at the altar discussing Henry in the opening scene. As Canterbury whispers to Ely about the offer he has made to the King "touching France," their two "birdlike heads,"[93] one above the other, almost touch in profile—an image that powerfully evokes the secret political deals going on behind the scenes.

The BBC tape is the least cut of all the filmed versions of *Henry V*: Barely 400 lines out of 3,313 have gone. This has the advantage of presenting the underplot with the Eastcheap characters in full (so that viewers can enjoy juxtapositions and contrasts with the main plot) and of revealing all the different facets of King Henry without foregrounding some at the expense of others. Thus we are given Henry's controversial command to kill the prisoners—cut in Olivier's and Branagh's films—as well as his angry threat, after he discovers the slaughter at camp, to kill any other Frenchmen his soldiers capture. (A close-up of the Boy lying dead, his nose and mouth bloodied, is an effective lead-in to this angry reaction.) The only mitigation of the brutal side of Henry comes in III. iii, where most of Henry's graphic vision of rape and murder at Harfleur (twenty-seven lines out of forty-three) is excised. In part because of Gwillim's appearance and demeanor (one critic describes him as a "peach"[94]), the Henry V of this production is likeable overall; we are shown glimpses of the ruthless soldier and the cunning politician, but inhuman toughness is not the dominant impression that emerges.

CONCLUSION: SOME CONTRASTS

While the films of Olivier and Branagh are splendid cinematic interpretations in their own right, all three versions of *Henry V* now on videotape offer insight into the play. The BBC/Time Life production is inevitably the least daring of the three, but it does not flatten out the character of Henry; David Gwillim's performance and those of most of the supporting actors repay study. Writing before Branagh's film was made, H. R. Coursen describes the BBC's traitors' scene at Southampton as "quite simply, one of the most powerful moments of drama I have ever witnessed. It transcended the medium of television."[95] Since most filmgoers will remember only Branagh's daring physical rendering of the scene, it is worth reconsidering the subtleties of the David Giles production on its own merits and not allowing it to be totally overshadowed by the more vigorous film. Later, after seeing Branagh's *Henry V*, Coursen found rewarding contrasts between the "cool and introverted" Henry acted by Gwillim and Branagh's "passionate, extroverted" protagonist, determining that each presentation is appropriate for its medium.[96] The BBC version also has the merit of inclusiveness and fidelity to the shape of Shakespeare's play since no scenes are cut. Moreover, it does justice to the tonal variety of the play, for it is easy to forget, after watching Branagh's intense and streamlined version, that *Henry V*'s humor extends beyond the Eastcheap sequences and the final scene. At least half the scenes in the play contain some comedy,[97] and several interludes during or immediately after Agincourt—Pistol capturing Monsieur le Fer, Fluellen confronting Williams and later chastising Pistol with a leek—provide comic relief from the grimmer realities of war. But two of these sequences are missing from Olivier's movie and all three from Branagh's.

The television studio and the small screen, however, are not conducive to a realistic depiction of war horrors; that is the area in which Branagh's movie triumphs. Like Olivier's, it supplies the battle sequences missing in Shakespeare's text, building a continuous sequence from the Crispin's Day speech to the climax of the "Non nobis" hymn. To Shakespeare's script Branagh adds the four-minute sequence (which he describes as "the greatest tracking shot in the world. . . . It was certainly bloody long"[98]) of the King carrying the Boy back across the battlefield—a recapitulation of the carnage of warfare, now viewed from the perspective of the soberly grateful but victorious English King. The closing shot of Henry's bowed and muddied head dissolves into the red and gold backdrop of the French court, a stunning transition from war to peace that is made possible only through cutting the Chorus to Act V and Pistol's encounter with Fluellen and his leek. This kind of streamlining is not an option in the BBC version, with its commitment to the full text.

In fact Branagh cuts about 1,820 lines (a little over half the play). This is about 100 lines more than Olivier leaves out: somewhat surprising, since Branagh's version, which includes the scene with the traitors and the execution of Bardolph, seems fuller. Inevitably some of the details that complicate the presentation of Henry in Shakespeare's play—"the often discomforting social and political constituents of Henry's situation,"[99] such as Fluellen's unflattering historical analogy between the King and Alexander the Pig—disappear in the streamlined adaptation. Nevertheless Branagh's film attains "clarity and immediacy"[100] in the plot line without sacrificing much in the way of subtlety; the opening council scene, for instance, is pared from 310 lines to 112, but it strongly conveys the underlying political machinations at court as well as Henry's emergence as a decisive ruler. Coherent and fast-paced, the movie takes us deep into Henry's medieval world and his campaign in France while it shows the King proving himself as a complex but successful leader. This is a "psychologically rich"[101] interpretation of the King (Branagh is fascinated with what makes world leaders tick); and Branagh's comment on trying to "realise the qualities of introspection, fear, doubt and anger" in a Henry who has "more than a little of the Hamlet in him"[102] suggests closer affinities with Alan Howard's RSC performance in 1975[103] than with either Olivier's or Gwillim's conception of the main character.

Branagh's film also gives depth to the minor characters by fully contextualizing them. The French, Henry's foils, are not caricatured as comically helpless or effete, as in Olivier's film. Paul Scofield's King appears deeply troubled but always dignified, and the Dauphin (Michael Maloney) is given credibility as a high-strung, impetuous young man who is eagerly seeking the approval of his peers. Katherine is no fairy-tale Princess but a flesh-and-blood woman, exuberant and self-assured as she enumerates body parts in English. The herald Montjoy (played by Christopher Ravenscroft) behaves arrogantly at first but develops genuine respect, even awe, for Henry over several meetings. Henry's English retainers, not surprisingly, are much more than ciphers. Individual perfomances are honest and daring. Exeter, played by the imposing Brian Blessed, not only uses his physical heft to convey power as the King's henchman and executioner, but displays a responsive concern for his young nephew, as when he reacts delightedly to Henry's rousing speeches at the breach and before Agincourt, supports him when he almost collapses after the surrender of Harfleur, and, although taken aback, doesn't question Henry's decision to march on from there to Calais. Before Michael Williams (played by his namesake) rises to the occasion as the king's conscience by the campfire, he is shown responding enthusiastically to the "yeomen" address at Harfleur and then compassionately helping the fallen Boy as they trudge through Picardy in the rain and mud. Robert Stephens portrays Pistol as a perfect mixture of sentimentality (tearily calling the King a "lovely bully" and weeping over Nym's corpse in the sequence added to the text) and craven meanness, as he vents his spite on Fluellen and later nastily outlines the depraved life he plans to lead after the war. Ian Holm does not overplay Fluellen as a comic character, but subtly captures his dignity, his pride in his nationality, and his passion for military protocol.

In contrast to the BBC studio production, Olivier's and Branagh's films offer compelling musical scores to complement visual images and underline emotion. William Walton's music (in the 1944 film) evokes both humor and majesty. Patrick Doyle's score for Branagh's movie is varied as well as subtle; among other arrangements it encompasses a tentative flute solo and bass chords for suspense, a terrific yet sinister fanfare for Henry's entrance to the council chamber and at Harfleur, a sentimental melody as the Eastcheap men depart for war, and a romantic cadenza (on strings) to underpin both Henry's Crispin's Day speech and the climax of his wooing of Katherine. The most memorable musical theme, the choral-orchestral arrangement of the "Non nobis" as the denouement of Agincourt, is introduced quietly at the first mention of war (and somberly carried by horns as the French King confirms that Henry has "passed the river Somme") before being given a plangent rendering on strings during the battle itself. A few critics have felt that the film's music conflicts with the naturalistic delivery of the poetry—for instance, when it swells under the Crispin's Day speech[104]—or that it is artificially superimposed on the spectacle, as when the grimy soldier Court (lipsynching of course) somewhat improbably launches into a flawless rendering of the "Non nobis" chant to introduce the closing symphonic arrangement. Most often, though, the music is an unobtrusive undercurrent to the speech; it enhances atmosphere and intensifies emotion without detracting from Shakespeare's poetry.

Both Olivier and Branagh aimed to make *Henry V* accessible to a wide audience (Branagh wanted to produce a "truly popular film," a "political thriller"[105] that would appeal to audiences brought up on Batman[106]), and both dispelled the myth of a boring Shakespeare. After more than fifty years Olivier's film obviously looks dated in comparison to Branagh's, and although Olivier was regarded as an innovator for refusing to recite Shakespeare's blank verse in a mannered way, Branagh is right to note that their acting styles, in terms of increased naturalism, belong to "different worlds."[107] Still, Olivier's version remains a "miracle of lucidity, order, and harmony."[108] On one level we can enjoy its formal beauty and its colorful, idealistic creation of past ages, both Shakespeare's London and Henry's Agincourt. It is ironic that Olivier's movie—on the face of it a chivalric pageant celebrating traditional values through Henry as the crusading hero of England—can be viewed as in some ways more politically subversive than Branagh's.[109] Above all, the presentation of King Henry as a performer, who begins and ends as an actor in the nonrepresentational Globe Theatre, may serve as a reminder of the way that kingship is constructed socially; it is power on display, dependent on an approving audience. After its self-reflexive opening, Branagh's film discourages the audience's willing suspension of disbelief. Only briefly an icon of power, this King Henry V is soon absorbed into the working day world of realistically conceived action.

NOTES

1. See Arthur Colby Sprague, *"Henry V,"* in *Shakespeare's Histories: Plays for the Stage* (London: The Society for Theatre Research, 1964), pp. 92–96; Sally Beauman, *The Royal Shakespeare Company's Centenary Production of* Henry V (Oxford: Oxford University Press, 1976), pp. 9–13; "Staging and Stage History," in Andrew Gurr (ed.), *Henry V, The New Cambridge Shakespeare* (1992), pp. 37–50; and Anthony Brennan, "Stage History," in *Henry V* (New York: Twayne, 1992), pp. xiv–xxxiv.

2. *The Empty Space* (New York: Atheneum, 1968).

3. Discussed in Scott McMillin, *Henry IV, Part i* (Manchester and New York: Manchester University Press, 1991), Chapter 4, "1964. The Royal Shakespeare Company: Peter Hall."

4. See Samuel Crowl, "Minding Giddy Business: Michael Bogdanov's *The Wars of the Roses*" in *Shakespeare Observed: Studies in Performance on Stage and Screen* (Athens: Ohio University Press, 1992), pp. 156–59; and T. W. Craik (ed.), *King Henry V, The Arden Shakespeare* (London and New York: Routledge, 1995), pp. 87–89.

5. See Sheldon Zitner, "Wooden O's in Plastic Boxes," *UTQ*, 51 (Fall 1981), 1–12, reprinted in J. C. Bulman and H. R. Coursen (eds.), *Shakespeare on Television: An Anthology of Essays and Reviews* (Hanover: University Press of New England, 1988), pp. 31–41, 31.

6. Terry Hands (director), in Beauman, *RSC Production*, p. 17.

7. Sheridan Morley in *Punch* wryly suggested that it was a device to prove that "cut-price Shakespeare simply doesn't work" (*RSC Production*, p. 256); Robert Speaight, "Shakespeare in Britain, 1975," *SQ*, 27.1 (1976), 15–23, thought that only the Chorus, not the whole opening scene, should be in modern dress (20); Peter Thomson, "Towards a Poor Shakespeare: The Royal Shakespeare Company at Stratford in 1975," *ShS*, 29 (1976), 151–56, found that performing Act I in modern dress made it difficult for the audience to identify the first two actors as bishops (156).

8. *RSC Production*, p. 150.

9. See Trevor Nunn's comments (as artistic director), in *RSC Production*, p. 5.

10. *RSC Production*, p. 31.

11. Ibid., p. 32.

12. Benedict Nightingale, *New Statesman*, in *RSC Production*, p. 253.

13. *RSC Production*, p. 232.

14. Benedict Nightingale, *New Statesman*, and Eric Shorter, *The Daily Telegraph*, in *RSC Production*, p. 254.

15. Richard David, *Shakespeare in the Theatre* (Cambridge: Cambridge University Press, 1976), notes Henry's "eye-shutting, teeth-clenching ordeal" in ordering Bardolph's execution (198).

16. *RSC Production*, p. 58.

17. Ibid., p. 14.

18. Ibid., pp. 73–74.

19. Ibid., p. 3.

20. Ibid., pp. 17, 55, 249.

21. Ibid., p. 73.

22. Ibid., p. 87.

23. Ibid., p. 56.

24. Ace G. Pilkington, *Screening Shakespeare from* Richard II *to* Henry V (Newark: University of Delaware Press), comments on this (15).

25. *Shakespeare on Film* (Bloomington: Indiana University Press, 1977), p. 21.

26. Roger Manvell, *Shakespeare and the Film* (New York: Praeger, 1971), quotes Peter Hall's comments in the *Sunday Times*, January 26, 1969, that Shake-

speare's reliance on the "associative and metaphysical power of words" makes him "inescapably uncinematic" (126–27).

27. In Clifford Leech and J.M.R. Margeson (eds.), *Shakespeare, 1971* (Toronto: University of Toronto Press, 1972), p. 191.

28. *On Acting* (New York: Simon and Schuster, 1986), p. 267.

29. Ibid., p. 275.

30. Ibid., p. 269.

31. Graham Holderness, *Shakespeare Recycled: The Making of Historical Drama* (London: Barnes and Noble, 1992), analyzes Olivier's projection of Henry as an actor (187–92) and its potentially "subversive" tendencies (187). Dudley Andrew, *Film in the Aura of Art* (Princeton: Princeton University Press, 1984), also notes how Olivier's film shows us the "power of the great man, the power of self-mastery generating crowd mastery" (139).

32. Peter S. Donaldson, "Claiming from the Female: Gender and Representation in Laurence Olivier's *Henry V*," in *Shakespearean Films/Shakespearean Directors* (Boston, Mass.: Unwin Hyman, 1990), provides a sustained analysis of this sequence (11–14).

33. *On Acting*, p. 271.

34. Ibid., p. 270. Anthony Davies, *Filming Shakespeare's Plays* (Cambridge: Cambridge University Press, 1988), points out the "complex and subtle manipulation of the spatial elements" so that "the visuals take on the credibility of cinema without losing the consciousness of theatre" (30).

35. *On Acting*, p. 273.

36. In *Filmguide to* Henry V (Bloomington: Indiana University Press, 1973), Harry M. Geduld comments on how formal arrangements make these characters "appear like illustrations within panels formed by scenic structures" (35).

37. Dudley Andrew describes how the battle is represented in the "full perfection of deep focus" (*Film in the Aura of Art*, p. 133).

38. This is argued by Dale Silviria, "The Romance of *Henry V*," in *Laurence Olivier and the Art of Film Making* (Rutherford, N.J.: Fairleigh Dickinson University Press, 1985), pp. 103–4.

39. Ibid., pp. 96–100.

40. *On Acting*, p. 275.

41. Ibid., p. 277.

42. Geduld, *Filmguide to* Henry V, states that 1,694 lines (out of a total of some 3,199) have been cut from the play (48). He gives a full analysis of the cuts and their significance on pp. 48–50.

43. Gordon Beaucamp, "*Henry V*: Myth, Movie, Play," *CollL*, 5 (1978), 228–38, 228.

44. From an interview with Laurence Olivier in 1955, quoted in Roger Manvell, *Shakespeare and the Film*, p. 38.

45. See the comments of James Agee, *Agee on Film: Volume I* (1958), included in Charles W. Eckert (ed.), *Focus on Shakespearean Films* (Englewood Cliff, N.J.: Prentice-Hall, 1972), p. 56.

46. Pilkington, "Laurence Olivier's *Henry V*," extensively analyzes the "filmic art" of Olivier's version (*Screening Shakespeare*, pp. 119–22).

47. See Jorgens, *Shakespeare on Film*, for comments on visual parallelism in Olivier's film (pp. 131–33).

48. See Manvell, *Shakespeare and the Film*, p. 39.

49. These are the terms that Geduld uses in *Filmguide*, pp. 59–60.

50. Ibid., p. 66.

51. *Henry V by William Shakespeare: A Screen Adaptation by Kenneth Branagh* (London: Chatto and Windus, 1989), p. 9.

52. "Kenneth Branagh—*Henry V*," in Russell Jackson and Robert Smallwood (eds.), *Players of Shakespeare 2* (Cambridge: Cambridge University Press, 1988), p. 97.

53. Branagh discusses his central idea of "allowing close-ups and low-level dialogue to draw the audience deep into the human side of this distant medieval world" in *Screen Adaptation* (10). Kenneth S. Rothwell, "Kenneth Branagh's *Henry V*: The Gilt [Guilt] in the Crown Re-Examined," *CompD*, 24.2 (Summer 1990), 173–78, also notes that the style of the film is "introspective and keyed to the mid or close shot" (173).

54. This is pointed out by Peter S. Donaldson, "Taking on Shakespeare: Kenneth Branagh's *Henry V*," *SQ*, 42 (1991), 60–71, 63–64.

55. See "Kenneth Branagh—*Henry V*," p. 98. One critic who analyzes the Stratford theater production as anti-war is Susan Collier, "Post-Falklands, Post-Colonial: Contextualizing Branagh as Henry V on Stage and on Film," *Essays in Theatre/Études Théatricales*, 10.2 (May 1992), 143–54. Harry M. Geduld, "A Royal Brotherhood of Death," *The Humanist*, July–August 1990, 43–44, also discusses Branagh's film as a "strong anti-war statement" after the Falklands war (43).

56. I admit to thinking, when I first saw the film, that this sequence (including slow-motion effects) went on for a bit too long. This is the verdict of Vincent Canby, "A Down-to-Earth Henry V Discards Spectacle and Pomp," *New York Times*, November 8, 1989, C19, who finds the battle scenes so "chaotic" and "exhausting" that it is difficult to tell which side won the day. Repeated viewing has convinced me of the coherence and relevance of all the details here, even down to the shots of Jamy doing the "gud service" he promised at Harfleur.

57. Samuel Crowl, "Fathers and Sons: Kenneth Branagh's *Henry V*," in *Shakespeare Observed*, also comments on how "Branagh's earthy, gritty Henry was built on getting at the man beneath the mask" (168).

58. One critic who explores the complexity of Branagh's interpretation is Sara Munson Deats, "Rabbits and Ducks: Olivier, Branagh and *Henry V*," *FLQ*, 20 (1992), 284–93. She interprets Olivier's as the "rabbit" (the ideal king) and

Branagh's as closer to the "duck" (the converse) of the rival gestalts of the play pointed out by Norman Rabkin.

59. On the evidence of pointed glances and gestures, it is also possible that Henry is "being manipulated by an unspoken conspiracy between Canterbury and *Exeter*" (see William Shaw, "Textual Ambiguities and Cinematic Certainties in *Henry V*," *FLQ*, 22.2 [1994], 117–28, 123).

60. The pastiche of quotations and wrenching of words out of context—in particular, Falstaff's interpolated "We have heard the chimes at midnight, Master Harry," which in *Henry IV, Part ii* forms part of his reminiscences with Justice Shallow and is never addressed to the Prince—are jarring notes in an otherwise superbly executed movie. This flashback does at least provide the audience with some important background information on the relationship between Prince Hal and Falstaff.

61. "Kenneth Branagh—*Henry V*," p. 103.

62. Ibid., p. 97.

63. Jill Forbes, "Olivier's and Branagh's *Henry V*," *Sight and Sound,* 58.4 (Autumn 1989), 258–59, complains about the quality of the sound recording here, amplifying and flattening Branagh's voice, "so that Henry addressing his troops before Agincourt sounds as if he were standing on the stage of the Albert Hall" (259). It is amusing to read Branagh's account of the difficulties of filming outside London: "Behind us were pylons, to one side was a modern housing estate, and on the other side was a reservoir. . . . As if this wasn't enough, the religious calm of the speech was regularly punctuated by the sonic horrors of the Heathrow flight path" (Kenneth Branagh, *Beginning* [New York: Norton, 1990], pp. 223–24).

64. "Kenneth Branagh—*Henry V*," p. 100.

65. *Beginning*, p. 142.

66. "Kenneth Branagh—*Henry V*," p. 97.

67. Amy Schwartz, "Henry Today," *Washington Post*, February 6, 1990, concludes that the film faithfully reflects the "complex intertwined pro- and anti-war themes in the actual lines," while Benedict Nightingale, "Henry V Returns as a Monarch for This Era," *New York Times*, November 5, 1989, quotes from Branagh: "The war seemed to be inevitable and regrettable and ugly and sad and exciting, intoxicating and seductive" (H18).

68. Stuart Klawans, "Films," *The Nation*, December 11, 1989, 724–26, calls this "an elegiac summation of everything that has been suffered in the movie" (726). Robert Lane, on the other hand, criticizes it as a strategy "to inoculate [Henry] against the moral stigma of having caused the violence" (" 'When Blood Is Their Argument': Class, Character and Historymaking in Shakespeare's and Branagh's *Henry V*," *ELH*, 61 [1994], 27–52, 40), while Michael Manheim, "The Function of Battle Imagery in Kurosawa's Histories and the *Henry V* Films," *FLQ*, 22.2 (1994), 129–35, finds that the "Non Nobis" music "may be taken as the essence of pure patriotism, or . . . the ultimate soporific needed to obscure the horrors of war" (134).

69. Charles H. Frey, "Branagh's *Henry V*," *MMLA Abstracts* (2 November 1990), in *SFNL*, 15.2 (April 1991), 2.

70. Jack Kroll, "A *Henry V* for Our Time," *Newsweek*, November 20, 1989, p. 78.

71. Graham Holderness, "Reproductions: *Henry V*," comments on how the entrepreneur's "conquest of new economic and artistic worlds continually endorses the cultural and ideological power of the old" (*Shakespeare Recycled*, p. 205).

72. Dympna Callaghan, "Resistance and Recuperation: Branagh's *Henry V*," *SFNL*, 15.2 (April 1991), 5–6, grimly concludes that Branagh's "realist aesthetic" suggests that "film is capable of realizing the reactionary political project that Renaissance mimesis was technically unable to discharge" (6).

73. "Invisible Bullets," in Jonathan Dollimore and Alan Sinfield (eds.), *Political Shakespeare* (Ithaca and London: Cornell University Press, 1985), p. 43.

74. *Beginning*, p. 139. Branagh's comment on the play as an "*ever-relevant* [italics mine] and compassionate survey of people and war" (*Screen Adaptation*, p. 12) is likely to raise the hackles of the cultural materialists. But no matter. Branagh aimed to please as wide an audience as possible.

75. Preface, *Shakespeare on Television*, p. ix.

76. *On Acting*, p. 369.

77. "The Player's Eye: Shakespeare on Television," *CompD*, 18.3 (Fall 1984), 193–202, 194.

78. Michèle Willems, "Verbal-Visual, Verbal-Pictorial or Textual-Televisual? Reflections on the BBC Shakespeare Series," *ShS*, 39 (1987), 91–102, 93.

79. H. R. Coursen, "The Bard and the Tube," in *Shakespeare on Television*, pp. 3–10, 6–7. Laurence Olivier also comments that "television is a more 'hearing' and 'listening to' medium than the cinema, where the picture is bigger and the eyes can wander only to darkness" (*On Acting*, p. 373).

80. Martin Banham, "BBC Televison's Dull Shakespeares," *CritQ*, 22.1 (1980), 31–40, in *Shakespeare on Television*, pp. 213–20, 214.

81. Jacqueline Pearson, "Shadows on the Shadow-Box: The BBC Shakespeare," *CritQ*, 21.1 (1979), 67–70, 67; see also "Critical Reception," in Susan Willis, *The BBC Shakespeare Plays: Making the Televised Canon* (Chapel Hill and London: University of North Carolina Press, 1991), pp. 50–57.

82. *The BBC Shakespeare Plays*, p. 17.

83. Ibid., p. 88.

84. Ibid., p. 102.

85. Paul M. Cubeta, "The Shakespeare Plays on TV: Season Two," *SFNL*, 5.1 (December 1980), compares the formal tableau to "figurines of unusual beauty" (quoted in *Shakespeare on Television*, p. 261).

86. *The BBC Shakespeare Plays*, p. 88.

87. Martin Banham, "BBC Television's Dull Shakespeares," *Shakespeare on Television*, p. 218.

88. C. M. Pearce, *Cahiers Elisabéthains*, 17 (April 1980), quoted in *Shakespeare on Television*, p. 260.

89. Samuel Crowl, "The Shakespeare Plays on TV: Season Two," *SFNL*, 5.1 (December 1980), quoted in *Shakespeare on Television*, p. 260.

90. See Pilkington, *Screening Shakespeare*, pp. 95–96.

91. Tim Hallinan, "Jonathan Miller on The Shakespeare Plays," *SQ*, 32.2 (1981), 134–45, 134.

92. Sheldon Zitner, "Wooden O's in Plastic Boxes," in *Shakespeare on Television*, p. 36.

93. Pilkington, *Screening Shakespeare*, p. 89.

94. Mark Crispin Miller, "The Shakespeare Plays," *The Nation*, July 12, 1980, in *Shakespeare on Television*, p. 262.

95. *The Leasing Out of England: Shakespeare's Second Henriad* (Washington, D.C.: University Press of America, 1982), p. 176.

96. *Shakespearean Performance as Interpretation* (Newark: University of Delaware Press, 1992), p. 172.

97. There are comedic sequences in I. ii, II.i, III. ii, III. iv, III. vii, IV.i, IV. iv, IV. vii-viii, V. i, and V. ii.

98. *Beginning*, p. 235.

99. Peter Lane, "When Blood Is Their Argument," p. 38.

100. "A Screen Adaptation," p. 10.

101. Peter S. Donaldson, "Taking on Shakespeare," p. 60.

102. *A Screen Adaptation*, pp. 9–10.

103. Alan Howard had played Hamlet for the RSC in the early 1970s, before taking on Henry V, and he comments,"When I first read *Henry V*, it struck me that Henry's situation was very much what Hamlet's might have been, if he had lived and had had to fight Fortinbras" (*RSC Production*, p. 53).

104. Jonathan Yardley, "The Metamorphosis of 'Henry,' " *The Washington Post*, February 26, 1990, considers it "decidedly inferior background music" (C2).

105. *A Screen Adaptation*, p. 10.

106. Graham Fuller, "Two Kings," *Film Comment*, November–December 1989, 2–7, quotes Branagh's wish to "take the curse of medievalism" off the play, so that contemporary Batman audiences "could conceivably be persuaded to see it" (6).

107. In the interview with Benedict Nightingale, Branagh describes his way of speaking Shakespeare's lines as "delivering the text in as realistic a way as possible and without denying its complexity, its richness, and the dramatic poetry that makes the hair stand up on the back of your head" ("Henry V Returns," H18).

108. Jorgens, *Shakespeare on Film*, p. 123.

109. See Holderness, "Reproductions: *Henry V*," in *Shakespeare Recycled*, pp. 187–89. Jill Forbes, "Olivier's and Branagh's *Henry V*," also points out that Branagh's version does not develop the "notion of ceremony" or play acting, which Marxist critics stress as "an essential component of Shakespeare's notion of kingship" (259).

BIBLIOGRAPHICAL ESSAY

The following survey does not attempt to provide an exhaustive bibliography on *Henry V*; instead it outlines the most important critical work on the play, emphasizing books over articles. Readers who would like to pursue in detail topics treated in this book—for example, the role of the Chorus (Chapter 1) or Kenneth Branagh's film of *Henry V* (Chapter 6)—are encouraged to consult the notes at the end of the relevant chapter to compile an additional list of articles and reviews.

SOURCE MATERIALS

Shakespeare's most prominent source for the play is the *Chronicles of England, Scotland, and Ireland*, by Raphael Holinshed (1587). Today's readers can refer to *Shakespeare's Holinshed*, selected and edited by Richard Hosley (New York: Capricorn Books, 1968), or can peruse the passages of Holinshed most relevant to *Henry V* in John Russell Brown's Signet edition of the play (New York and Toronto, 1965; 1988). Geoffrey Bullough presents and analyzes the sources of *Henry V* in *Narrative and Dramatic Sources of Shakespeare*, vol. 4 (London, 1966). This volume contains another important source, *The Famous Victories of Henry V*, which is also given in full in Maynard Mack's Signet edition of *Henry IV, Part i* (1965). J. H. Walter reviews other possible sources of the play in his Arden edition of *Henry V* (London: Methuen, 1954). To better understand opposing political viewpoints in the Renaissance that are relevant to *Henry V*, students will find helpful Machiavelli's *The Prince* (1514), translated by George Bull (Harmondsworth: Penguin Books, 1961), and Thomas Elyot's *The Book named the Governor*, published in the Everyman edition (London: Dent,

1962). This treatise, which had been reprinted at least seven times by 1580, presents the ruler in an ideal light, as does Erasmus's *Institutio Principis Christiani* (1516), *The Education of a Christian Prince* (translated by Lester K. Born [1936; New York: Norton, 1968]). The significance (by omission) of Erasmus's "pacificist and anti-imperialist ideas" to *Henry V* is argued by Andrew Gurr, "*Henry V* and the Bees' Commonwealth," *ShS*, 30 (1977), 61–72.

HENRY V AND ITS HISTORICAL CONTEXTS

Criticism of the play from the mid-1940s to the 1960s, and often beyond, is indebted to E.M.W. Tillyard's *Shakespeare's History Plays* (1944; London: Chatto and Windus, 1959). Tillyard argues that what unifies Shakespeare's two tetralogies is the orthodox "providential" version of events found in his sources, especially Hall's *Chronicle* (1548). This is English history written from the standpoint of the Tudor myth: The reign of Henry V is viewed as a brief albeit glorious respite in the cycle of crime and punishment that begins with the murder of Richard II (when Bolingbroke usurped the throne to become Henry IV) and ends with the death of Richard III and the accession of Richmond, the Tudor Henry VII, who brings stability to the kingdom. Lily B. Campbell, *Shakespeare's Histories: Mirrors of Elizabethan Policy* (San Marino, Calif.: The Huntingdon Library, 1947), finds, too, that Shakespeare's plays endorse conventional notions of order in the state. Irving Ribner, *The English History Play in the Age of Shakespeare* (1957; New York: Barnes and Noble, 1965), sees a somewhat more complex view of history explored in Shakespeare's plays but also argues that within the tetralogies Henry V is presented as an ideal king, a "Renaissance mirror for princes" (p. 192).

The providential view of history in Shakespeare's plays was attacked as oversimplified by Wilbur Sanders, *The Dramatist and the Received Idea* (Cambridge: Cambridge University Press, 1968), and by Henry A. Kelly, *Divine Providence in the England of Shakespeare's Histories* (Cambridge, Mass.: Harvard University Press, 1970), both preludes to more sustained attacks on Tillyard's views in the 1980s. Particularly important in emphasizing "ambivalence"—the conviction that Shakespeare did not subscribe uncritically to the "Tudor myth system of order" but "had to undermine it, . . . to vex its applications with sly or subtle ambiguities"—is A. P. Rossiter's "Ambivalence and the Dialectic of History" (1951), in *Angel with Horns* (London: Longman, 1961, p. 59). No one today is in danger of taking Tillyard's interpretation as the last word on the subject of Shakespeare's history plays. Nevertheless, his book, which opened up important historical perspectives on the drama, still repays study.

Since the 1980s, the older historical approach to drama has often been superseded by the new historicist one, with its commitment to treating history as a text (open to different interpretations and deconstructions) and to Renaissance dramatic literature as part of an ongoing cultural debate. Before the term "new historicist" was coined, Philip Edwards' *Threshold of a Nation: A Study of English and Irish Drama* (Cambridge: Cambridge University Press, 1979) implicates *Henry V* in the expansionist quest of Elizabethan England to subjugate Ireland. Ten years later, in *Shakespeare and the Popular Voice* (Cambridge, Mass.: B. Blackwell, 1989), Annabel Patterson connects the two versions of *Henry V*, the Quarto and Folio texts, with the contest between Queen Elizabeth I and the Earl of Essex for popular support around the time that Essex was leading his military expedition to Ireland (1599). In " 'Vile Participation': The Amplification of Violence in the Theater of *Henry V*," *ShS*, 42 (Spring 1991), 1–32, Joel B. Altman also employs a new historicist approach; he searchingly examines the public anxiety over the Irish struggle to account for why Shakespeare's play was designed to excite "violence and release" in its theater audience. Also thought-provoking, though more general in their analyses of how the ideology of power informs the play, are Stephen Greenblatt's "Invisible Bullets: Renaissance Authority and Its Subversions," in *Shakespearean Negotiations* (Berkeley and Los Angeles: University of California Press, 1988), and Jonathan Dollimore and Alan Sinfield, "History and Ideology: The Instance of *Henry V*," in John Drakakis (ed.), *Alternative Shakespeares* (London and New York: Methuen, 1985). Both of these articles are discussed in detail in Chapter 5. An important book that emphasizes how different ideological biases inform the interpretation of history and the reading of the history plays, including *Henry V*, is Phyllis Rackin, *Stages of History: Shakespeare's English Chronicles* (Ithaca: Cornell University Press, 1990). Other studies that cover *Henry V* while examining the notion of history as a constructed "story" are Barbara Hodgson, *The End Crowns All* (Princeton: Princeton University Press, 1991), which focuses on the question of closure in the plays, and Robert C. Jones, *These Valiant Dead* (Iowa City: University of Iowa Press, 1991), which explores how Henry helps create his own myth. In *Shakespeare Recycled: The Making of Historical Drama* (London: Barnes and Noble, 1992), Graham Holderness discusses how *Henry V*, among Shakespeare's other history plays, has been appropriated by and reproduced within our modern culture.

CRITICAL STUDIES

Many formalist critics have discussed Shakespeare's histories as dramatic literature, exploring aesthetic and humanist concerns rather than promoting a particular view of history or ideology. Some of these are mentioned later in this essay. In addition, the following studies written within this mode contain chapters on *Henry V* that offer valuable insights into the play: Hugh M. Richmond, *Shakespeare's Political Plays* (New York: Random House, 1967); Robert Ornstein, *A Kingdom for a Stage: The Achievement of Shakespeare's History Plays* (Cambridge, Mass.: Harvard University Press, 1972); Moody E. Prior, *The Drama of Power: Studies in Shakespeare's History Plays* (Evanston, Ill.: Northwestern University Press, 1973); Larry S. Champion, *Perspectives on Shakespeare's English Histories* (Athens: University of Georgia Press, 1980); Alexander Leggatt, *Shakespeare's Political Drama: The History Plays and the Roman Plays* (London and New York: Routledge, 1988); and E. Pearlman, *William Shakespeare: The History Plays* (New York: Twayne, 1993). Two anthologies that gather up important pre-1970 criticism are Ronald Berman (ed.), Henry V: *Twentieth Century Interpretations* (Englewood Cliffs, N.J.: Prentice-Hall, 1968) and Michael Quinn (ed.), Henry V: *A Casebook* (London: Macmillan, 1969).

Since 1970 interest has grown in how the history plays comment on their own theatrical strategies and dramatic art. The fullest exponent of this metadramatic approach is James L. Calderwood, *Metadrama in Shakespeare's "Henriad"* (Berkeley; Los Angeles; London: University of California Press, 1979), and there are useful insights into how the language of *Henry V* functions as a pragmatic instrument in Joseph A. Porter, *The Drama of Speech Acts* (Berkeley; Los Angeles; London: University of California Press, 1979). Also in the metadramatic mode, John W. Blanpied explores how the dramatist's art evolves in *Henry V* in *Time and the Artist in Shakespeare's English Histories* (Newark: University of Delaware Press, 1983).

HENRY'S CHARACTER AND THE NATURE OF THE PLAY

Critics who consider the play a great achievement usually warm to the character of Henry V, or at least think that he is portrayed as an admirable king. In their editions of the play, both J. Dover Wilson (New Cambridge, 1947) and J. H. Walter (Arden, 1954) defend Henry as an ideal monarch in the epic vein, while Charles Williams,"*Henry V*," in Anne Ridler (ed.), *Shakespeare Criticism, 1919–1935* (London: Oxford University Press, 1936), praises Henry's straightforward honor and "legerity of spirit" (p. 188). In just a few pages of his *Shakespeare* (London: J. Cape, 1936), J. Middleton Murry captures the imaginative energy he finds in Shakespeare's portrayal of the "ideal of kingship," where "organic and creative order is embodied in Harry the king" (pp. 184–85). Such undivided enthusiasm is now somewhat rare, although M. M. Reese, *The Cease of Majesty* (London: E. Arnold, 1961), provides a careful analysis of how the play shows Henry doing "everything . . . expected of the perfect king" (p. 321). More recently, Michael Goldman, *Shakespeare and the Energies of Drama* (Princeton: Princeton University Press, 1972), points out Henry V's compelling charisma, and C. G. Thayer, *Shakespearean Politics: Government and Misgovernment in the Great Histories* (Athens: Ohio University Press, 1983), does not "doubt for a moment" that Shakespeare "expected his audience to love" this great national hero (p. 146).

Not all commentators share this conviction. Several claim that *Henry V* is a perfunctory treatment of England's brief glory under a successful ruler. In "From *Henry V* to *Hamlet*" (1933), in Peter Alexander (ed.), *Studies in Shakespeare* (London: Oxford University Press, 1964), Harley Granville Barker puts this view across well, asserting that Henry V is the "perfect man of action" but that "there seems to be very little that is dramatically interesting for him to do" (p. 79). This is echoed in Tillyard's chapter on *Henry V* (1944) and carried further in Rossiter's labeling *Henry V* a "propaganda-play on National Unity" ("Ambivalence: The Dialectic of the Histories" [1951], p. 57). James Winny, too, finds that "Shakespeare's conception of the ideal king . . . and his creative powers were at odds" (*The Player King: A Theme of Shakespeare's Histories* [London: Chatto and Windus, 1968], p. 174).

Henry has many detractors. In the nineteenth century, William Hazlitt, in *Characters in Shakespeare's Plays* (1818), indicts him as an "amiable monster," while at the beginning of this century, W. B. Yeats finds Henry's "rough energy" and "coarse nerves" unappealing (*Ideas of Good and Evil*, 1903). Mark van Doren, *Shakespeare* (New York: Henry Holt, 1939), dismisses the hero as too "hearty" and strident, just as the style of the play is overinflated. The "ironic" reading of the play—the argument that Shakespeare deliberately presents Henry as deeply flawed and even as a "hypocrite"—began in earnest with Gerald Gould, "A New Reading of *Henry V*," *The English Review*, 29 (July 1919), 42–55. Harold C. Goddard, *The Meaning of Shakespeare* (Chicago and London: University of Chicago

Press, 1951), provides the fullest and liveliest interpretation of Henry as a Machiavel, while John C. Bromley, *The Shakespearean Kings* (Boulder: Colorado Associated University Press, 1971), damns Henry as a "combination of crudity and ferocity" (p. 90). In "*Henry V*: Another Part of the Critical Forest," *JHI*, 37.1 (1976), 3–26, Gordon Ross Smith uses historical details, such as Mortimer's superior claim to the throne, to deconstruct the notion of Henry as an impeccable monarch.

More common now than these polarized approaches, for or against Henry, is the justification of Henry's character in political terms. The following critics perceive Henry as a strong king whose skills in leadership inevitably diminish his human qualities: John Palmer, *Political Characters of Shakespeare* (London: Macmillan, 1945); Una Ellis-Fermor, *The Frontiers of Drama* (London: Methuen, 1945; 1964); Derek Traversi, *Shakespeare: From* Richard II *to* Henry V (Stanford, Calif.: Stanford University Press, 1957); Michael Manheim, *The Weak King Dilemma in the Shakespearean History Play* (Syracuse, N.Y.: Syracuse University Press, 1973); and Alvin Kernan, "The *Henriad*: Shakespeare's Major History Plays," in *The Revels History of Drama in English*, vol. 3 (London: Methuen, 1975). In an effort to do justice to the ambivalence of the play, many commentators emphasize how *Henry V* affords both celebratory and ironic perspectives on the King. Allan Gilbert, "Patriotism and Satire in *Henry V*," in Arthur D. Mathews and Clark M. Emery (eds.), *Studies in Shakespeare* (Coral Gables, Fla.: University of Miami Press, 1953); Honor Mathews, *Character and Symbol in Shakespeare's Plays* (Cambridge: Cambridge University Press, 1962); and Zdeněk Stříbrný, "*Henry V* and History," in Arnold Kettle (ed.), *Shakespeare and His Changing World* (New York: International Publishers, 1964), offer some early discussions of this doubleness in the play. Several studies that analyze how the adulatory Chorus counterpoints the realistic action of the play, such as Edward I. Berry, "True Things and Mock'ries: Epic and History in *Henry V*," *JEGP*, 78 (1979), 1–16, do likewise. Anne Barton also addresses the play's conflicting presentations of the King in "The King Disguised: Shakespeare's *Henry V* and the Comical History," in Joseph G. Price (ed.), *The Triple Bond* (University Park: Pennsylvania State University Press, 1975), pp. 92–117. Most important in clarifying the dual perspective and evaluating its significance is Norman Rabkin, "Either/Or: Responding to *Henry V*," in *Shakespeare and the Problem of Meaning* (Chicago and London: University of Chicago Press, 1981). Recently Graham Bradshaw has advocated going beyond an "either/or" approach and instead meeting the play's challenge to apprehend different perspectives simultaneously (Chapter 1 of *Misrepresentations: Shakespeare and the*

Materialists [Ithaca and London: Cornell University Press, 1993]). The commentaries of Barton and Rabkin are reprinted in Harold Bloom (ed.), *William Shakespeare's* Henry V: *Modern Critical Interpretations* (New York: Chelsea House, 1988), a useful collection of criticism after 1970.

HENRY V IN THE THEATER AND ON FILM

Henry V has almost always proved successful on stage. Arthur Colby Sprague, *Shakespeare's Histories: Plays for the Stage* (London: The Society for Theatre Research, 1964), surveys early theater productions of the play, while both Andrew Gurr, in his New Cambridge edition of *Henry V* (Cambridge University Press, 1992), and T. W. Craik, in the Arden Shakespeare *King Henry V* (London and New York: Routledge, 1995), take us up to 1989 in their detailed sections on the play in performance. A fascinating account of the memorable 1975 production by the Royal Shakespeare Company, from the point of view of directors, actors, and reviewers, is contained in Sally Beauman, *The Royal Shakespeare Company's Centenary Production of* Henry V (Oxford: Oxford University Press, 1976). Over the years the *Shakespeare Survey* has provided accounts of this and other important British productions of *Henry V*, while the *Shakespeare Quarterly* covers productions of Shakespeare's plays worldwide. Anthony Brennan counterpoints his careful discussion of *Henry V* (New York: Twayne, 1992) with references to American and British theater and film versions of the play. Drawing attention to what producers have cut as well as what they have emphasized, he urges that "all of the strands of the text," the full complexity of *Henry V*, be staged (p. 2).

Film critics have found much to praise in Laurence Olivier's movie version of *Henry V* (1944). Jack J. Jorgens illuminates its structure in *Shakespeare on Film* (Bloomington: Indiana University Press, 1977); Dale Silviria analyzes its aesthetic form in *Laurence Olivier and the Art of Film Making* (Rutherford, N.J.: Fairleigh Dickinson University Press, 1985); and Peter S. Donaldson treats the cultural issues of "Gender and Representation in Laurence Olivier's *Henry V*" in *Shakespearean Films / Shakespearean Directors* (Boston, Mass.: Unwin Hyman, 1990). Harry M. Geduld's *Filmguide to* Henry V (Bloomington: Indiana University Press, 1973), with its detailed account of how the film was made, is indispensable for anyone studying the movie. Likewise, Kenneth Branagh's Henry V *by William Shakespeare: A Screen Adaptation* (London: Chatto and Windus, 1989) is an excellent introduction to his film, while in "Kenneth Branagh—*Henry V*," in Russell Jackson and Robert Smallwood (eds.), *Players of Shakespeare 2*

(Cambridge: Cambridge University Press, 1988), the actor-director shares his ideas on the character of Henry as he played him in the 1984–85 RSC production—perceptions that also informed his 1989 film. Samuel Crowl discusses Branagh's film in *Shakespeare Observed: Studies in Performance on Stage and Screen* (Athens: Ohio University Press, 1992). Two essays (out of numerous reviews and articles) that compare Olivier's and Branagh's versions of *Henry V* in a particularly helpful way are Peter S. Donaldson, "Taking on Shakespeare: Kenneth Branagh's *Henry V*," *SQ*, 42 (1991), 60–71, and Sarah Munson Deats, "Rabbits and Ducks: Olivier, Branagh, and *Henry V*," *FLQ*, 20 (1992), 284–93.

Now that Shakespeare has entered the age of television and is enshrined in the BBC/Time Life video series "The Shakespeare Plays," several commentators have considered the opportunities and drawbacks afforded by this medium. Susan Willis analyzes the production side of the BBC *Henry V*—its choice of style, sets, and actors—in her *The BBC Shakespeare Plays: Making the Televised Canon* (Chapel Hill and London: University of North Carolina Press, 1991). In his *Screening Shakespeare from* Richard II *to* Henry V (Newark: University of Delaware Press, 1991), Ace C. Pilkington examines in detail both the BBC *Henry V* and Olivier's version. An excellent collection of essays, including excerpts from reviews of the BBC *Henry V*, has been compiled by J. C. Bulman and H. R. Coursen in *Shakespeare on Television: An Anthology of Essays and Reviews* (Hanover: University Press of New England, 1988).

INDEX

Names of characters in *Henry V* appear in **bold type**.

About the Author

JOAN LORD HALL is Lecturer in English and the Writing Program at the University of Colorado, Boulder. She received degrees in English language and literature at University College, London, and Girton College, Cambridge. She has published several articles on Renaissance drama and is the author of *The Dynamics of Role-Playing in Jacobean Tragedy* (1991).

ISBN 0-313-29708-8

EAN

90000>

9 780313 297083

HARDCOVER BAR CODE